HEIDEGGER'S *BLACK NOTEBOOKS*

HEIDEGGER'S
BLACK NOTEBOOKS

RESPONSES TO
ANTI-SEMITISM

EDITED BY
ANDREW J. MITCHELL
AND PETER TRAWNY

Columbia University Press
New York

Columbia University Press
Publishers Since 1893
New York   Chichester, West Sussex
cup.columbia.edu
Copyright © 2017 Columbia University Press

Library of Congress Cataloging-in-Publication Data
Names: Mitchell, Andrew J., 1970–, editor.
Title: Heidegger's Black notebooks: responses to anti-Semitism / edited by
Andrew J. Mitchell and Peter Trawny.
Description: New York: Columbia University Press, 2017. | Includes bibliographical
references and index.
Identifiers: LCCN 2017009182 | ISBN 9780231180443 (cloth: alk. paper) |
ISBN 9780231180450 (pbk.: alk. paper) | ISBN 9780231544382 (e-book)
Subjects: LCSH: Heidegger, Martin, 1889–1976. Schwarze Hefte. |
Heidegger, Martin, 1889–1976—Notebooks, sketchbooks, etc. | Antisemitism.
Classification: LCC B3279.H48 S36234 2017 | DDC 193—dc23
LC record available at https://lccn.loc.gov/2017009182

Columbia University Press books are printed on permanent
and durable acid-free paper.

Printed in the United States of America

Cover design: Lisa Hamm

CONTENTS

ACKNOWLEDGMENTS

A s the majority of the essays gathered here stem from the Emory University conference "Heidegger's 'Black Notebooks': Philosophy, Politics, Anti-Semitism," the editors would like to thank the Emory Conference Center Subvention Fund, the Center for Faculty Development and Excellence, the Office of the Provost, the Office of the Dean of Emory College of Arts and Sciences, the Hightower Fund, the departments of philosophy, comparative literature, German studies, and French and Italian, the Graduate Institute of the Liberal Arts, and the Tam Institute for Jewish Studies for their generous assistance in making the conference possible. The editors would also like to thank the graduate student assistants to that conference, Katherine Davies, Lily Levy, and Christopher Merwin, for their dedication and effort.

Hans Ulrich Gumbrecht's article first appeared in German in the *Frankfurter Allgemeine Zeitung*, April 25, 2015, https://blogs.faz.net/digital/2015/ 04/25/herrlich-volklicher-wille-was-zeigt-sich-in-heideggers-schwarzen-heften-838/.

Finally, at Columbia University Press, we are grateful to our editor Wendy Lochner for her encouragement, support, and patience with this project from the very beginning.

ABBREVIATIONS

Referentences to the works of Martin Heidegger are provided paren-
thetically in the text by *Gesamtausgabe* volume (*GA*), with German pagination provided first, followed by a slash and the English
pagination of published translations where extant. The only exception to
this is *Being and Time* (*GA* 2) where no English pagination is provided, but
rather the *Gesamtausgabe* pagination is followed by the German pagination of the single edition published by Niemeyer (included as marginal
pagination in all three of the English translations of *Being and Time*). Modifications to published translations are noted by "tm," modifications to
emphasis by "em." Where no English translation pagination is provided,
translations are by the author unless otherwise specified.

MARTIN HEIDEGGER IN THE *GESAMTAUSGABE* (FRANKFURT: VITTORIO KLOSTERMANN, 1976 TO DATE)

GA 2   *Sein und Zeit*. Ed. Friedrich-Wilhelm von Herrmann, 1977.
English translation: *Being and Time*, trans. Joan
Stambaugh, rev. Dennis J. Schmidt (Albany: State
University of New York Press, 2010). Cited by the single
edition pagination of *SZ*.

GA 3   *Kant und das Problem der Metaphysik*. Ed. Friedrich-Wilhelm von Herrmann, 1991. English translation: *Kant and the Problem of Metaphysics*, 5th ed., enlarged, trans. Richard Taft (Bloomington: Indiana University Press, 1997).

GA 5   *Holzwege*. Ed. Friedrich-Wilhelm von Herrmann, 1994, 7th ed. English translation: *Off the Beaten Track*, ed. and trans. Julian Young and Kenneth Haynes (Cambridge: Cambridge University Press, 2002).

GA 6.1   *Nietzsche I*. Ed. Brigitte Schillbach, 1996.

GA 7   *Vorträge und Aufsätze*. Ed. Friedrich-Wilhelm von Herrmann, 2000.

GA 9   *Wegmarken*. Ed. Friedrich-Wilhelm von Herrmann, 1996, 3d ed. English translation: *Pathmarks*, ed. William McNeill, various trans. (Cambridge: Cambridge University Press, 1998).

GA 10   *Der Satz vom Grund*. Ed. Petra Jaeger, 1997. English translation: *The Principle of Reason*, trans. Reginald Lily (Bloomington: Indiana University Press, 1994).

GA 12   *Unterwegs zur Sprache*. Ed. Friedrich-Wilhelm von Herrmann, 1985.

GA 13   *Aus der Erfahrung des Denkens*. Ed. Hermann Heidegger, 1983.

GA 16   *Reden und andere Zeugnisse eines Lebensweges*. Ed. Hermann Heidegger, 2000.

GA 18   *Grundbegriffe der aristotelischen Philosophie*. Ed. Mark Michalski, 2002. English translation: *Basic Concepts of Aristotelian Philosophy*, trans. Robert D. Metcalf and Mark B. Tanzer (Bloomington: Indiana University Press, 2009).

GA 24   *Die Grundprobleme der Phänomenologie*. Ed. Friedrich-Wilhelm von Herrmann, 1989, 2d ed.. English translation: *The Basic Problems of Phenomenology*, rev. ed., trans. Albert Hofstadter (Bloomington: Indiana University Press, 1982).

GA 25   *Phänomenologische Interpretation von Kants "Kritik der reinen Vernunft."* Ed. Ingtraud Görland, 1995, 3d ed.. English translation: *Phenomenological Interpretation of Kant's "Critique of Pure Reason,"* trans. Parvis Emad and

Kenneth Maly (Bloomington: Indiana University Press, 1997).

GA 26   *Metaphysische Anfangsgründe der Logik im Ausgang von Leibniz.* Ed. Klaus Held, 1990, 2d ed. English translation: *The Metaphysical Foundations of Logic,* trans. Michael Heim (Bloomington: Indiana University Press, 1984).

GA 29/30   *Die Grundbegriffe der Metaphysik: Welt – Endlichkeit – Einsamkeit.* Ed. Friedrich-Wilhelm von Herrmann, 1992, 2d ed. English translation: *The Fundamental Concepts of Metaphysics: World, Finitude, Solitude,* trans. William McNeill (Bloomington: Indiana University Press, 1995).

GA 34   *Vom Wesen der Wahrheit. Zu Platons Höhlengleichnis und "Theätet."* Ed. Hermann Mörchen, 1997, 2d ed. English translation: *The Essence of Truth: On Plato's Cave Allegory and "Theaetetus,"* trans. Ted Sadler (New York: Continuum, 2002).

GA 36/37   *Sein und Wahrheit.* Ed. Hartmut Tietjen, 2001. English translation: *Being and Truth,* trans. Gregory Fried and Richard Polt (Bloomington: Indiana University Press, 2010).

GA 38   *Logik als die Frage nach dem Wesen der Sprache.* Ed. Günter Seubold, 1998. English translation: *Logic as the Question Concerning the Essence of Language,* trans. Wanda Torres Gregory and Yvonne Unna (Albany: State University of New York Press, 2009).

GA 39   *Hölderlins Hymnen "Germanien" und "Der Rhein."* Ed. Susanne Ziegler, 1989, 2d ed. English translation: *Hölderlin's Hymns "Germania" and "The Rhine,"* trans. William McNeill and Julia Ireland (Bloomington: Indiana University Press, 2014).

GA 40   *Einführung in die Metaphysik.* Ed. Petra Jaeger, 1983. English translation: *Introduction to Metaphysics,* 2d ed., trans. Gregory Fried and Richard Polt (New Haven: Yale University Press, 2014).

GA 42   *Schelling: Vom Wesen der menschlichen Freiheit.* Ed. Ingrid Schüßler, 1988. English translation: *Schelling's Treatise on*

the Essence of Human Freedom, trans. Joan Stambaugh
(Athens: Ohio University Press, 1985).

GA 47   *Nietzsches Lehre vom Willen zur Macht als Erkenntnis.* Ed.
Eberhard Hanser, 1989.

GA 53   *Hölderlins Hymne "Der Ister."* Ed. Walter Biemel, 1993, 2d ed.
English translation: *Hölderlin's Hymn "The Ister,"* trans.
William McNeill and Julia Davis (Bloomington: Indiana
University Press, 1996).

GA 54   *Parmenides.* Ed. Manfred S. Frings, 1992, 2d ed. English
translation: *Parmenides,* trans. André Schuwer and
Richard Rojcewicz (Bloomington: Indiana University
Press, 1992).

GA 56/57   *Zur Bestimmung der Philosophie.* Ed. Bernd Heimbüchel,
1999, 2d ed. English translation: *Towards the Definition
of Philosophy,* trans. Ted Sadler (New York: Continuum,
2008).

GA 60   *Phänomenologie des religiösen Lebens.* Ed. Claudius Strube,
1995. English translation: *The Phenomenology of
Religious Life,* trans. Matthias Fritsch and Jennifer Anna
Gosetti-Ferencei (Bloomington: Indiana University
Press, 2004).

GA 65   *Beiträge zur Philosophie (Vom Ereignis).* Ed. Friedrich-
Wilhelm von Herrmann, 1994, 2d ed. English
translation: *Contributions to Philosophy (Of the Event),*
trans. Richard Rojcewicz and Daniela Vallega-Neu
(Bloomington: Indiana University Press, 2012).

GA 66   *Besinnung.* Ed. Friedrich-Wilhelm von Herrmann, 1997.
English translation: *Mindfulness,* trans. Parvis Emad and
Thomas Kalary (New York: Continuum, 2006).

GA 67   *Metaphysik und Nihilismus.* Ed. Hans-Joachim Friedrich, 1999.

GA 69   *Die Geschichte des Seyns.* Ed. Peter Trawny. 1998, English
translation: *The History of Beyng,* trans. Jeffrey Powell
and William McNeill (Bloomington: Indiana University
Press, 2015).

GA 77   *Feldweg-Gespräche.* Ed. Ingrid Schüßler, 1995. English
translation: *Country Path Conversations,* trans. Bret W.
Davis (Bloomington: Indiana University Press, 2010).

GA 79   *Bremer und Freiburger Vorträge.* Ed. Petra Jaeger, 1994.
          English translation: *Bremen and Freiburg Lectures:*
          Insight Into That Which Is and Basic Principles of
          Thinking, trans. Andrew J. Mitchell (Bloomington:
          Indiana University Press, 2012).

GA 94   *Überlegungen II–VI.* Ed. Peter Trawny, 2014.

GA 95   *Überlegungen VII–XI.* Ed. Peter Trawny, 2014.

GA 96   *Überlegungen XII–XV.* Ed. Peter Trawny, 2014.

GA 97   *Anmerkungen I–V.* Ed. Peter Trawny, 2015.

MARTIN HEIDEGGER IN SINGLE EDITIONS

NHS   "Über Wesen und Begriff von Natur, Geschichte und Staat,"
          in *Heidegger-Jahrbuch 4: Heidegger und der*
          Nazionalsozialismus: Dokumente, ed. Alfred Denker and
          Holger Zaborowski (Freiburg: Karl Alber, 2009), 53–88.
          English translation: *Nature, History, State 1933–1934,*
          trans. Gregory Fried and Richard Polt (New York:
          Bloomsbury, 2013).

SZ   *Sein und Zeit,* 17th ed. (Tübingen: Max Niemeyer, 1993).

WDR   "Wilhelm Diltheys Forschungsarbeit und der gegenwärtige
          Kampf um eine historische Weltanschauung," *Dilthey*
          Jahrbuch 8 (1992–93): 143–80. English translation:
          "Wilhelm Dilthey's Research and the Current Struggle
          for a Historical Worldview," in Theodor Kisiel and
          Thomas Sheehan, eds., *Becoming Heidegger: On the Trail*
          of His Early Occasional Writings, 1910–1927, 238–74
          (Evanston: Northwestern University Press, 2007).

ZS   *Zollikoner Seminare: Protokolle, Zwiegespräche, Briefe,* ed.
          Medard Boss (Frankfurt: Vittorio Klostermann, 1987).
          English translation: *Zollikon Seminars: Protocols—*
          Seminars—Letters, trans. Franz Mayr and Richard Askay
          (Evanston: Northwestern University Press, 2001).

MARTIN HEIDEGGER IN OTHER ENGLISH TRANSLATIONS

EL   Martin Heidegger and Herbert Marcuse, "An Exchange of Letters," trans. Richard Wolin, *New German Critique* 53 (1991): 28–32. German original: *GA* 16:430–31.

EP   *The End of Philosophy,* trans. Joan Stambaugh (New York: Harper and Row, 1973).

HMT   *Heidegger: The Man and the Thinker,* ed. Thomas Sheehan, trans. various (New Brunswick, NJ: Transaction, 2010).

MHNS   *Martin Heidegger and National Socialism: Questions and Answers,* ed. Günther Neske and Emil Kettering, intro. Karsten Harries, trans. Lisa Harries (New York: Paragon House, 1990).

N1   *Nietzsche: The Will to Power as Art,* in *Nietzsche,* vols. 1–2, ed. and trans. David Farrell Krell (San Francisco: Harper and Row, 1991).

PLT   *Poetry, Language, Thought,* trans. Albert Hofstadter (New York: Harper and Row, 2001).

QCT   *The Question Concerning Technology and Other Essays,* trans. William Lovitt (New York: Harper and Row, 1977).

EDITORS' INTRODUCTION

I n March of 2014 the first three volumes of Heidegger's *Black Notebooks* were published amid international controversy. These black oilcloth notebooks were kept privately by Heidegger from 1930 into the 1970s. Heidegger himself arranged for them to be published last of all in his *Gesamtausgabe* (Collected Edition). The first three volumes, entitled *Considerations*, were soon followed by a fourth volume, entitled *Remarks*. These four volumes comprise the notebooks Heidegger kept during the war years, and their publication is provoking an international reappraisal of Heidegger. For what these volumes from the war years reveal is something never before seen in Heidegger's published writings: anti-Semitic content cast in the terms of his, anti-Semitism within his very thinking of the history of being.

Anti-Semitism is an attitude or pattern of behavior that is directed against Jews, sprung from rumor, prejudice, and pseudoscientific sources (whether from race theory or simply racist), functioning affectively and/or administratively, and leading to a) defamation; b) universal vilification; c) isolation: professional prohibitions, ghettoes, camps; d) expulsion: emigration; e) annihilation: pogroms, mass executions, death camps. Additionally, today, we also deem anti-Semitic anything that is supposed to characterize the Jew as "Jew."[1] In short: anti-Semitism is "the expression of hostility and hatred against Jews."[2]

The controversy surrounding the *Black Notebooks* was thus of a new kind. Previous revelations brought the depths of Heidegger's involvement with National Socialism (Farías) to light. Further attempts to read his Nazism back into *Being and Time*, however, proved speculative at best. Next came the issue of unpublished seminars from Heidegger's time as rector (Faye). These were supposedly so damning as to never be published. Arguments on their basis, however, were undermined by deceptive scholarship. More, the seminars have all been published, as scheduled, and readers are free to assess such claims for themselves. In the wake of these, we were simply left with the fact that Heidegger was a member of the NSDAP.

But even granting this fact, however short or long one wishes to make it, one aspect of the National Socialist milieu was still missing from Heidegger, that of anti-Semitism. To be sure, a letter from 1934 exists where Heidegger remarks in passing about "the Jew Fränkel," subsequently published letters to his wife find him commenting on the "Jewification" of German culture in 1916.[3] But for a National Socialist, this did not seem like much. Such comments were easy to dismiss as reflecting entirely on the man Martin Heidegger. They were not philosophical utterances, properly speaking, but offhand moments in private communications. One could still argue that the philosophy was untouched.

With the *Black Notebooks* things are different. Now for the first time we find anti-Semitic remarks: not concerning particular individuals in Heidegger's professional memoranda, nor in private, youthful letters to his wife, but as written into his mature thinking of the 1930s. During these years, Heidegger's thinking undergoes a shift (a "turn") whereby history (*Geschichte*) assumes an increased ontological importance. Being itself is thought as something "given" or "sent" to us, something that we receive only in part. These various dispensations of being make up the epochs of an ontological history. Heidegger's name for this is the "history of beyng" (taking recourse to an outmoded spelling so as to call attention to this new understanding) and the approach to thinking concomitant with it, "beyng-historical thinking." The text that inaugurates this period in Heidegger's thought where the history of beyng comes to the fore is the posthumously published work, *Contributions to Philosophy (Of the Event)*, composed between 1936–38.

The *Contributions* concern themselves, in part, with a new "narrative" for Heidegger's thinking after the abandonment of the project of *Being and*

Time or "fundamental ontology" more generally. The *Contributions* present the history of philosophy as a metaphysical tradition in need of an overcoming. Heidegger now speaks about the "first beginning" of metaphysics, the inauguration of Western philosophy as we know it, and of the "other beginning," which concerns the advent of a nonmetaphysical thinking of difference. The parts in this narrative, however, Heidegger assigns nationally. It was the ancient Greeks who were the people of the first beginning. The metaphysical tradition they inaugurated has played itself out and now stands ready for an overcoming on the part of that philosophical and poetic people, the Germans. To be sure, Germanic Hellenism is a well-worn tradition, but Heidegger goes a step further in that he fleshes out the international landscape in greater detail. As we know from the *Introduction to Metaphysics* of 1935, Heidegger felt Germany to be caught in a pincer grip between Russia and America. Since this book's 1953 publication, such was the general cast of the narrative: Greeks at the first beginning, Germans struggling against Russians and Americans for the other beginning. The *Black Notebooks* now add a new antagonist to the mix, the Jews.

Russian and American are both national identifiers, but "the Jew" is not. Heidegger sees the Jews as elements of what he terms "world Judaism" (*Weltjudentum*).[4] In the *Contributions* Heidegger presented "machination" as responsible for the objectification of contemporary life and the predominance of lived experience. In the *Black Notebooks* the agent of machination (or is it not the other way around?) is world Judaism. World Judaism is understood to be at war with National Socialism. Heidegger sees this as a kind of metaphysical opposition, a war between two opponents who have created each other so as to continue the battle. Rather than this "vulgar" National Socialism locked in conflict with world Judaism, Heidegger vows allegiance to what he calls "spiritual National Socialism."

Given this worry over world Judaism, we can identify (at least) three kinds of anti-Semitism operative in the remarks on Jews within the *Black Notebooks*:

1.   the idea that Jews would be purely calculative in their thinking. This hackneyed stereotype shows itself in all its ugliness when Heidegger attaches philosophical criticisms of his teacher Husserl to the fact that Husserl was Jewish. As a Jew, Husserl would necessarily think calculatively and thus be excluded from "the region of essential decisions" (*GA* 96:46).

2.   the idea that Jews live by a principle of race. This is a keystone of Heidegger's thinking of Judaism, that the Jews would be just as racist as the National Socialists. On this basis, Heidegger comes to think world Judaism and the National Socialists as somehow united in a metaphysical opposition seeking each other's annihilation.

3.   that Jews would be relentlessly devoted to the task of uprooting all beings from being. The stereotype of the wandering Jew here reaches ontological proportions, spreading their own homelessness to all they encounter in an ontological uprooting of beings from being. The Jews become agents of, if not equivalent to, the ontological process of machination (*Machenschaft*), the objectification of all that is.[5]

In the wake of the *Black Notebooks'* publication, one question has leapt to the fore: to what extent are these anti-Semitic statements integral to Heidegger's thinking? The question is difficult to answer. The remarks are found in notebooks whose status within Heidegger's oeuvre is rather curious. These are private notebooks never published during his lifetime. Indeed, they were meant to be published last in his *Gesamtausgabe*, and kept under close protection until then.[6] The *Notebooks* also make greater reference to current events than anything else we have from him. But while the *Black Notebooks* are unlike Heidegger's other writings, this does not mean they are entirely divorced from them or from the thinking that publicly presented itself in those pages. It is worth recalling that the *Contributions* are filled with references to the *Black Notebooks* (to *Considerations* II–VIII). Further, when Heidegger surveys his own authorship in the 1937–38 text "The Wish and the Will (On Preserving What Is Attempted)" and presents his own list of the key materials on hand, he includes, alongside the various lecture courses, seminar notes, and individual lectures that he lists, some of the *Considerations* from the *Black Notebooks* (GA 66:420/371). It seems that Heidegger considered them groupable with the selected best of his philosophical authorship.

While the status of the *Notebooks* has not been settled, this has not proved an obstacle to judgments about them. Two vociferous camps have emerged in response to the question of how integral anti-Semitism is to Heideggerian thought, those who exonerate and those who condemn.

One of the typical strategies of those who would exonerate Heidegger is a quantitative argument. Taken together, all the remarks about Jews and

Judaism in the *Black Notebooks* make up no more than a handful of pages in the eighteen hundred pages of *Notebooks* published thus far. The argument then is that mountains are being made of molehills. A few scattered remarks do not undermine the overwhelming amount of thought and work expressing no such anti-Semitic sentiments (or even any concern about Jews) at all. There are simply too few such remarks to be of any importance in assessing Heidegger on the whole.

The quantitative argument is often tied to a second exoneration strategy, that of the difference between the philosopher and the man. The limited number of remarks regarding Jews are attributed to the personal opinions of Heidegger the man; they are independent of the thinking of Heidegger the philosopher. They are the lamentable, though understandable, failings of a man to escape the prejudices of his times.

Both these approaches are thoroughly flawed, however. Even apart from the sorites paradox of just how many remarks it would take to render a text or author anti-Semitic, regarding the quantitative argument we might first ask what constitutes an "anti-Semitic" remark? How do we delimit such a thing? One of the more infamous statements in the *Black Notebooks* comes as the ninth point in a ten point list: "9. World Judaism, spurred on by the emigrants let out of Germany, is everywhere elusive. In all the unfurling of its power, it need nowhere engage in military actions, whereas it remains for us to sacrifice the best blood of the best of our own people" (GA 96:262). Does this mean only the ninth point would be anti-Semitic, or is the whole list not anti-Semitic? The individual points situate themselves within larger contexts, to isolate the exact words as anti-Semitic is to overlook the enabling conditions for such remarks, the contexts, and even the manner of thinking itself. In a text, no statement stands alone, but is made possible by the surrounding context. And what of cases where no anti-Semitic statements are uttered. Is it possible that one could create the conditions for anti-Semitic remarks, encourage those remarks, but without ever uttering any such remark, and nonetheless still be found anti-Semitic?

With regard to the remarks concerning only the man Heidegger and not the thinking, such a distinction is difficult to maintain. To be sure, it is Heidegger himself who assures us that the biography of a philosopher (or poet) is not important for understanding that philosophy (in philosophy: "our only interest is that he was born at a certain time, that he worked, and that he died"; in poetry: "The poem was written by Georg Trakl. Who the author is remains unimportant here" *GA* 18:5/4; *GA* 12:15/PLT 193). But as far as the *Black Notebooks* are concerned, we are not dealing with biographical details, but with genuine philosophical texts. The *Black Notebooks* are part of the *Gesamtausgabe*, a carefully curated presentation of Heidegger the thinker. They are found in the fourth division of the *Gesamtausgabe*, a division titled "Indications and Sketches" (*Hinweise und Aufzeichnungen*), which contains seven thick volumes of seminar notes and the nine volumes of the *Black Notebooks*.

A text from the mid-1970s, *The Legacy of the Question of Being*, reflects on the *Gesamtausgabe* as a whole and specifically the fourth division in a section titled "A Dangerous Error."[7] Regarding the title of the fourth division, Heidegger explains that "here one expects, according to the common conception, incidental notes, loose sheets, if not even 'materials' for a supposed 'work' to be completed as a continuous text. One thereby forgets that across the entire edition [*Ausgabe*] it is everywhere a matter of only a 'path' [*Weg*], indeed only a trail and footbridge to the field of this path of the one question of being."[8] The fourth division of the *Gesamtausgabe*, i.e., the *Black Notebooks*, are part of the path pursuing that one question. Even more, the fourth division is understood as a kind of distillate of that path: "division 4 attempts to present what is decisive along the path that has been granted for decades."[9] It is hard to believe that Heidegger has his seminars in mind here, rather than the notebooks. To say that the *Black Notebooks* concern the man and not the thinking, or are even incidental to Heidegger's thinking as such, would be deeply mistaken. To view the fourth division as a set of fixed results rather than a path (and to then attribute these results to the man or exclude them from the path of Heidegger's lifelong thinking) would be "the greatest possible distortion of the arrangement of the Collected Edition [*Gesamtausgabe*]."[10] The *Black Notebooks* do not allow themselves to be so easily dismissed.

The second camp responding to the *Black Notebooks* has largely used them as confirmation of their condemnation of Heidegger as a lifelong anti-Semite. This condemnatory stance is as much a failure to read Heidegger as that of his exonerators. The *Black Notebooks* show that during the war years, in private notebooks, Heidegger expressed anti-Semitic positions in the language of his philosophical thinking of the time. There are no records of anti-Semitic views expressed by Heidegger after the war, in the subsequent *Black Notebooks* or elsewhere. Does the absence of such utterances prove the absence of the prejudice? Of course not. But it does not confirm its existence, either. This is not to say that there is no anti-Semitism where unexpressed, something with which the condemners would surely agree. Anti-Semitism can still be operative even without being fully present in incriminating statements. But to claim that this potential for anti-Semitism is the same as overt anti-Semitism is intellectually lazy at best. The specter of anti-Semitism simply demands our greater vigilance.

None of the published writings express overtly anti-Semitic views. But the being-historical treatises, *Contributions* and the like, in light of the *Black Notebooks*, are susceptible to being developed in anti-Semitic directions. That anti-Semitic viewpoints can be grafted onto a philosophy does not make that philosophy itself anti-Semitic, much less what follows from that philosophy (to say nothing of the thoughts of that philosopher twenty years later). This tells us more about the nature of anti-Semitism than it does about Heidegger.

When anti-Semitism is capable of being found anywhere, even where no overt marker of it exists, then anti-Semitism is no longer something that can be evaluated in terms of its presence or absence within a text. Perhaps there is no text that can resist an anti-Semitic appropriation (or interpretation) and this is just a fact about texts. But what follows from this is that a response to anti-Semitism that seeks to identify whether a certain text *is or is not* anti-Semitic is doomed from the start. Whatever its "results," it will miss just what it seeks, misrecognizing its victim as either uncontestably honorable or irretrievably evil. Accordingly, the problem of anti-Semitism is bigger than any particular anti-Semites. It becomes a question of nonpresence and the proper relation to this.

What is called for is a response similar to that which Derrida offers in regard to Heidegger's reading of Nietzsche, where the issue is not to defend against these kinds of charges but to strategically surrender to them so that this relation might emerge: "Therefore, rather than protect Nietzsche from the Heideggerian reading, we should perhaps offer him up to it completely, underwriting that interpretation without reserve; in a *certain way* and up to the point where, the content of the Nietzschean discourse being almost lost for the question of being, its form regains its absolute strangeness, where his text finally invokes a different type of reading, more faithful to his type of writing."[11]

In our terms, rather than protect Heidegger from the condemnatory anti-Semitic reading, we should instead "offer him up to it completely" so as to allow the strangeness of the *Black Notebooks* and the decades of work that follow to be heard. This is not exoneration so much as a crucible to see what is capable of withstanding or resisting the anti-Semitic interpretation as well as what is not. For we are here speaking of someone whose thinking transformed the twentieth and twenty-first centuries of thought and scholarship within philosophy and beyond. If *he* is to be an anti-Semite, then let us be sure we understand *him*. Heidegger's thinking is the key to his anti-Semitism and to getting beyond it, properly understood.

Obviously, the two positions outlined in the foregoing are extremes, split along an axis of all or nothing, entirely anti-Semitic from start to finish or absolved of all failings. In a sense these are comfortable positions, unambiguous and self-assured. They hardly require the difficult work of textual analysis and interpretation. They seek to end all discussion of Heidegger's anti-Semitism by resolving the issue one way or the other. All such resolutions are at the same time calls to cease thinking.

But what if thoughtful reading did not work in this way? What if it were *unethical* to conclude? Concluding one way or the other does away with our responsibility to investigate and think. If this means that final conclusions (much less final solutions) can never be reached, then so be it. Positions are always revisable. This is the world we inhabit, an ambiguous world never wholly exonerated nor condemned. Such are the only conditions in which responsibility makes any sense. The all-or-nothing logic promulgated by exonerators and condemners alike is exactly analogous to Heidegger's own "being-historical Manichaeism," in accordance with which Heidegger considered the history of being to pose a choice between *either* the unworld of machination (and with it world Judaism and with it [vulgar] National Socialism) *or* the new beginning, a preservation of beings in beyng (vs. machinational uprooting).[12]

Perhaps Heidegger's failing was to embrace a metaphysical antagonism where his thinking otherwise was always able to discover paths of relation and difference that avoided stark opposition. In any event, Heidegger's anti-Semitic statements are contemporaneous with his assumption of just such a being-historical Manichaeism. The paradox is that, if anti-Semitism is tied to this oppositional construction in Heidegger's thinking, then the best defense against such a construction *is Heideggerian thought itself.*

If Heidegger's anti-Semitism is indeed tied to his being-historical Manichaeism, then it is tied to a position operating with an oppositional logic (the insistence on a decision between being vs. beings), which is to say that Heidegger's anti-Semitism is tied to a *metaphysical* position. To overcome this anti-Semitism, then, will require overcoming metaphysics. But this is precisely what Heidegger has taught us. It is Heidegger himself who showed that an overcoming of metaphysics is no inversion of the same, nor a renunciation of metaphysics in the name of a "new" beginning, but instead a conversion (*Verwindung*) from metaphysics into a sense of non-oppositional difference (broadly speaking). Heidegger's anti-Semitism cannot be beaten by insisting on one side or the other (exonerate or condemn), rather the nature of that anti-Semitism itself is only properly addressed by a "converted" (*verwunden*) thinking. From this perspective, Heidegger's anti-Semitism would be part of the metaphysical tradition, one perhaps even unbeknownst to him, that would have to be overcome. And it is only from this nonmetaphysical perspective that we can adequately address *Heidegger's* anti-Semitism.

But once we accept this, then we also accept never being able to be done with the question of Heidegger's anti-Semitism; we agree to remain alert to its traces even where no overt marker exists. For if this anti-Semitism is tied to metaphysics, and conversion (*Verwindung*) is no simple doing away with metaphysics, then there will be an ineradicable anti-Semitic remainder, the remainder of metaphysics, that we will never be able to discount or dismiss—indeed, it is a remainder we shall even have to protect and keep from getting lost, once the initial rush over the *Black Notebooks* has subsided.

This is something distinct from either exonerating or condemning. It is to continue thinking and reading, interpreting and responding. It is a way of holding Heidegger up to the mirror of his own thought. It is, to quote Habermas, "to think with Heidegger against Heidegger."[13]

The majority of the papers gathered here are from the Emory University conference on the *Black Notebooks* held in September of 2014, the first such conference in the U.S.[14] Essays by Hans Ulrich Gumbrecht and Slavoj Žižek were added later. The intention of the conference was to bring together a variety of viewpoints on the issue from across disciplines. Roughly speaking, the first group of articles deals with topics within the *Black Notebooks* and their operative contexts, the second group focuses on issues in assessment more broadly.

Our volume begins with a new essay by Peter Trawny, "The Universal and Annihilation: Heidegger's Being-Historical Anti-Semitism," taking up one of the most disturbing motifs in the *Black Notebooks*, the idea of "annihilation," more specifically "self-annihilation," more specifically still, the notion of a "Jewish" self-annihilation.

Historical background on the nature of Heidegger's anti-Semitism is provided by Sander Gilman in his "Cosmopolitan Jews vs. Jewish Nomads: Sources of a Trope in Heidegger's *Black Notebooks.*" Gilman situates Heidegger's claims of "worldless" anti-Semitism in a long tradition of anti-Semitic German worries over cosmopolitanism. The idea of worldlessness expressed here is likewise at the center of Eduardo Mendieta's essay, "Metaphysical Anti-Semitism and Worldlessness: On World Poorness, World Forming, and World Destroying," where Mendieta concludes that Heidegger's onto-poetic-geopolitical anti-Semitism leads to a bestialization of the Jew. Bettina Bergo's essay, " 'Sterben Sie?': The Problem of Dasein and 'Animals' . . . of Various Kinds," delves further into this bestialization by examining Heidegger's changing views on animals and, more specifically, the difference between animals and Dasein. Bergo does so against the background of the National Socialist biology of the time.

Heidegger's anti-Semitism is entangled with his views on modernity, including the influence of Marx and the importance of technology. Richard Polt's essay, "Inception, Downfall, and the Broken World: Heidegger Above the Sea of Fog," focuses on the way in which Heidegger's notion of a "first beginning" of metaphysics likewise entails a "downfall" (*Untergang*), which Heidegger understands as "modernity." Heidegger first viewed National Socialism as a possible escape from this downfall, only to become increasingly critical of the ideology. Michael Marder's contribution, "The Other 'Jewish Question,'" reads Heidegger against Marx's famed 1843 text "On the Jewish Question." Where Marx proffered emancipation from religion, Heidegger sees only a Jewish solution to a Jewish problem. Marder points out how, for all his emphasis on questioning, Heidegger fails to question his conception of Jews and Judaism. Martin Gessmann, in his "Heidegger and National Socialism: He Meant What

He Said," examines the critique of *Being and Time* in the *Black Notebooks* as well as the paths leading from *Being and Time* to the anti-Semitism of the *Notebooks,* specifically through a growing worry over technology. He argues that a new shift in technology is afoot and that our reading of Heidegger will have to contend with this.

With the publication of the *Black Notebooks,* how does our conception of Heidegger and relation to his thinking change? Our volume concludes with reflections on this question. Hans Ulrich Gumbrecht's "'The Supreme Will of the People': What Do Heidegger's *Black Notebooks* Reveal?" argues that the *Notebooks* indeed confirm all our worst fears about Heidegger, but they also show something perhaps equally distressing, Heidegger's banality. Peter E. Gordon's "Prolegomena to Any Future Destruction of Metaphysics: Heidegger and the *Schwarze Hefte*" takes up the issue of how to read Heidegger in light of the *Notebooks.* Where Heidegger called for a destruction of the history of metaphysics, Gordon calls for a destruction of Heidegger. Heidegger's work then becomes a "field of ruins" where we are free to critically appropriate his insights while remaining aware of the prejudices connected to them. Tom Rockmore, in "Heidegger After Trawny: Philosophy or Worldview?," examines Trawny's diagnosis of Heidegger's being-historical anti-Semitism in order to argue for anti-Semitism throughout Heidegger's entire career. His "philosophy" is ultimately inextricable from such a biased "worldview." Robert Bernasconi, in "Another Eisenmenger? On the Alleged Originality of Heidegger's Anti-Semitism," argues that Heidegger's anti-Semitism is not a new "being-historical" strain, but the standard, traditional variety. He lobbies for a more careful reading of Heidegger and his racism, rather than simple dismissal, emphasizing our obligation to confront the prejudices of the history of philosophy rather than to ignore them or denounce them from a position of presumed moral superiority. Last, in "The Persistence of Ontological Difference," Slavoj Žižek argues that Heidegger's greatness lies in the openings he provides for rethinking materialism, suggesting that the import of this adherence politically outweighs anything we find in the *Black Notebooks.*

HEIDEGGER'S *BLACK NOTEBOOKS*

1

THE UNIVERSAL AND ANNIHILATION

Heidegger's Being-Historical Anti-Semitism

PETER TRAWNY

TRANSLATED BY IAN ALEXANDER MOORE

AND CHRISTOPHER TURNER

U niversal topography—a virtual landscape, formed by universal features, unfolded in universal terms. Production and transport, information and value are conditions of this universal space, where people can act without the particular restraints of nationality, race, or sex. There is no universal topography without democratic ideas of basic equality, rationality, and transparency. It is manifest in universal institutions: the UN with its base in New York, for example, is a necessary institution of universal topography.

Heidegger's *Black Notebooks* appear to testify to the genesis of this universal topography. It is a genesis from out of a difficult confrontation, if not a battle. For we are familiar with the topography of Heidegger's thinking, a narrative topography that moves along the places of philosophy and poetry: "Greece," "Germany," and the "Ister," the Danube, that connects them. Yet Heidegger's topography is more refined. For example, when he speaks of the "*birth*land of the upper Donau-valley," which he distinguishes from the "clamorous Allemani" (*GA* 96:199–200). Or when, in contrast to "Europe," there appears the "West" or "Evening-Land" (*Abend-Land*) (*GA* 94:273).

This topography is enlarged in the *Black Notebooks* by many other places—or should I say, rather, nations, powers, imperia?—first of all

"Russia," the country on the side of the "Germans," which is to be distinguished from the Soviet Union, i.e., from "Bolshevism," just as "Germany" is to be distinguished from "National Socialism." Then "America," as heir to "England," a power that is interpreted in explicitly being-historical terms. "France," too, appears on the side of "England," i.e., as an enemy in the battles of the Second World War. Even the "Asiatic" is named, impartially alongside *Chinesentum* or "Chinese-dom," "chinoiserie," which at the time was a commonplace defamation that saw in China merely a land of massive exploitation. And likewise "Judaism," "Jewry," and "world Judaism."

During the Second World War, which is perhaps actually only a continuation of the first, this topography is brought into a specific order, not to say a specific battle formation (τάξις). On the one side, the agents of so-called machination: America, England, Bolshevism (communism understood in being-historical terms), and Judaism (also Christendom); on the other side, the places of the "beginning": Greece, Germany, and Russia. The topography splits into the representatives of a narrative topography (Greece—Germany—Russia) and those of a universal topography (Rome—America—England—Judaism). Both topographies are irreconcilably opposed to one another, for where there is a universal topography there can be no narrative.

The topographic order is determined in two ways. On the one hand, we can recognize in this arrangement the front lines of the war. In the *Überlegungen* (*Considerations*), written between 1938 and 1941, Heidegger attentively follows what is happening in the war. He is interested in the "'historiographic' incidents" (*GA* 96:261). On the other hand, the topography proves to be a staging of the drama of the history of being. The front lines are inscribed into a narrative in which the "beginning" and the "end" form the two most important dimensions. The beginning is ascribed to German thinking and poetizing—always with recourse to the pre-Socratic Greeks—while the end is ascribed to the powers of machination.

To put it differently: the topographic order of the history of being forms a border, a front, on which the places of the "beginning" are opposed to the places of the "end." To put it still differently: the topographic order in Heidegger's thinking around the Second World War puts topography itself on the line, the possibility of a topography that speaks of "another beginning" and/or an "annihilation" and "self-annihilation," a beginning and an end of "place" and "locality" themselves. I could thus say: the beginning is place itself, the end (in the sense of *Verendung*, "coming to an end," "perishing"), the annihilation of place. The annihilation consists in nothing other than in a *universal* that transforms the "places" of the world into what Marc Augé has called "non-places."[1]

Yet already here, at the beginning of my lecture, in which I only just presented my thesis, namely, that in Heidegger there is a front between "place" and the "universal," I must raise an objection against myself. In Heidegger there is no concept of the universal as I am using it here. By universal, I understand an unconditionally valid field of meanings. If, for example, we take Plato's idea of the good, we can understand that the idea of the good holds not only in Greece or in Germany, thus not only in a specific topography but also in every possible topography—indeed perhaps even beyond the topographical as such. The human being distinguishes the good from the bad, regardless of where or when (I am intentionally expressing myself somewhat vaguely). Heidegger, however, appears to understand something different by the term *universal*, as we shall see.

A meaning is universal when it is understood always and everywhere. The universal is accordingly a meaning that holds independently of a particular language, independently of a particular history, independently even of social conditions. The meanings of mathematics, technology, and that is also to say of science, and possibly even the meaning of capital, are all universal. Nature, too, is universal. And yet the meaning of the distinction between good and bad, the meaning of freedom (in various senses), even the meaning of love, are all universal as well. The body and gender could also be universal.

My thesis is that, among these universals, Heidegger recognizes only that of mathematics and science, i.e., technology. Indeed, at bottom, he did not even recognize this as a universal, but rather thought of it as a "destining" of beyng. He thus inscribed into the front, between beginning and end, that between "place" and "nonplace," between "home" and "homelessness." And machination appeared as the "principle of destruction," which—as calculation, technology, and perhaps even capital—makes every form of particular localization impossible.

There is only a front where war prevails. Yet even as regards war, and especially the Second World War, we must keep that double determination between a "historiographic" and a "being-historical" interpretation constantly in view. On the historiographic level, in the relation between beginning and end, at issue are "decisions" and a "destruction," indeed "a devastation, whose domination can no longer be infringed on by the catastrophes of war and the wars of catastrophe," yet, and this for me is more important, this "can be witnessed" (*GA* 96:45). War—construed "being-historically"—is no longer military conflict, but rather the attestation of a "decision" whereby "all become slaves of the history of beyng" (*GA* 96:141). War is thus no longer a matter of military victors and vanquished.

War attests to the following "being-historical" occurrence: "[By means of machination] *all* imperialism, *collectively*, and that is to say in all its mutual escalation and friction, is driven to a *consummate completion* [*Vollendung*] *of technology*. Its final act will be the earth blowing itself up and current humanity disappearing. Which is no misfortune, but rather the first purification *of being* from its deepest deformation by the predominance of beings" (*GA* 96:238). The war of the "imperia" is testament to a "consummate completion of technology," that is, in my view, testament to an inevitable implementation of the universals of technology, science, and capital. According to Heidegger, however, this must stage itself in a war that takes place precisely as a "first purification *of being*," i.e., as the "annihilation" of "current humanity." The earth that blows itself up becomes the earth of a being-historical "decision" in which *either* the end of the first beginning—an end that is clearly thought by Heidegger in different ways— is able to take place as the end of "inceptuality" in general *or* the "other beginning" of "another history" is able to take place. In short, the history of being proves to be an *apocalyptic reduction*—such that, in the end, where annihilation shows itself, we will discover whether there shall be merely an end . . . or yet another beginning.

The apocalyptic reduction is not a transcendental but a historical (*geschichtlich*) reduction; its "subject" is the history of being itself. In the context of this narrative the apocalyptic reduction reveals what for a long time was concealed: the possibility of a history beyond the significations of metaphysics. In this sense the unique "event of appropriation" (*Ereignis*) is in itself the apocalyptical reduction.

In the first section, I will attend to the question concerning the universal in Heidegger's thought, though, as previously mentioned, Heidegger never thought of this as a "universal," even in the medieval sense of the term (as *universalia*). In the second, I show how, within the universal itself,

Heidegger caught sight of a "being-historical" potential for annihilation that threatened not only the beginning and the inceptual but Heidegger's own thinking as well.

——— ∞∞∞ ———

Heidegger was never so close to the philosophical concept of universality as around the time he published *Being and Time*. Heidegger speaks programmatically of a "universal ontology," that is, of an "absolute science," as a *"transcendental science"* (*GA* 24:16/12, 15/11, 23/17). At this time Heidegger more or less identifies "universal" with "transcendental." The transcendental here is of course neither that of Kant nor Husserl. Instead, transcendental science has the task of grasping the "transcendence" of Dasein. Already in *Being and Time* Heidegger had characterized "being" itself as "the *transcendens* pure and simple" (*GA* 2:51/*SZ* 38).

Transcendence as a "surpassing" ("On the Essence of Ground," *GA* 9:137/107) toward the specific "freedom" of Dasein—this transcendence was thought in the later lecture courses of the 1920s in terms of Plato (possibly under the influence of Paul Natorp's 1903 book *Plato's Theory of Ideas*).[2] Thus Heidegger at one point says: "What we are seeking is the ἐπέκεινα τῆς οὐσίας," that which is "beyond being" (*GA* 24:404/285)—a noteworthy formulation, because it shows—perhaps uniquely in its own way—that the philosopher had come closer to a Platonic understanding of the universal. It is worth noting that here he entered a vicinity that will continue to occupy us: the vicinity of a philosopher who, precisely in stark contrast to him, spoke of an *Autrement qu'être ou au-delà de l'essence*, someone for whom—in strong contrast to Heidegger—Platonism and Neoplatonism harbored a persistent attraction.[3] I am speaking, of course, of Emmanuel Levinas.

Within the sphere of Heidegger's thinking, a universal ontology must be able to transcend the realm of the ontic. Beings must be able to be abandoned in a "surpassing" toward being. In this sense, only being can be universal. It is precisely this thought, however, that Heidegger employs differently in the history of being. "Being" is reserved topographically for the Greeks and Germans; it is, so to speak, dispersed into the narrative of the history of being. In contrast, beings—as pursued solely and exclusively by machination—become "universal" quantities.

This can be seen above all in the *Anmerkungen* or *Remarks*, the *Black Notebooks* that were written in large part after the war. Now—and is this an accident?—Heidegger begins to meditate on the concept of the universal. Yet the result of this meditation more or less confirms the interpretation we have just proposed.

There is a universal that unfolds in the modern era on the basis of the "rationality" of the "mathesis universalis," which consequently "solidifies" as "'technology'" (*GA* 97:42). When this "process" becomes "universal on a planetary scale," it eliminates "every sort of exit from its course." It is "on the whole, without ground or prospect, to become once again the point of departure for a change into something else" (*GA* 97:42). "Here," Heidegger says, is "the mere complete ending," i.e., the uninterrupted continuation of the end. Consequently, Heidegger considers the universal—that field of general meanings that holds for every human as human—to be a hindrance of the beginning, indeed, to be the impossibility of inceptuality itself.

Yet even this meaning of the universal, which Heidegger ascribes solely to "'technology,'" i.e., to "machination," is called into question. An "agent" who "expands his horizon and even [makes it] universal," posits "in absolute terms only the inevitable relativity of his own horizon of action" (*GA* 97:8). Even in universality the radically finite thinking of finitude catches sight of something merely relative. Now it may be that Plato thought the universal in the ideas, nevertheless Plato remains a philosopher who, under the conditions of his finitude, became the witness to a finite theory. But let us be careful. Heidegger speaks of an "agent." The subtext is clear: it is the Allies, chiefly the "Americans," who, with their assertion of a universal meaning of "justice," appear to be representatives of a universal topography, who only factically, i.e., with the might (*Gewalt*) of the victor, establish universal validities.

The concept of the universal is therefore replaced by that of the "international." "'Sciences' are, like technology and as techniques, necessarily international" (*GA* 97:59). Yet there is no "international thinking," "but rather only the universal thinking emerging in the uniquely one" (*GA* 97:60). This thinking, however, "in order to remain close to the origin," is "necessarily a destinal dwelling in the singular homeland and singular people." Time and again one reads: "The uni-versal—[is what] comes from the uniquely one of beyng itself" (*GA* 97:60).

This displacement of the semantic field is interesting, though difficult to interpret. Does Heidegger's program of a "universal ontology" perhaps return here in a modified way? Is not "being" or even "beyng itself" actually the "uniquely one"? Without doubt, Heidegger inscribes the "universal" in this sense (emphasizing its united and unified character) into his "being-historical" topography, insofar as the Germans now become the true representatives of the "uni-versal." Thus we also read: "the respectively singular destinal homeness [*Heimattum*] of rootedness in the soil [*Bodenständigkeit*] is the rootedness [*Verwurzelung*] that alone grants growth into the universal" (*GA* 97:60). Recall that for Heidegger in the 1920s it was already the case that only "being" was the "*transcendens* pure and simple" (*GA* 2:51/SZ 38). Only "being" could appear as a universal.

Thus in Heidegger's juxtaposition of science and technology, on the one hand, as "international" and, on the other hand, thinking as universal, the "ontological difference" appears to return, i.e., the thought that only philosophy can be universal, because it thinks being precisely in the sense of transcendence, while the individual sciences can be assigned to beings, and that now means to the "international." And if the Greeks and the Germans are just about the only ones who know what "thinking" means and what it calls for, then it is only consistent to claim that this "singular people" has an understanding of the "universal."

Yet the displacement of the semantic field (*Bedeutungsfeld*) of the universal is a displacement *in* the meaning of the universal itself. With Heidegger's determination of the "uni-versal" as the "uniquely one of beyng itself"—although and perhaps precisely because Heraclitus and Parmenides (but also, and above all, Plato and Aristotle and a fortiori Plotinus) already thought "being" as the "one" (or at least ascribed the meaning of ἕν to it)—with this determination, all the narrative features of "beyng itself," of the "history of beyng," flow into the universal, so that little to nothing remains of its Platonic institution as a context-independent semantic field. When Heidegger ventures the remark that "poetry too" is "universal," he sacrifices the Platonic determination of the concept of the universal to his own being-historical determination, i.e., as uniquely one of beyng itself in the context of a narrative topography (or, better here, topology).

I return now to Heidegger's thought that modern rationality, with its tendency to unfold on a "planetary, universal scale," passes over into a "mere complete ending" (*GA* 97:42). It was precisely this possibility that, during the war, Heidegger had left open in what we are terming his apocalyptic reduction. It was a matter, then, of the decision between complete ending and the "coming" of the uniquely one of beyng itself. Heidegger's thinking circled around this decision—and one would do well not to ignore the fact that, in this circling, it went utterly astray.

The apocalyptic reduction in Heidegger operates with the concepts of ending, destruction, annihilation (or self-annihilation), and devastation. I would like to distinguish these concepts roughly in the following way: "ending" (*Verendung*) is a persistent relegation of history into an "end," thus a persistent "coming to an end" (*Enden*); "destruction" is the violent alteration of an order, after the "destruction" something still exists, yet it is something that is different from the previous order; "annihilation" is the violent conversion of something into nothing; "devastation" is, like "ending," something that makes any "beginning" impossible, whether this likewise holds for any ending remains undecided.

I will refer, above all, to the concept of "annihilation" (particularly "self-annihilation"), yet also to that of "destruction." But first, within the framework of the apocalyptic reduction, I should explain when and why Heidegger introduced these concepts. In addition, I will also show how they are deployed in the narrative topography mentioned previously—they are deployed on the side of universal topography.

The narrative of the history of being operates, as I said, with the forms of beginning and end. At the end of the first beginning, it is decided whether an other beginning will happen or whether the end will continue, as it were, without end. The end of the first beginning, however, is thought of as the being-historical epoch of universal "machination" (in my sense), i.e., of technology. Machination thereby proves to be an extremely efficient "destining" of beyng. It produces an *immanence* that ultimately no longer contrasts with any transcendence. In the immanence of "machination" there is no longer any outside from which this immanence could be interrupted and thus be opened up onto something different. Heidegger's thought of the "coming" of a "last God" presents the possibility of an opening up of the immanence of "machination" through the interjection of another place.

THE UNIVERSAL AND ANNIHILATION 9

But there is another scenario for depicting the rupture or, rather, collapse of the immanence of "machination." The Second World War, interpreted being-historically as a continuation of the first, appeared as a "total mobilization" (Ernst Jünger) of all the technological means of domination and violence. Never before had there been such an immense "annihilation"—above all among the civilian population. Here Heidegger could quite possibly have in mind the old story about an all-consuming "world conflagration" (which the Stoics knew from Heraclitus), the story of an apocalypse of "being." With this, the immanence of machination could be interrupted from within; *machination would annihilate itself.*

Thus we read at one point: "The highest level of technology is attained when, as consumption, it has nothing left to consume—but itself. In what shape does this self-annihilation come to pass? We should expect it on the basis of the incessant pursuit of the ever 'new' that is inherent to its essence—i.e., increasing consumption" (*GA* 97:18). The self-annihilation of technology in the shape of the Second World War, considered being-historically, should bring about the collapse of machination and thereby reach the decision for the other beginning. The "purification of being" should liberate the world from beings—and this means from existing human beings—in order to allow for "Da-sein." History ends in an apocalyptic reduction. It should become manifest therein how the history of beyng continues on (if it does continue on).

Heidegger deploys the thought of a front between what we are terming a "narrative" topography and a "universal" topography, not so that narrative topography would actually triumph over the universal, but so that the universal would "annihilate itself." Now, the problem begins with the fact that Heidegger—as I have shown—assigns protagonists to both topographies: the world of poetry and of philosophy is inhabited by the "Greeks," the "Germans," and the "Russians"; the world of "machination" is represented by the "Americans," the "English," the "Bolsheviks," "National Socialists," and "Judaism" (to which "Christendom," *mutatis mutandis*, also belongs). I will concern myself in what follows particularly with the last-named representative of universality, Judaism.

In *Überlegungen* XIV Heidegger comes to speak of "England." He asks himself why "we recognize so late that, in truth, England is and is able to be *without* Western [*abendländische*] bearing" (*GA* 96:243). The reason for this is that England began "to establish the *modern* world," but modernity is "oriented in its essence toward the unfettering of the machination of the entire globe" (*GA* 96:243). Even the intention pursued by several Nazis (above all, early on, by Hitler), to realize hegemonically advanced claims to power in common with England, is rejected. England "from within Americanism and Bolshevism, and this means at the same time also from within world Judaism" plays out an "historical process" all the way "to the end" (*GA* 96:243). In this, the "role of *world Judaism*" is—as a "kind of humanity" that is "*utterly unattached*"—to take over "the uprooting of all beings from being as its world-historical 'task'" (*GA* 96:243).

"World Judaism" is thereby introduced as a distinctive representative of machination in the narrative of beyng. Already the term *world Judaism* signals a problem. It is not unusual for Heidegger to wish that his words be understood "literally." Accordingly, the talk here would simply be of the "Judaism of the world." In any case, Heidegger speaks in other passages expressly of the "worldlessness" of Judaism. Aside from the difficulty of understanding this ascription (if one does not want to return to the "world-lessness" of inanimate nature, for instance, of stones, *GA* 29/30), the possibility of taking the concept of world Judaism "literally" has taken care of itself.

In that case, however, there remains only the context of a broader narrative that was quite influential at the beginning of the twentieth century, the context of the so-called *Protocols of the Elders of Zion*. The *Protocols of the Elders of Zion* are a fiction, in all likelihood created by the czarist intelligence service within the ambit of the Dreyfus affair, according to which a "world Judaism," acting on a global scale and in secret, surreptitiously pursues world domination by modern means, such as the "international press." In my opinion, Heidegger did not read the *Protocols*. Yet he did not have to. They were continually present in Hitler's speeches and in the propaganda of the "Third Reich." A different source for the concept of "world Judaism" can be ruled out. The *Protocols of the Elders of Zion* are the "absolute reference point" (Wolfgang Benz) for the term *world Judaism*.[4]

World Judaism can only serve the "unfettering of the machination of the entire globe" by taking on, in its *"utterly unattached"* manner, "the uprooting of all beings from being as its world-historical 'task'" (*GA* 96:243). It is an anti-Semitic stereotype, which disregards the reality of the twenties and thirties, that Judaism is a "world Judaism," that the Jews lived primarily "internationally." This stereotype points to the diaspora, i.e., to the dispersal of Judaism from the time of its flight from Egypt. Yet most German and European Jews lived a thoroughly settled life for generations in a fixed place. Assimilation was initially more important to them than "Zionism."

Hence, so I conjecture, Heidegger writes and underscores that "world Judaism" is acting *"utterly unattached."* World Judaism is therefore in this respect, but also in regard to thinking—and for Heidegger this is paramount—"unattached." Thus it can organize the "unfettering of the machination of the entire globe" by carrying out the "uprooting of all beings from being." This "uprooting," however, fosters "machination."

Heidegger elsewhere makes clear what this uprooting ensures in machination. He attributes to the Jews a "marked gift for calculation." "Calculating" or "reckoning" refers to the mathematical-technological matrix of the universal topography. Mathematics and technology are a universal form for grasping beings (cf. measuring and counting, for instance). Mathematics and technology produce everything, without regard for any rootedness. Swedish electricity is not distinguished from Finnish electricity (the voltage is again only a mathematical-technological distinction). The number ten is as valid in Japan as it is in Italy.

If I now recall that I earlier distinguished the being-historical finalities of "ending," "destruction," "annihilation," and "devastation," then it can be easily understood that Heidegger attributes a destructive role to world Judaism within the history of beyng in its struggle with metaphysics. One of the perhaps most important anti-Semitic passages in the *Black Notebooks* runs as follows: "Jewry [*Judenschaft*] is the principle of destruction in the period of the Christian West, i.e., of metaphysics. [It is] that which is destructive in the inversion of the completion of metaphysics—i.e., of Hegel's metaphysics by Marx. Spirit and culture becomes the superstructure of "life"—i.e., of the economy, i.e., of organization—i.e., of the biological—i.e., of the 'people'" (*GA* 97:20). The "Jews" destroy the metaphysical structure of the "Christian West," insofar as this structure is completed [*vollendet*] in Hegel's philosophy. Marx, who claimed to have set Hegel on his head, blazes the trail that leads directly into machination, and that means, now, the machination of the Third Reich. For, the sequence "superstructure of 'life'—i.e., of the economy, i.e., of organization—i.e., of the biological—i.e., of the 'people' " gets straight to the point: Marx, the destructive Jew, is the one who paves the way for National Socialism.

(Hitler, whose anti-Semitism is brutally biologistic, speaks in *Mein Kampf* of the "destructive principle of the Jew"—in relation to Mommsen's infamous formulation of the Jews as the "effective ferment of cosmopolitanism and national decomposition."[5] And "the Jew," that is for Hitler anyways, is always also "the Marxist.")

This thought appears in several passages. Thus he stresses at one point that "*With their marked gift for calculation*, the Jews 'live' according to the principle of race, and indeed have done so for the longest time, for which reason they themselves most vigorously resist its unrestricted application" (*GA* 96:56)—an infamous remark, in my eyes. Even here the National Socialists with their Nuremburg race laws become epigones of the persecuted Jews.

But we are yet to grasp the apocalyptic reduction. The mathematical-technological essence of Judaism—cofounded by Marx—is also drawn into the maelstrom of the "self-annihilation" of machination. Heidegger's remarks on annihilation are polysemous and thus difficult to interpret. "Annihilation" is not "self-annihilation." Thus I will distinguish between "annihilation" and "self-annihilation" in keeping with the apocalyptic reduction of the history of being.

Heidegger speaks of an "annihilation" in the lecture course, *On the Essence of Truth*, from the winter semester, 1933–34, thus an exoteric text. He interprets the famous fragment 53 of Heraclitus, according to which πόλεμος is the father and king of all things, some of whom he makes into gods, others into human beings, some into slaves, others into freemen. This saying is frequently interpreted by Heidegger at this time.

Πόλεμος is understood as "standing against the enemy" (*GA* 36/37:90/72–73). The "enemy" is "each and every person who poses an essential threat to the Dasein of the people and its individual members" (GA 36/37:90–91/73). The "enemy" by no means needs to be "external," i.e., it does not need to manifest himself in the form of a hostile nation. Rather, it could "seem as if there were no enemy." For, it is a "fundamental requirement to find the enemy, to expose the enemy to light, or even first to make the enemy" (GA 36/37:91/73). Accordingly, whether the enemy actually exists or not is a matter of indifference. Dasein needs an enemy. (I would like to call attention to the fact that the saying of Heraclitus in no way says anything like this.)

The enemy could "have attached itself to the innermost roots of the Dasein of a people and can set itself against this people's own essence and act against it" (GA 36/37:91/73). The enemy is thus an enemy of "essence." Hence the "struggle" will be "all the fiercer and harder and tougher." For "it is often far more difficult and wearisome to catch sight of the enemy as such, to bring the enemy into the open" and "to prepare the attack looking far ahead with the goal of total annihilation" (GA 36/37:91/73).

The "enemy of essence" is faced with "total annihilation." The discourse is brutal. Heidegger obviously wants to accommodate himself to the new ruling powers. For, the semantics of this formulation was and is topically current. The enemy is the *parasite* that has "attached itself to the innermost roots of the Dasein of a people." Is it even necessary to characterize the enemy any further?

Here Heidegger is silent. Yet in a later passage he says: "Marxism cannot be defeated once and for all unless we first confront the doctrine of ideas and its two-millenia-long history" (GA 36/37:151/118). Accordingly, perhaps it is "Marxism" after all that is regarded as the "enemy of essence." I already indicated that Marx, as a member of "Jewry," cofounded the "principle of destruction" in the history of metaphysics. Precisely that, however, is said here, approximately ten years prior to the passage in the *Black Notebooks*: defeating Marxism "once and for all" demands a confrontation with the whole history of metaphysics since Plato. (I believe that all the Marxists among the "Heideggerians" must once again engage themselves with Heidegger's understanding of Marx.)

EXCURSUS

In his essay "Heidegger, Gagarin, and Us," which appeared in 1961, Emmanuel Levinas attempts to lay out the most important difference between Judaism and Heidegger (including the "Heideggerians," explicitly named as such). These concern the topographical ordering of the world emphasized by Heidegger and the destruction of this order in technology as affirmed by Judaism.

"One's implementation in a landscape, one's attachment to *Place*," that is the "very splitting of humanity into natives and strangers."[6] In this perspective "technology" is "less dangerous than any spirit [*génies*] of a Place." Technology "does away with the privileges of this enrootedness and the related sense of exile," which refers to it. Technology "wrenches us out of the Heideggerian world and the superstitions surrounding *Place*."[7]

In contrast, the astronaut Gagarin has shown us how we can leave place behind. Thus we read: "For one hour, man existed beyond any horizon—everything around him was sky or, more exactly, everything was geometrical space. A man existed in the absolute of homogeneous space."[8] In the year 1961 Yuri Gagarin had orbited the earth for 106 minutes in the spacecraft, *Vostok 1*.

What is crucial is that Levinas attributes the idea of replacing "place" with "homogeneous space" to Judaism. "Judaism has not sublimated idols—on the contrary, it has demanded that they be destroyed. Like technology, it has demystified the universe. It has freed Nature from a spell. Because of its abstract universalism, it runs up against imaginations and passions. But it has discovered man in the nudity of his face."[9]

Levinas also speaks of a "destruction." In Heidegger's eyes it has to do with the destruction proceeding from universalism (on my interpretation), with the "destruction" of machination, which is still not "annihilation." It is a little uncanny to see to what extent Levinas affirms the apocalyptic reduction of the history of being. He is the one who, coming from the other side, inscribes the confrontation of a "universalist" Judaism with a place-bound Heideggerianism into the apocalyptic reduction.

Heidegger reckons all that into the history of metaphysics. Sometime at the beginning of the 1940s he notes the following concerning Platonism: "The positing of the ἀγαθόν [the good] as the τελευταία ἰδέα [ultimate idea] *over* ἀλήθεια [truth] and the ἀληθές [true] as γιγνωσκόμενον [what is known] is the first and that means the step actually going the farthest toward the standardized production of long-range fighter planes and toward the invention of radio communication technology, with the help of which the former are deployed in the service of the unconditional mechanization of the globe and of the human being that is likewise prefigured by that step" (*GA* 67:164). I admit that I personally like this passage very much. It appears to be an immediate application of the history of being to a topical and acute phenomenon.

In brief and to sum it all up: Plato's doctrine of ideas—bound up with a denigration of ἀλήθεια in Heidegger's eyes—is the origin of each and every "standardized production." For the simple reason that everything produced requires a model. This model is provided by Plato in the ideas. This, by the way, is also the argument for why Heidegger conceives Marxism as a kind of Platonism: Platonism is the origin of production.

However, what is here produced "in a standardized manner" are "long-range fighter planes" and "radio communication technology." Heidegger thereby correctly grasps that airplanes presuppose radio communications. Yet to this extent Platonism is the "step that goes the farthest" because it brings the "long-distance fighter planes" far into enemy territories.

Is it a coincidence that Levinas speaks of Gagarin's spacecraft, *Vostok 1,* and Heidegger speaks of "long-distance fighter planes"? According to Heidegger, both serve "destruction," both have left the earth behind and move within universal space. It suggests that for Heidegger the Platonic idea and Judaism are connected. Augustine, by the way, in the eighth book of *De Civitate Dei,* wonders whether Plato could have known the prophets and among them especially the prophet Jeremiah. He comes to a negative conclusion but nevertheless says that he would *almost* like to accept the assertion that Plato must have known those books. Judaism, Platonism, Christianity—three forms of universalism that Heidegger attacks, at least in the *Black Notebooks.*

⸙

The history of being, however, accomplishes the complete apocalyptic reduction, where no enemy exists any longer and history itself carries out the decision. With this, annihilation becomes "self-annihilation." And self-annihilation can happen to everyone and everything, according to Heidegger. The universal is total, it makes no exceptions. At one point Heidegger speaks of the "self-annihilation" of communism, i.e., of the communism thus thought by him being-historically, according to which there is no difference between Bolshevism and Americanism. He then speaks, after the war, of the "self-annihilation" of the Germans and—still before the end of the war—of the "self-annihilation" of the " 'Jewish' " (*GA* 97:20).

I want to emphasize the oscillation in the word *self-annihilation*. Oscillating words are, admittedly, ubiquitous in Heidegger, yet here one must be precise. "Self-annihilation" does not need to be understood everywhere as "physical" annihilation. Rather there is a "self-annihilation of humanity" (*GA* 96:181) that consists in the fact that the modern subject as the "last man" (Nietzsche) passes over into its ending. On the other hand, however, there is a "self-annihilation" of the "adversary," with respect to which "politics" in its "modern essence" must do nothing other than put the "adversary into play" in a "position," wherein there is no other option but "self-annihilation" (*GA* 96:260). One has the impression that in this passage he identifies the "adversary" with "Americanism," yet we read: "One uncovers 'Americanism' as a political adversary now for the first time and late enough and only halfway" (*GA* 96:260).

However, I am not claiming that the oscillation of the concept of self-annihilation yields an equivalence of meaning. Rather, every single case must be considered—and in addition one must heed *when* Heidegger speaks of the self-annihilation of the "Jewish," for example, and of the self-annihilation of the Germans. At this point the testimonial character of the *Black Notebooks* must not be ignored. As is the case in the lecture courses, it is important to see when Heidegger takes up which variation in the narrative of the history of being.

The apocalyptic reduction turns out to be the self-annihilation of technology. In the universal topography we thus encounter a being-historical unity of Americanism, England, Bolshevism, communism, National Socialism, and Judaism or world Judaism. All these protagonists of the history of being are determined by a "marked gift for calculation": a gift, admittedly, that Heidegger attributes to the Jews (*GA* 96:56). They move within a worldless world in long-range fighter planes and spacecraft. They are agents of machination.

Before the end of the war, before the "end" that Heidegger attempted to interpret being-historically, "self-annihilation" concerns these agents of machination. At stake is the other beginning. The decision demands that this beginning must transpire without victor and vanquished. The difference between victor and vanquished recedes immediately into "technology." It must annihilate itself by carrying away all those agents along with it.

The end of the war shows that the agents of universalism have prevailed. Now machination drives the Germans to self-annihilation. Heidegger speaks of a "killing-machinery" that has changed "the German people and country into a single *Kz* [*Konzentrationslager*, concentration camp]" (*GA* 97:100). The self-annihilation of machination has yet to transpire, which can only have as its consequence the self-annihilation of the Germans.

But how are we to understand the "self-annihilation" of the "Jewish"? The question remains as to whether in such a formulation, around the year 1942, we must not think of the physical annihilation of the Jews. The question remains as to how we shall treat the narrative interpretation of this annihilation—as "self-annihilation" of "machination" with respect to the "decision" between "end" and "beginning." The question remains as to whether it is justifiable within this "self-annihilation" to equate the self-annihilating annihilator with the annihilated. The question remains as to whether the annihilator is someone annihilated. The question remains as to whether the annihilated is also an annihilator. It remains to be said, that . . .

2

COSMOPOLITAN JEWS VS. JEWISH NOMADS

Sources of a Trope in Heidegger's *Black Notebooks*

SANDER L. GILMAN

The current scandal surrounding Heidegger concerns the presence of anti-Semitic content in the *Black Notebooks* that he kept during the war years. Defenders have stressed the small quantity of such utterances across thousands of pages, accusers that they reflect on the entirety of Heidegger's philosophy. The remarks in the *Notebooks* are termed philosophical or even being-historical expressions of anti-Semitism by some; others find them to be banal stereotypes. In any event, anti-Semitism is nothing new with Heidegger. In fact, our understanding of Heidegger himself may now depend on hearing these remarks within their proper historical context. For the Jewish "worldlessness" that he decries on being-historical grounds is inseparable from the anti-Semitic figure of the wandering or nomadic or homeless Jew. A look at the history of anti-cosmopolitan, antimodern anti-Semitism from the Enlightenment on may help us better situate Heidegger's remarks.

The history of cosmopolitanism from the Enlightenment to the twentieth century focused on the double strand of a positive or a negative image of mobility.[1] The Jews were the litmus test for this in German-speaking central Europe: were they "aliens," a beneficent or at least a malleable population because they were mobile, or were they "predators," a threat to established or evolving national identity because of their mobility? This discourse, with all the ambiguities on both sides of the issue, was reflected in the idea of a cosmopolitan versus a nomadic people. And the Jews, from the Old Testament to the present, were taken as the exemplary cases for each position.

From the Baroque idea that the Jew was the original Gypsy to the Enlightenment discourse about the movement of peoples through the debates within Zionism in the nineteenth and twentieth centuries about the rootedness of the Jew, the antithetical idea of the movement of the Jews as an indicator of potential integration or isolation from the national state remains a factor in defining the cosmopolitan.

Cosmopolitanism and its sister concept nomadism, again and again, have taken on quite different meanings when their referent is the Jews. Once this litmus test is applied, both cosmopolitanism and nomadism are clearly revealed as symbolic manifestations of the anti-Semitic stereotype, which associates Jews with capital. Such a history of the cosmopolitan points toward the ambivalence of these very concepts when applied in the present day to specific categories of social and geographic mobility, whether these refer to the Jew, the asylum seeker, the migrant, the undocumented immigrant. The marginal and excluded of Enlightenment Germany may have transmuted into the global citizen of the twenty-first century in some instances, but the aura of the corrupt and corrupting, of the rootless and the transitory, of the foreign and the unhoused always remains beneath the surface and shapes the sense of what it means to be cosmopolitan and global. And as such it impacts upon the self-image of those so defined.

The universal claim of globalization and its surrogate cosmopolitanism is that all human beings share certain innate human rights, including the free movement of peoples across what are seen as the superficial boundaries of nation, class, race, caste, and perhaps even gender and sexuality.[2] The tension between the universal and local meanings of cosmopolitanism, however, originally arose in the Enlightenment, as did the common use of the term itself. Standard etymologies in various European languages note that it is a Greek term, its modern use having been borrowed from the French and brought into English as early as the sixteenth century, by the necromancer John Dee to denote a person who is "a Citizen . . . of the . . . one Mysticall City Vniuersall."[3] However, it only became common usage in English in the early nineteenth century. In German the term *Weltbürger* (world citizen) was likewise generated in the early sixteenth century to provide an alternative to the French cosmopolitisme and *cosmopolite*. The

French Academy documents cosmopolitisme in its dictionary of 1762, but that is the first "official" recognition of a much older usage. As in English, the earlier German usages are sporadic. Erasmus seems to have been the first to use it in the early sixteenth century in a letter to Ulrich Zwingli referring to Socrates who, when asked of what city he was a citizen, replied that he was a "Weltbürger (κοσμοπολίτην *sive mundanum*)."[4] The term only came into wider use in the German Enlightenment, thus earlier than in English. It seems to have been Jakob Friedrich Lamprecht who popularized the term in German with his periodical entitled *Der Weltbürger* (1741–42). A wide range of Enlightenment figures quickly followed suit, though G. E. Lessing used the term *cosmopolitan* (rather than *Weltbürger*) in 1747. Functioning as the litmus test for the cosmopolitan in the German Enlightenment in all these cases is the status of the Jews.

One of the major Enlightenment thinkers, Abbé Grégoire, attacked the facile use of a universal claim of cosmopolitanism before the National Assembly during the French Revolution:

> A writer of the last Century (Fénelon) said: I love my family better than my self: I love my country better than my family but I love mankind better than my country. Reason has criticized both those extravagant people who talked about a universal republic and those false people who made a profession out of loving people who lived in a distance of two thousand years or two thousand leagues in order to avoid being just and good towards their neighbors: systematic, de facto cosmopolitanism is nothing but moral or physical vagabondage.[5]

For Grégoire, the local case was the question of the universal emancipation of French Jewry as citizens, trumping their specifically Jewish identity, an idea of which he was a powerful advocate.[6] For the Enlightenment, and it is with the Enlightenment that this tale begins, it is the Jews in Paris, not in the distant past nor in faraway Palestine, that are the litmus test for true French cosmopolitanism. Anything else is merely "vagabondage," moral or physical nomadism. True cosmopolitanism was defined by attention to the immediate and the proximate, a topic much debated at the time. But it is immediately contrasted with the merely nomadic.

The first major German literary advocate of cosmopolitanism, Christoph Martin Wieland, who devoted several essays to cosmopolitanism in the 1780s, most famously "The Secret of Cosmopolitan Order" in 1788, writes: "Cosmopolitans . . . regard all the peoples of the earth as so many branches of a single family, and the universe as a state, of which they, with innumerable other rational beings, are citizens, promoting together under the general laws of nature the perfection of the whole, while each in his own fashion is busy with his own well-being."[7] Wieland, like the *philosophes*, sees this as a transcendental category, trumping the local. Wieland is himself paraphrasing Friedrich II's oft-cited note of June 1740 concerning Huguenot and Catholic toleration but not emancipation: "Each should be blessed in their own manner" ("Jeder soll nach seiner Façon selig werden"), a toleration grudgingly extended in 1750 to Prussian Jewry.[8] Wieland's own Enlightenment views on the Jews are clear: he mocks, in his *Private History of Peregrinus Proteus* (1781), the pagan whose grandfather "had a boundless aversion for Jews and Judaism; his prejudices against them, were, perhaps, partly unjust, but they were incurable," yet equally detested Christians who "passed for a Jewish sect."[9] Enlightenment thought more generally promoted a stable cosmopolitanism, a universalist sensibility rooted in the nation. Religious affiliation, especially that of the Jews, was rejected for its particularity. Wieland's cosmopolitanism thus contests the religious exclusivity of both Christians and Jews over the universal.

Jewish cosmopolitanism is contested when it is defined in terms of capital; when it is uncontested, any discussion of capital is avoided. Indeed, any discussion of the fantasies about some type of unitary definition of Jewish cosmopolitanism necessarily hangs on the very meaning associated with capital and its function within the new nation-state. The fantasy of the Jews is one of a people (or nation or race) driven solely by their own economic motivation. It is Shylock's curse, which the historian Derek Penslar so elegantly presents as a core reference for Jewish identity in modernity.[10]

The Jews as an abstraction and as a social reality come to be the litmus test in the Enlightenment through which these notions' potentials and difficulties can be analyzed.[11] When cosmopolitanism is examined under this lens, we have a double focus: first, the role that the abstraction, "the Jews," played in formulating theories of the acceptability of, or dangers in, the movement of peoples beyond and across national boundaries and, second, the response of actual individuals who define themselves as Jews to such attitudes and meanings. This is a forerunner of what the British scholar of geography, Ulrike Vieten, calls the "novel form of *regional*

cosmopolitanism [that] is underway in Europe."[12] But it has deeper historical roots. As the meanings of all of these concepts (cosmopolitanism,
boundary, Jews, as well as capital) shift and evolve, so too do the responses
of those generating them and seeing them as applicable or inapplicable to
their particular circumstances as these change.

If we are to examine the debates about the Jews as the touchstone
of cosmopolitanism in the Enlightenment, and specifically within the
German-language Enlightenment, then two conflicting definitions of the
Jews must first be separated. First, the Jews are a people who ascribe to a
particular religious belief and practice and who are at least potentially able
to freely follow their beliefs in the new, enlightened world of the European
national state. Second, the Jews are seen as the concrete manifestation of
the exploitative force of capital, whose rise parallels the very establishment
of such states, at least in the eyes of these commentators.

J. G. Herder (1744–1803) is thus torn between these two poles. In his
Ideas for a Philosophy of the History of Mankind (1784–91) he defines the
nation as "a group of people having a common origin and common institutions, including language"; the nation-state represents the union of the
individual with the national community; each people is unique; polyglot
entities are "absurd monsters contrary to nature."[13] The Jews must join the
body politic by integrating their linguistic practice into that of the natu-
rally occurring nation-state. But can they? According to Herder, "The Jews
of Moses are properly of Palestine, outside of Palestine there can be no
Jew."[14] Yet "a time will come when no person in Europe will inquire whether
a man be a Jew or a Christian. Jews will live according to European laws
and contribute to the state" (486). Nevertheless, "each nation has its center
of happiness in itself, like every sphere its center of gravity," he writes in
Also a History of Mankind (1774). In his *Theological Letters* (1780–81), he
too approvingly quotes the remark made by François de Salignac de La
Mothe Fénelon, archbishop of Cambrai, which was later invoked by Abbé
Gregoire (and virtually every other Enlightened commentator on cosmopolitanism), "I love my family more than myself; more than my family my
fatherland; more than my fatherland humankind." Yet for Herder it is the
status of the nation, of the fatherland, that is at the core of any and all questions of individual identity and thus individual happiness. While Herder
sees the Jews as one of the "cultures" of the ancient world, it was the Jewish
Volksgeist that defined the rise of protocapitalism.[15] Given that Herder most

probably coined the term *nationalism* (*Nationalismus*), Jewish cosmopolitanism came to define its antithesis.

The "nation" in question is not a racial entity, but rather a linguistic and cultural one (indeed, in the *Ideas for a Philosophy of the History of Mankind* (1784–91) and elsewhere Herder rejects the very concept of a biologically defined race). Herder's views reflect those of the time, as expressed by Johann Georg Schlosser in the critical poem "Der Kosmopolit" (1777): "It is better to be proud of one's nation than to have none." Are the Jews a nation or merely wandering cosmopolitans?[16] If a nation, can or should they become part of another nation? Or are they, as Johann Gottlieb Fichte notoriously stated in his 1793 pamphlet *A Contribution to Correcting the Public's Judgments About the French Revolution,* a threat: "In nearly all the nations of Europe, a powerful, hostile government is growing, and is at war with all the others, and sometimes oppresses the people in dreadful ways: It is Jewry!"[17] The Jews are a "state within the state," incapable of any integration and thus damned to wander the world.[18] Truly vagabondage.

According to Herder, writing in the *Ideas,* even if the Jews had stayed "in the land of their fathers, and in the midst of other nations, . . . they would have remained as they were; for and even when mixed with other people they may be distinguished for some generations downward."[19] The "more secluded they live, nay frequently the more they were oppressed, the more their character was confirmed" (36). In fact, he suggests that, ideally, "if every one of these nations had remained in its place, the Earth might have been considered as a garden, where in one spot one human national plant, in another, another, bloomed in its proper figure and nature" (36). The movement of peoples interferes with the natural function of language in defining people. But the reality of history is that almost every people on earth, as Herder points out, "has migrated at least once, sooner or later, to a greater distance, or less" (36). The impact of this migration is shaped by the "time when the migration took place, the circumstances by which it was occasioned, the length of the way, the previous state of civilization of the people, the reception they met with in their new country, and the like" (36).

And yet Herder sees the very origin of "the coining of money" as one of the contributions of the "many little wandering hordes" in the Middle East, "according to the Hebrews" (317). As the Jews spread across Europe, "in the manner that they spread abroad as a people" they held its nations in thrall thanks to their command of money. They did not invent usury, Herder states, but "they brought it to perfection" (335). The Jews move among and across the nations like everyone else, yet Herder is happy to quote from Kant's lectures on practical philosophy: "Every coward is a liar; Jews, for example, not only in business, but also in common life."[20] On this point, Herder and Kant agree.

Yet the Enlightenment had an alternative manner of speaking about the Jews as a people that offers a different history of the concept of cosmopolitanism. For Christian Enlightenment thinkers, cosmopolitanism was the hallmark of the enlightened subject rooted in a particularist universality. Jews, confined to their backward particularity, could not by definition achieve this status. Herder, in his *Ideas*, provided a rather standard Protestant reading of the Hebrew Bible (the *Tanakh*) that presented the Jews as a nomadic people. Whether this was ever historically true or not, it is clear that the texts assembled into what came in Christianity to be called the Old Testament are the product of city-states. Whether the Jews were or were not just one of "many little wandering hordes," as Herder describes them, is the question, but it is clear that the Old Testament, at least in Genesis, represents a nostalgia for a simpler time and space that came to be defined in the Enlightenment as "nomadic."[21] Herder lists all the innovations of these nomads; among them is the invention of "trade by weight and measure": capitalism.[22]

For Herder, the nomad represented not only earlier stages of Jewish development but also described the Jews as still existing in the present in what he saw as a throwback to their nomadic past. This is found in the overlapping history of the Sinti and Roma and the Jews. It should be noted that some early German commentators, such as Wilhelm Ernst Tentzel at the close of the seventeenth century, correctly argued that the "Gypsies" had come from South Asia even if they were uncertain of their exact origins (Tentzel's guess was Ceylon).[23] However, those theologians who were focused on converting the Jews looked closer to home. The Christian Hebraist Johann Christoph Wagenseil asserted in 1705, in his *Benachrichtigungen Wegen Einiger die Gemeine Jüdischheit Betreffenden Sachen* (Reports regarding a few matters concerning the Jewish community), that the first Gypsies (*Zigeuner*) were indeed Jews who fled into the forests after having been accused in the fourteenth century of poisoning wells. Saying that they had come from Egypt, they cheated the peasants there by claiming to be able to effect wondrous cures, tell the future, and prevent fires. Eventually they returned to the cities and again became sedentary and declared themselves Jews. But vagabonds, thieves, and beggars had joined them and they continued their nomadic ways. As proof, he contends that the Gypsies were unknown before the fourteenth century, that the language of today's Gypsies is full of Hebrew words, and that their amulets use kabbalistic formulas.[24] In Johann Jakob Schudt's infamous *Jüdische Merckwürdigkeiten* (1714) there is a long chapter that claims that Wagenseil was simply wrong and that the Jews were condemned to their wanderings in Egypt for having rejected Jesus and Mary on their flight to Egypt.[25] He follows this with a long digression on the Eternal Jew, the shoemaker Ahasverus, or Cartaphilus, condemned to wander the world because of his rejection of Christ. Learning the language of each country he visits, he must wander, as Christ condemned him to do, until the Second Coming.[26] The Jews, according to Schudt, are, like the Turks, "sanctimonious cheats" because of their usury.[27] In both cases the economic role of the Jews as pseudonomads is integral to these contradictory images. Whether authentic or not, the Jews are nomadic in the same way as the Sinti and Roma, even if they are not "Gypsies" per se.

The Enlightenment saw nomads as not using their given space productively. As early as the mid eighteenth century, in *Wilhelm Meister,* Goethe would see the nomad through the lens of the colonist in his explanation of why it is seductive for Germans to seek adventures abroad. The novel's protagonist, Lenardo, speaks of the enticement of "immeasurable spaces [that] lie open to action" and of "great stretches of country roamed by nomads."[28] In the present, nomads have no value and must be replaced by those who do, but this is a false promise that may lead to the corrosion of the Europeans' national identity.

In this Enlightenment view, nomads add no value to the land today and thus seem to need to be replaced by members of a national community. But it is these self-same nomads in the past that were the starting point for the national state and for its most egregious exploitative feature, capital. Karl Marx, in his *Capital.* wrote that "nomad races are the first to develop the money form, because all their worldly goods consist of moveable objects and are therefore directly alienable; and because their mode of life, by continually bringing them into contact with foreign communities, solicits the exchange of products."[29] The nomad is implicitly cast as the

Urcapitalist, the Jew, whose drive in the modern world is shaped by his inheritance from the desert (this is also analogous to the explanation for the rise of monotheism among the Jews: the need for a portable God after the destruction of the Temple).[30]

In contrast to Marx, Georg Simmel, in the *Philosophy of Money* (1900), explains that "as a rule, nomadic peoples hold land as common property of the tribe and assign it only for the use of individual families; but livestock is always the private property of these families. As far as we know, the nomadic tribe has never been communistic with regard to cattle as property. In many other societies too movables were already private property while land remained common property for a long period thereafter."[31] Not so much *Urcapitalists* as *Urcommunists*, perhaps?

Two decades before, the Russian Zionist Leon Pinsker argued in his German-language pamphlet *Auto-Emancipation* (1882) that the statelessness of the Jew in the age of nationalism condemns him to be a nomad. For the Jewish people "produces in accordance with its nature, vagrant nomads; so long as it cannot give a satisfactory account of whence it comes and whither it goes; so long as the Jews themselves prefer not to speak in Aryan society of their Semitic descent and prefer not to be reminded of it; so long as they are persecuted, tolerated, protected or emancipated, the stigma attached to this people, which forces it into an undesirable isolation from all nations, cannot be removed by any sort of legal emancipation."[32] For Pinsker (1821–91), these are nomads living as "Jew peddlers" because they refuse to acknowledge their own rootedness in the desert as true nomads.

If the nation-state has its roots in a nomadic world before capital, and if the cosmopolitan symbolically represents the dangers (and advantages) of capital, we can turn to a major Jewish thinker of the late nineteenth century for a sense of the linkage between the two concepts. The great Jewish Hungarian scholar of Islam Ignaz Goldziher's detailed 1876 study of the constitution of Jewish mythology adds a further nuance to our sense of the ambivalent image of the cosmopolitan hovering between advantage and danger.[33] For Goldziher (1850–1921), "the national level [of Jewish mythopoeia] can be sorted out of the mix. It was Abraham, not yet rethinking these tales in national terms, who was not yet a cosmopolitan figure, but as an individual [who formed these tales]" (59). In this portrayal of the biblical Abraham, individuality—the particular—and cosmopolitanism—the universal—are portrayed as dichotomous. Abraham is an individual, not a cosmopolitan, for he is part of "the nomadic level that found its element in a continual wandering from grazing pasture to grazing pasture, in the continual changing of their abode, before it was historically grounded in the completion of its movement to agriculture" (64). Like the Arabs, whom Goldziher idealizes, the Jews (here he cites Philo) "glorify their nomadic life" (103). The Jews detest artisan labor (*Handwerk*), no matter how intense "their desire for money," as below their status as nomads (105). They are thus inherently different in their storytelling from the ancient Greeks and the Aryan inhabitants of South Asia: "The Hellenes and the Indians have their primary figures of myth being of a cosmopolitan character, for Zeus and Indira have no specific national character, even though now and then they are specifically local. The figures of Hebrew myth in this period become the national ancestors of the Hebrew people, where myth is raised to become the national prehistory of the Hebrew people before its settlement in the land of Canaan" (306). Here the national and the cosmopolitan appear as diametrically opposed. Jewish tales are restrictedly national and local, rather than cosmopolitan and global. They are the product of the world of the nomad, at least as imagined from the point of view of the biblical national Jewish state, which remained local, unlike the transcendental worlds of Greece and India.

Nomadism is also pressed into service to explain the origin of the Jews' "natural" relationship to cosmopolitanism and to capital. The German economist Werner Sombart, in his classic response to Max Weber's *The Protestant Ethic and the Spirit of Capitalism* (1905) wrote in *The Jews and Modern Capitalism* (1911) of the "restless wandering Bedouins [who] were the Hebrews" who established in "this promised land" an "economic organization" where "the powerful and mighty among them after having conquered large tracts of land instituted a sort of feudal society. Part of the produce of the land they took for themselves, either by way of rent in kind, by farming it out to tax-collectors, or by means of the credit nexus."[34] In other words, they were protocapitalists, but of a particularly nasty kind—the origin of the stereotyped Jewish banker in the world of the nomad. For Sombart, the contemporary Jew is an extension of the earlier nomad as far as the Jews' character and relationship to capital is concerned.

Max Weber responds in *Ancient Judaism* (1920–21), where he argues against such a view.[35] He accepts that there is a narrative (but not historical) succession of "the stages of the three Patriarchs from the 'nomad' Abraham to the 'peasant' Jacob."[36] However, he refutes the idea that the nature of Jewish usury stems from any biblical claims to divine approbation in Deuteronomy 28:43–44, which reads: "The stranger that is within thee shall get up above thee very high; and thou shalt come down very low. He shall lend to thee, and thou shalt not lend to him: he shall be the head, and thou shalt be the tail." For Weber, "the medieval and modern money and pawn usury of the Jews, the caricature in which this promise was fulfilled, was certainly not intended by the holy promise." Rather, Weber reads this as being symbolic of the triumph of city over countryside, "which prevailed in every typical polis throughout early Antiquity from Sumerian-Accadian times."[37] While a particular quality of the Jews, it is one no different from that of other peoples living in the cosmopolitan world of the ancient city with its myth of agrarian settlement.

The Jews are nomads, Herder and his reading of the Bible say so, and the essence of the Jew is captured by his nomadism in the present-day world of the nineteenth-century pan-European anti-Semite. In the seminal anti-Semitic work written by Richard Wagner's son-in-law, Houston Stewart Chamberlain, *Foundations of the Nineteenth Century* (1912), the history of the Jew in the distant past is again the history of the Jew today: "Of all the histories of the ancient world there is none that is more convincing, none more easily to be realized, than that of the wanderings of the patriarch Abraham. It is a story of four thousand years ago, it is a story of yesterday, it is a story of today." But it is the history of a degenerate people, Chamberlain argues, for "any change in the manner of living is said to have a very bad effect on the high qualities of the genuine and purely Semitic nomads. The learned [A. H.] Sayce, one of the greatest advocates of the Jews at the present day, writes: 'If the Bedouin of the desert chooses a settled life, he, as a rule, unites in himself all the vices of the nomad and of the peasant. Lazy, deceitful, cruel, greedy, cowardly, he is rightly regarded by all nations as the scum of mankind.'"[38] And it is the history of an impure race as well: "As a matter of fact the current opinion is that the Semite and even that purest Bedouin type are the most absolute mongrels imaginable, the product of a cross between negro and white man!"[39] Mixed races, Chamberlain suggests, have no spaces left for them so they simply wander.

As early as 1887, the Austrian-German Orientalist Adolf Wahrmund had cast the Jew-as-nomad as the essential capitalist: "Thus we have the typical image of the private enterprise of the nomad, that continues until today, in the form of the wandering merchants and dealers who cross the land selling junk, stocks, and . . . thus rob our peasants and return on the Sabbath with their plunder home to wife and children."[40] The very nature of capitalism is that of the "parasitic" nomad and the essential nature of the Jew.

However, the Jews are not very good nomads insofar as they violate one version of the Enlightenment's underlying assumptions concerning the claims of cosmopolitanism, namely the Greek concept of ξενία, *xenía*. As the German journalist Otto Gildemeister noted in 1921, "Even the highest law regarding the safety of the stranger (*Gastfreundschaft*) is not recognized by these nomads. Thus Jewess Jael murders Sisera after having been tempted into a tent and served milk. Trusting her he goes to sleep. Then Jael drives a stake into his temple and mocks his mother when she comes to seek her son."[41] "True nomads" are ideals against which the Jews are often set from the Enlightenment onward.[42]

The ancient Jews violate the rules of many of the nomads described in the *Lebensraum* theorist Friedrich Ratzel's *History of Mankind* (1896), where the Jews are seen as originally

> nomads like their kinsmen in Arabia and Syria. . . . Their oldest books know nothing of fixed altars and their sacrifices are always of cattle. They took to a settled life on conquering and dividing the land of Canaan. But the promised land was only an oasis. . . . The misfortunes of the national ruin, however, brought about a purification which in a race aesthetically deficient, but spiritually proud and austere, tended to strengthen the conception of a deity all powerful and all-knowing, and at the same time jealous and severe.[43]

It is only through "contact with the Greeks, fundamentally Aryan, yet touched by a Semitic spirit, who, independently of the Jews, had gone through a process of spiritual refinement in the direction of truth, knowledge, and beauty, [that] Christianity developed into a power capable of transforming races."[44] Any quality of value possessed by the Jews comes only with being filtered through a Greek sensibility and the resultant creation of a modern consciousness. For Ratzel, the Jews' initial contribution to Western culture may have been a sort of primitive monotheism (as opposed to Christianity), but their long-term impact is on "above all the economic life of other nations."[45]

In the nineteenth century the philosopher Ernest Renan saw in the Jews the survival of "nomadic instincts" and the "nomadic nomos" of the Jews into modern times, while René Guenon would write of the "perverse nomadism of the Jews."[46] It is the character of the Jews as nomads in the present day that defines Renan and Guenon's claim. And one can here quote Felix Delitzsch, of "Babel und Bibel" infamy, in 1920, when he notes concerning the continuity of Jewish nomadic character from the biblical period that "it is obvious that such a people, which is deliberately landless or an international people, presents a great, a frightening danger for all other peoples of the earth."[47] Jews were aggressive nomads and remain so today.

However, the Jews are also terrible at being nomads because, well, they are Jews. Adolf Hitler states this baldly in *Mein Kampf*, echoing his reading of Chamberlain:

> Since the Jew never possessed a state with definite territorial limits and therefore never called a culture his own, the conception arose that this was a people that should be reckoned among the ranks of the nomads. This is a fallacy as great as it is dangerous. The nomad does possess a definitely limited living space; only he does not cultivate it like a sedentary peasant, but lives from the yield of his herds with which he wanders about in his territory. The outward reason for this is to be found in the small fertility of a soil that simply does not permit of settlement. The deeper cause, however, lies in the disparity between the technical culture of an age or people and the natural poverty of a living space.[48]

The Jews are only symbolic nomads in the modern world. If the Jews are nomads in this pejorative sense, it means they are, in the present world, parasites on settled, non-nomadic national peoples. Echoing Wagner's claim that the Jews lack the ability to create original art, the psychologist C. G. Jung stated in 1934 in a lecture in Hitler's Berlin that

> the Jew who is something of a nomad, has never yet created a cultural form of his own, and as far as we can see never will, since all his instincts and talents require a more or less civilized nation to act as a host for their

development. Aside from certain creative individuals, the average Jew is already much too conscious and differentiated to be pregnant with the tensions of the unborn future. The Aryan unconscious has a higher potential than the Jewish; that is the advantage and the disadvantage of a youthfulness not yet fully estranged from barbarism.[49]

It is not what one does but who one is that defines the nomad, defines the cosmopolitan, symbolizing the role identity is seen to play in the world one inhabits.

Martin Heidegger said more or less the same thing in a seminar in 1933–34: "For a Slavic people, the nature of our German space would definitely be revealed differently from the way it is revealed to us; to Semitic nomads, it will perhaps never be revealed at all" (NHS 82/56). This was echoed in 1941 in his so-called *Black Notebooks*, when he defined the Jews not as a people but as a state of mind: "The question of the role of World Jewry is not a racial but rather a metaphysical one about the type of human specificity, that is in all cases can be extrapolated as a world-historical 'goal' from the rootlessness of the Becoming from Being" (GA 96:121).[50] Jews, now as a state of mind, cannot grasp the very notion of a national or particularist space. This is the key to post-Ratzel views of the scientific relationship between a people and their geographic space. Ratzel argued that space defined character and, while this was an older claim having its roots in German Idealism (*pace* Herder), he rested it on scientific claims of physiology, space, and mind. According to such a view as translated by Heidegger, the Slavs have their ideology of pan-Slavism, which is rooted in their national identity and geographic space. The Jews, and here Heidegger clearly rejects a Zionist model for Jewish identity rooted in the land, have no such possibility of identification. His image of the Jew is that of the perpetual wanderer and the eternal capitalist.

If there is a trope that ties Heidegger to the straightforward rhetoric of classical nineteenth-century anti-Semitism, one he shared with Karl Marx, it is the notion that such a metaphysical representation of the Jews is made concrete by their economic exploitation: "One of the most secret forms of the *gigantic, and perhaps the oldest, is the* tenacious skillfulness in calculating, hustling, and intermingling through which the worldlessness of Jewry is grounded" (GA 95:97). That such views are not unique to Heidegger after 1933 is self-evident:

Even though the spirit of *egotism, self-aggrandizement,* and *ruthless greed* had already become the *driving force* behind economic activities by the time of the 1789 revolution as a result of the prevailing doctrine of Freemasonry and had dismissed the Christian doctrine of the individual's inherent *obligation to the common good* as antiquated and backward, there were still certain internal reservations non-Jews had to overcome before they could adopt without any qualms the Jewish economic methods that fed into capitalism. So non-Jewish devotees of capitalism always came in a few lengths behind their unscrupulous Jewish forerunners in the capitalist race.[51]

Here there is a consistency within racial anti-Semitism as a continuation of the religious charges of usury against the Jews. Thus the Jews corrupted Western society with a model of capitalism that is Jewish to its metaphysical core. Thus Adolf Hitler, in a letter from 1919 written to a former soldier about the very nature of the Jews, repeats the substance of what he learned about Jews in the dosshouses of Vienna before the war, which echoes throughout the autobiographical account of his education as an anti-Semite in *Mein Kampf* (1925–26). "His power is the power of money, which multiplies in his hands effortlessly and endlessly by way of accrued interest, and which forces the *Volk* under the most dangerous of yokes whose ultimately tragic consequences are concealed by the initial attraction of gold and glitter. Everything men strive after as a higher goal—be it religion, socialism, or democracy—is to the Jew but a means to an end, a way for him to satisfy his lust for money and domination."[52] It is the rootlessness of capital, able to move seamlessly across all boundaries, both geographic and moral, that defines the Jew.

For such thinkers, Jewish nomadism is a permanent stain on the Jewish character, in contrast to the stability of the German (or even the Slav). This is a standard trope of Nazi rhetoric. Joseph Goebbels, in his talk "Communism with the Mask Off," delivered on September 13, 1935, observed that Jewish cosmopolitanism was the core of contemporary "Judeo-Bolshevism" as "Bolshevism is not merely anti-bourgeois; it is against human civilization itself. In its final consequences it signifies the destruction of all the commercial, social, political and cultural achievements of Western Europe, in favor of a deracinated and nomadic international cabal that has found its representation in Judaism."[53] That the Jews are simultaneously a race and not a race, nomadic as well as cosmopolitan, is reflected in the eclectic arguments of the Nazis about the Jews: they represent all forms of evil.

That this by the 1940s is part of the rationalization that provided the rhetoric not only for exclusion but—given Hitler's earlier statement on January 30, 1939, about the Jewish Bolshevik responsibility for any further war and its implications for the survival of the Jews—for genocide. The press specialist of the "Anti-Komitern" section of the Foreign Office, Karl Baumböck, wrote in 1942 that "with ice-cold, diabolical calculation, they unleashed a new world war that they hoped would defeat the national-authoritarian nations. After destroying these nations, the way would once again be open to establish Jewish domination of the remaining nations. The immutable and lunatic goal of world Jewry is and remains the domination of every nation on its own territory, by firmly lodging itself in nations' organs and exercising complete control of their soil, their money, and all their goods."[54] Heidegger's version of this claim in September 1941 states that "at the start of the third year of the planetary war.—Common sense would like to calculate history, and longs for a 'balance sheet.' . . . World Jewry, spurred on by the emigrants who have been let out of Germany, is intangible everywhere and, as much as it develops its power, never has to take part in warlike activities, whereas the only thing left for us is to sacrifice the best blood of the best of our own people" (*GA* 96:261–62). It is the German Jews specifically who are at the forefront of the destruction of Germany through their planned world conflagration.

When at that moment Heidegger (and an entire cohort of Weimar intellectuals in thrall to the Nazis such as Gottfried Benn) turns against the "intellectuals"—a trope of anti-Semitism reaching back to the Dreyfus affair—he too echoes the rhetoric of the party in their attack on rootless intellectuals, now literally driven from pillar to post:

> This island of whining, faultfinding, bloodless intelligentsia floating in a sea of swirling renewal and change is admittedly growing smaller by the month and far more seldom seen. Nevertheless, even if there are scarcely a hundred thousand of them left in Germany today, they are all the more numerous in foreign countries, which, for the New Germany, is perhaps as pertinent. There they are in league with German outcasts, emigrants, and the sacked [*An-die-Luft-Gesetzten*] and thus remain vicious enemies.[55]

The reality of the war is the rationale for seeking its causes. If World War I was caused by a Jewish "stab-in-the-back" on the home front (Erich Luden-dorff) and not the ineptitude of its leadership; then World War II must also have its roots in the further betrayal of Germany by pseudo-Germans, the German Jewish exiles. Such a metaphysical definition of the Jews demands that there be only a nomadic mindset that may mask itself as national identity but which is permanently opposed to the true grounded spirit of the rooted Aryan.

Jewish thinkers about nomadism, on the other hand, saw it as a transitional phase to some further (and improved) state. The image of the Jew makes this concrete, impacting upon how Jews themselves understand their own function in the society they inhabit. It is no wonder that Max Brod, writing in Martin Buber's periodical *The Jew* in 1916, complained: "One should not inject us with being a centrifugal force in society and then marvel at the findings of 'nomadism' and 'critical destruction' in our corpse."[56] It is this internalization of the cosmopolitan and the nomad that has come to define the Jew in the post-Enlightenment world, indeed even into the twenty-first century.

Modern Jewish historians, such as Jacob Neusner in *Self-Fulfilling Prophecy: Exile and Return in the History of Judaism*, have argued for a material understanding of diaspora.[57] For Neusner, it is the model of wilderness and land, the dialectic between tent and house, nomadism and agriculture, wilderness and Canaan, wandering and settlement, diaspora and state. The Welsh Congregationalist W. D. Davies has argued, in *The Territorial Dimension in Judaism*, that this dichotomy is well-balanced in the Bible, that for every quote praising wilderness as the decisive factor in Judaism, there could be found a counterpart in praise of the Land of Zion.[58]

Galut, on the other hand, is often understood as the experienced reality of being in exile, albeit one structured by the internalization of the textual notion of the diaspora and tempered by the daily experience (good or bad) of life in the world. The Jew experiences the daily life of exile through the mirror of the biblical model of expulsion, whether it be the expulsion from the Garden of Eden or freedom from slavery in Egypt. Galut has formed the Jewish self-understanding of exile. The voluntary dispersion of the Jews (*galut* or *golah*) is articulated as being inherently different from the involuntary exile of the Jews (diaspora). These two models exist simultaneously in Jewish history in the image of uprooted and powerless Jews on the one hand and rooted and empowered Jews on the other. It is possible to have a firm, meaningful cultural experience as a Jew in the diaspora or to feel alone and abandoned in the *galut* (as well as vice versa)—two people can live in the very same space and time and can experience that space and time in antithetical ways. Indeed, the same person can find his or her existence bounded conceptually by such models at different times and in different contexts.

Heidegger had no sense for galut. Certainly the term appears nowhere in his work. He also had no sense for diaspora as a textual condition. For all the subtlety and nuance of his thinking on other matters, when it comes to the Jews he falls into the well-worn tracks of anti-Semitic hysteria from centuries past. If these are the Jews who are agents of the worldless, so much the worse for the very world and rootedness he seeks to defend.

3

METAPHYSICAL ANTI-SEMITISM AND WORLDLESSNESS

On World Poorness, World Forming, and World Destroying

EDUARDO MENDIETA

One's implementation in a landscape, one's attachment to Place, *without which the universe would become insignificant and would scarcely exist, is the very splitting of humanity into natives and strangers. And in this light technology is less dangerous than the spirits [genies] of the* Place. *Technology does away with the privileges of this enrootedness and the related sense of exile. It goes beyond this alternative. It is not a question of returning to the nomadism that is as incapable as sedentary existence of leaving behind a landscape and a climate. Technology wrenches us out of the Heideggerian world and the superstitions surrounding* Place. *From this point on, an opportunity appears to us: to perceive men outside the situation in which they are placed, and let the human face shine in all its nudity. Socrates preferred the town, in which one meets people, to the countryside and trees. Judaism is the brother of the Socratic message.*

—EMMANUEL LEVINAS, "HEIDEGGER, GAGARIN AND US"

In our actual world Heidegger was a Nazi, a cowardly hypocrite, and the greatest European thinker of our time. In the possible world I have sketched he was pretty much the same man, but he happened to have his nose rubbed in the torment of Jews until he finally noticed *what was going on, until his sense of pity and his sense of shame were finally awakened. In that world he had the good luck to have been unable to become a Nazi, and so*

*to have had less occasion for cowardice and hypocrisy. In our actual world,
he turned his face away, and eventually resorted to hysterical denial. This
denial brought on his unforgivable silence. But that denial and silence do
not tell us much about the books he wrote, nor conversely. In both worlds,
the only link between Heidegger's politics and his books is the contempt for
democracy he shared with, for example, Eliot, Chesterton, Tate, Waugh
and Paul Claudel—people whom, as Auden predicted, we have long since
pardoned for writing well. We could as easily have pardoned Heidegger his
attitude towards democracy, if that had been all. But in the world without
Sarah, the world in which Heidegger had the bad luck to live, it was not all.*

—RICHARD RORTY, "ON HEIDEGGER'S NAZISM"

INTRODUCTION: IN HEIDEGGER'S SHED

According to the editors of Martin Heidegger's *Gesamtausgabe*, the
Schwarze Hefte were meant to be published as the final volumes of the
series, which, as we know, is not the case. There are some volumes from
other sections of the *Complete Edition* that have yet to appear. As in the
past, the editors have either reversed or contravened Martin Heidegger's
directions, to the extent that we know what Heidegger himself may or may
not have specified. It should not go unnoted that, notwithstanding the
secrecy and tight control that is exercised over the *Nachlass*, there have
been leaks over the last four decades about the contents of some of the
unpublished manuscripts (the *Contributions*, for instance); nevertheless,
the content of these *Hefte* was kept secret up until the moment they began
to be edited for publication. This in itself is remarkable. Just as it is remarkable that Heidegger kept them and allegedly had intended to publish them
as if they were a final testament or confession. Peter Trawny has written a
wonderful book that aims to provide philosophical reasons for why Heidegger may have decided to publish them at all. I thus recommend his *Freedom to Fail: Heidegger's Anarchy*.[1]

Before I touch on the theme of this chapter, I think it is important to
reflect on Heidegger's *Gesamtausgabe* as an exemplar of what I would like
to call "the philosopher's workshop," but which, in Heidegger's case, should
be more properly be called "the philosopher's shed" because of Heidegger's

rejection of the urbane and refined and avowed preference for the rural and rustic. A workshop or shed is where we tend to keep our tools, some tables, perhaps bits and pieces of half-begun, half-finished, broken down or abandoned projects. A workshop is where we do our tinkering, where we experiment, try things out, get our fingers cut, burned, and bruised. It is also the place were we go to hone our skills at something. Workshops are also filled with the debris produced by our practicing at perfecting some skill. As you all know, the *Gesamtausgabe* is divided in four parts: in the first part we find the texts published during Heidegger's life. The second is made up of all the lecture courses he gave from 1919 to 1944, divided according to the university were he was teaching. The third is made up of the many unpublished manuscripts Heidegger labored on, lectures, and notes, which evidently were intended as books, sequels, responses to published works, etc. The last section contains notes and recordings or protocols of seminars he gave, most of which came from his own hand, except in cases where his manuscripts have been corroborated and complemented with students notes. In addition, the publisher Karl Alber will be publishing, in three sections, Heidegger's correspondence, which is made up of an estimated ten thousand letters.[2] The output is simply staggering. I hazard to speculate that to this "five-part" *Gesamtausgabe* we could anticipate or project a sixth part, one made up of the typescripts of some of the lecture courses and lectures Heidegger delivered before the end of the war. For instance, we know that many of the lecture course manuscripts that have been published in the *Gesamtausgabe* were edited using extant versions of different manuscripts. Take an example: the lecture course from the summer of 1934, first announced as The State and Science, became *Logic as the Question Concerning the Essence of Language* (*GA* 38). The editor of the *Gesamtausgabe* volume claims in his editorial note that the volume was reconstructed from three different sources, excluding an extant one, Helene Weiss's manuscript. It is indeed peculiar that the editor of *GA* 38 makes a point to discredit a manuscript that is actually very close to the one now published as part of the authorized *Gesamtausgabe*.[3] Just as we have different published variations of Kant's lectures on anthropology and geography, there may be a time when we will have different versions of Heidegger's lectures. Note, for instance, that Theodore Kisiel has reconstructed from different manuscripts what Heidegger may have or may not

have said about "the greatness of the NS" or the "greatness of this movement" in his 1935 course *Introduction to Metaphysics*.[4]

I note all of this because I want to make a point about something that
philosophers like Heidegger, who kept busy workshops and sheds, teach us
about the nature of philosophy, which is often occluded or even rejected:
philosophy is a praxis that requires relentless exercise, and thinking as writing and writing as thinking constitutes one, and only one, of the ways in
which philosophy is practiced. As someone who is not a Heidegger scholar
per se, but who has studied him closely and intensely since graduate school
with what I would call a morbid and terrified fascination, I came to
respect the intensity of Heidegger's passion for thinking and for working
on his thinking through his writing. This is exemplified in his *Schwarze
Hefte*. Their status is ambiguous, as the genre to which they belong is not
entirely clear. They were notebooks in which clearly Heidegger put down
very personal, highly controversial, and potentially incriminating thoughts.
In this sense they represent a sort of "philosophical diary" inasmuch as
Heidegger is writing out thoughts that he does not feel confident about
publicly voicing, but which at the same time have a temporal and occasional character. Many of the "considerations" and "reflections" in these
notebooks are directly addressed to current events in Heidegger's life and
times. In this regard the annotations are historically and biographically
indexed, as when Heidegger reflects on his year as *Rektor*. The *Notebooks*
remind us that thinking takes place in time, and that time is preserved in
the history of a thought, the temporality of a thinking. The notebooks are
thus a testament to Heidegger's conviction about the temporality of thinking
itself. In fact, he wrote indexes to each so as to keep track of certain key ideas.

But the *Hefte* are also just "notebooks" in which Heidegger jots down
ideas that he will elaborate on later, in greater detail and in a less "personal"
way, in the book manuscripts, such as the *Beiträge*. As we read over the
four volumes published so far, we can see that some of the annotations are
brief, elliptical, and aphoristic. Some are no more than a couple of sentences. But a few go on for pages. And there are not only Heidegger's own
indexes but also elaborate internal cross-referencing, which means that
Heidegger was rereading and reevaluating the developing coherence or
integrity of his "considerations," "reflections," and "indications." In this
sense the notebooks are not just a diary, a record of what was thought or

what took place, but also literally a writer's workshop. In the notebooks Heidegger is fashioning a language, formulations, and phrasings that then get worked over in other words and into more developed texts. Trawny notes in his *Heidegger and the Myth of a Jewish World Conspiracy* that while the notebooks contain annotations that seem like attempts and first approximations of certain Heideggerian formulations, they also do not have the unfinished character of someone's rushed diary, in which ideas have been, as it were, written in a condensed and hermetic way for later completion or articulation.[5] Thus these *Hefte* are also texts that have a finished character that a diary or even a traditional notebook does not have, and we must approach them with the utmost seriousness and treat them with perhaps the same hermeneutical care that we devote to works like *Besinnung* and the *Beiträge*.[6]

These preliminary considerations set the stage for a more substantive discussion of why these notebooks were kept secret and why they have reignited a new wave of debates concerning Heidegger's Nazism and anti-Semitism—or what we should call, following Domenico Losurdo, anti-Judaism.[7] In what follows I will first identify at least seven ways in which Heidegger's anti-Semitism is articulated in some of the remarks found in these notebooks and I will try to show why Heidegger's anti-Semitism is a metaphysical form of it, what Peter Trawny and others call a "being-historical anti-Semitism."[8] Then I will turn to the vexed relationship between Heidegger's metaphysical, being-historical, or linguistic racism and his metaphysical anti-Semitism by discussing the relationship between the animal and those "people" who are neither historical nor whose language is a privileged site for the disclosure of *Seyn*. These are peoples for Heidegger whose being cannot claim to be being-historical and who are unable to appreciate or respond to the givenness of Seyn. It should be noted at the start that reading these *Hefte* is an uncanny and discomfiting experience, for by reading them we are brought to the razor's edge between the abyssal profundity of risky thinking and the depthless banality of philosophical kitsch—we are riveted at that edge of undecidability: whether to scream in outrage or to burst out in laughter.

METAPHYSICAL ANTI-SEMITISM, I.E.,
ONTOPOETIC-GEOPOLITICAL ANTI-SEMITISM

In approaching Heidegger's anti-Semitic comments in his *Hefte*, as well as in his correspondence and personal communications, I should like to begin with three important clarifications.

First, I take it that there is neither vulgar nor sophisticated racism, just as there is neither crass nor classy anti-Semitism, with one being supposedly more excusable, acceptable, or tolerable than the other because of its degree of "culture." All forms of racism and anti-Semitism are as culpable and undesirable as the virulent, pedestrian, and unthinking forms we have painfully learned to immediately reject and denounce. Heidegger was an anti-Semite, even as he tried to give his anti-Semitism philosophical height, weight, and sophistication by dressing it in the philosophical regalia of the language of being and metaphysics.

Second, however, we also have to acknowledge that Heidegger's anti-Semitism was not a form of biological racism. As many have eloquently demonstrated, Heidegger was an inveterate critic of all forms of biologism and biologistic racism. Yet anti-Semitism does not require biologism. In fact, this is what makes anti-Semitism a distinct form of discrimination, namely that it endures and continues to be so entrenched because it does not fit within the schema of received, Western racialist thinking. The Jew does not belong first and foremost to a race. But the Jew also is not simply defined by a universal faith or traveling belief that has no homeland and no blood ties. While the Jew is a product of miscegenation from the outset, he or she is also held together and defined by blood ties that are always proclaimed and reclaimed in the name of a faith practice—a ritual, a belonging to a community of faith. Jews are thus neither a race nor simply an ethnicity. Jews are perhaps the hyper-race because of their blood lineage, held together by an avowed commitment to live by their faith. This is to say that one can be a committed anti-Semite even if one does not have a shred of racism, or, rather, biologistic racism. It is for this reason that, along with Beral Lang, notwithstanding Robert Bernasconi's skepticism about the term, I would speak of *metaphysical* racism and *metaphysical* anti-Semitism, that is, forms of invidious distinctions that are matched and connected to very effective forms of discrimination, at times turning into forms of violent exclusion and extermination.[9] By metaphysical anti-Semitism, however, I mean something that can be made more concrete by disaggregating it as an ontopoetic-geopolitical anti-Semitism.

The third preliminary reflection qualifies the prior one and takes up some of the themes that have emerged in the essays gathered in the present volume. Still, I will briefly illustrate with an example. Robert Bernasconi has been engaged in a debate with Pauline Kleingeld about whether and when Kant ceased to be a racist.[10] As we begin to read and make sense of the *Hefte*, some may want to begin to debate a similar question about Heidegger. Some will ask, when did Heidegger cease to be an anti-Semite, if he ever did? I would like to suggest, in response to Tom Rockmore's text, that we can discern at least three stages of Heidegger's anti-Semitism and/or anti-Judaism.[11] In view of the evolution of Heidegger's anti-Semitism, it will become clear that he is not simply anti-Semitic but anti-Judaist as well. He develops a specific way of thinking about Jews, rather than simply the Semitic tribes.

There is a first stage that seems to stretch from the 1910s and 1920s up through 1933, which we might call pedestrian or *das Man* anti-Semitism. A second stage spans the *Rektoratsrede* to the end of the war. Following Trawny, we call this being-historical anti-Semitism, *seinsgesischtchilicher Antisemitismus*, or philosophical anti-Semitism. This anti-Semitism belongs to the period when Heidegger is engaged in his own form of "private National Socialism." But we can also talk about a third stage that would reach from the end of the war to Heidegger's death in 1976, and this belongs to the period of the fourfold, the thinking of *Gelassensheit*, the period of waiting to be saved by a god. We could call this "Letting be anti-Semitism," "Releasement anti-Semitism," or "postmetaphysical" racism. But this is just a very preliminary chronology.

I will now argue that we can discern at least seven ways in which Heidegger justifies or rationalizes his anti-Semitism during the 1930s and early 1940s, the period when he writes some of the remarks we are now forced to consider:

First, Heidegger thinks and argues that one has to identify the Jew with the completion of Western metaphysics. The alleged Jewish world conspiracy is but the culmination of Western metaphysics, just as the forces of the gigantic and of machination are expressions of the same world-historical process. For this reason, it could be argued that, for Heidegger, the Jew is

Nietzsche's "Last Man," the embodiment of the culmination of metaphysics, understood as the fateful self-giving of Being.

Second, and along these lines, the Jew is representative of the empty rationalism and universalism that defines modernity and of the culmination of Western calculative thinking. As a vociferous critic of liberal and humanistic universalism, which is based on an anthropocentrism, Heidegger identifies the Jew with the cosmopolitan and democratic principles of a calculative thinking that stands in opposition to grounded, world-historical, localized, meditative thinking. If, as we read in the texts from the mid-1930s, in particular the 1933–34 seminar on *Nature, History, State*, "relatedness to space, that is, the mastering of space and becoming marked by space, belong together with the essence and the kind of Being of a people," then this relatedness and being marked by space is alien, inaccessible, and incomprehensible to "Semitic nomads" (NHS 81/55, 82/56).

Third, Heidegger takes the historical prejudice that associates Jews with money and gives it a "being-historical" sense. The Jew is the embodiment of the domination of calculation and machination that for Heidegger characterized modernity. The Jew is to calculation as number is to machination, i.e., the reduction of that which truly presences, being, to the empty, deterritorializing, and dehistoricizing formalism of number.

Fourth, the Jew, inasmuch as he or she personalizes "number," the empty measuring of quantity that displaces and dislocates, likewise personifies the rootless nomadism of the cosmopolitan and enlightened liberal subject. Stuart Elden has provided an extremely useful summary of Heidegger's thinking about number. It would be relevant to quote him extensively so as to see how it is that the philosophical reflection on number prepares the ground for the peculiar personification of Jewishness as quantity. Now quoting Elden (who is summarizing discussions of Aristotle's physics in *GA 9, Wegmarken; GA 10, Der Satz vom Grund*; and *GA 69, Die Geschichte des Seyn*):

1. Mathematics is an abstraction, an extraction from, an extractive looking at [*Heraussehen*] being. There is therefore a *Khorizein*, a separating, between mathematics and being.
2. Arithmetic's *monas*, the unit is *athetos*, unpositioned, geometry's *stigme*, the point, is *thetos*, positioned.

3.   Mathematical objects are positioned but do not have a place. For the Greeks, the objects they are abstractions from have a place. The modern concept of space is not present in either.

4.   Place has a *dunamis*. This should be understood ontologically: every being has *its* place. Place is something belonging to beings as such: it is their capacity to be present.

5.   The extension of material is not sufficient to understand place.

6.   Motion is tied up with place. Only what is movable is in a place, but place itself does not move.

7.   Everything perceivable has stretch, size, *megethos*. This is understood as *synekhes*, the *continuum*. This is a succession, not only where the ends meet in one place, but where the ends of one are identical with the next.

8.   This is the crux of the difference between arithmetic and geometry: the mode of their connection is different . . .

9.   Therefore, though points can be extracted from a line, these points do not constitute the line. The line is more than a multiplicity of points, the surface more than the multiplicity of lines, the solid more than a multiplicity of surfaces.[12]

The Jew, qua personification of number, embodies the worldlessness and baselessness that stands opposite a "metaphysical" people who belongs to the homeland and whose autochthony is rooted and nourished by the soil of a "we" that affirms and decides for itself in and through its state. Additionally, since this "we" that affirms itself through its state is a historical decision, indeed, is *the* historical decision par excellence, it could be argued that, conversely, this worldlessness and this being without a proper home also mean that the Jew would be without history, would be outside the time of the decisive. The Jews, at least during the time Heidegger was writing, had neither a homeland nor a state. Thus, for Heidegger, they could not be epochal, make history, rather they just leave a mark in time as an event of nature. They were in time but not in history. One can also extrapolate, given the Jews' relationship to their different adopted languages, including German, that Heidegger would see Jewish polyglotism as an additional mark of their worldlessness and baselessness. The Jew belongs to no language and thus lacks the most elemental ground of all: a world-historical language. They are not privy to the poietic-ontological gift of a metaphysical people. As Maurice Olender argued in his wonderful book

The Languages of Paradise: Race, Religion and Philology in the Nineteenth Century: "Language not only defined the human being; it was also the primordial instrument of political association."[13] Heidegger subscribed to this belief as well, but for him the politics of language and language as the site of the political become the ground for political exclusion.

Fifth, the Jew is the personification of the principle of race thinking that is ultimately based in Judeo-Christian and Renaissance humanism. The Jew lives by the principle of race thinking, and it is for this reason that Jews are both the target of racialism's most virulent application and also, by the same token, those who seek to limit its application while nonetheless deploying it for their own ends. But, to underscore, Heidegger is here transposing biological racism onto what Marion Heinz has called "existential-ontological racism." As she writes, "In the place of biologistic theories of the worthlessness of the Jewish people, Heidegger affirms a racism founded on existential ontology within his theory of the Jews as aliens and enemies of the life of the German people."[14] This existential-ontological racism places Jews within what Trawny has called a "being-historical Manichaeism,"[15] in which the metaphysical people confront the antimetaphysical people. As a metaphysical foe and menace, the Jew instigates the sacrifice of the blood of the metaphysical people, while the Jew uses others as proxies for his or her world-historical criminality.

Sixth, the Jew is added to the pincers that grip central Europe, in general, and Germany, in particular, so that we now have a tripartite world-historical tongs made up of Americanism, Bolshevism, and world Jewry. The formulation articulated in *Introduction to Metaphysics* is now updated to say: "Europe lies in the pincers of Russia, America, and the Jews, which are metaphysically the same, namely in regard to their world-character and their relation to the spirit." (cf. *GA* 40:48–49/50). Jews are now also part of the "dawning spiritlessness, the dissolution of spiritual powers, the deflection of all originary questioning about grounds and the obligation to such grounds" (*GA* 40:49/50). Additionally, we have to see how these 1935 claims are updated in the *Schwarze Hefte* and how they are also articulated in the *Beiträge*, where we find explicit articulations of the assimilation of Jewishness to Bolshevism and Christianity (*GA* 65, §19).

Seventh, and following on the prior elevation of Jews to a world-historical phenomenon, the Jew, Jewry, and Jewishness are now viewed in terms of an ontological-geopolitical struggle. They are now a foe in an ontological-geopolitical conflagration and metaphysical confrontation. Jacques Derrida, in *Of Spirit*, had written:

> Geopolitical, then: Europe, Russia, and America are named here, which still no doubt means just Europe. But the dimension remains properly geopolitical. Thinking the world is determined as thinking the earth or the planet. . . . Geopolitics conducts us back again from the earth and the planet to the world and to the world as a world *of spirit*. Geopolitics is none other than a *Weltpolitik* of spirit. The world is not the earth. On the earth arrives an obscuring of the world (*Weltverdüsterung*): the flight of the gods, the destruction of the earth, the massification of man, the pre-eminence of the mediocre.[16]

The Jew is now not just part of this *Welpolitik*, but the prime instigator and framer of it. Jews become the acme of Americanism and Bolshevism, with their social leveling and their despiritualization of the world as well as their enframing and machination of the earth.[17] Kisiel's further elaborations on Heidegger's philosophical-cum-metaphysical geopolitics, however, allow us to see more clearly what is at stake in the assimilation of the Jew to the *Weltpolitik* of spirit. Kisiel argues that when we read the texts from the mid-1930s carefully, *Introduction to Metaphysics* in particular, we can see that Heidegger's philosophical geopolitics displaces itself along three levels: geographical, spiritual, and poietic-ontological.[18] I would argue that the Jew, within this *Welpolitik or* ontological geopolitics, is metastasized into the groundless and rootless cosmopolitan subject that contributes to the despiritualization of the world or rather to the desertification of the world (*Verwüstung*). The Jew is excluded while occluding the poietic-ontological site of the disclosure of being in the most metaphysical of languages: German. If we consider Heidegger's reflections from the late 1920s and 1930s on the world-forming essence of Dasein, to which I will turn in the last part of this chapter, then we could add that the Jew is a destroyer of worlds. While the Greeks and Germans are world formers, the Americans, Russians, and Jews turn out to be world destroyers.

HEIDEGGER'S ANTI-SEMITIC BESTIARY

In the rest of this chapter I want to explore the relationship between Heidegger's reflections on the animal and what I have called his *ontopoetic-geopolitical* anti-Semitism. Elsewhere I explore what I call Heidegger's bestiary and analyze the relationships that Heidegger establishes between time, history, language, the "who" of a people, and the state vis-à-vis his conception of the animal.[19] Heidegger's bestiary, I argue, turns out to be a political bestiary as well.[20] I want to begin with two important quotes from the 1929 course *The Fundamental Concepts of Metaphysics*. The first citation reads:

> As we said, man is not merely a *part of the world* but is also master and servant of the world in the sense of *"having"* world. Man has world. But then what about the other beings which, like man, are also part of the world: the animals and plants, the material things like the stone, for example? Are they merely parts of the world, as distinct from man who in addition *has* world. . . . We can formulate these distinctions in the following theses: [1.] the stone (material object) is *worldless*; [2.] the animal is *poor in world*; [3] man is *world-forming*.
>
> (GA 29/30:263/177)

The second reads:

> Who forms the world? Man according to our thesis. But what is man? Does he form the world in the way that he forms a choral society, or does he form the world as essentially man? Is this "man" as we know him, or man as one whom for the most part we do not know? Man insofar as he himself is made possible by something in his being human? Could this making-possible precisely consist in part in what we are proposing as world-formation? For it is not the case that man first exists and then also one day decides amongst other things to form a world. Rather world-formation is something that occurs, and only on this ground can a human being exist in the first place. Man as man is world-forming. This does not mean that the human being running around in the street as it were is world-forming, but that the *Da-sein in* man is world-forming. We are deliberately employing the expression "world-formation" in an ambiguous

manner. The Dasein in man *forms* world: [1.] it brings it forth; [2.] it gives an image or view of the world, it sets it forth; [3.] it constitutes the world, contains and embraces it.

(*GA* 29/30:413–14/285)

In these quotes humanity, or more specifically the Dasein of the human, is defined as that type of being that forms worlds in three ways: it creates them; it creates or produces images, or representations, of them in such a way that Dasein can survey them as a totality, as the other of itself; and third, once it constitutes them, Dasein can embrace them or take possession of a world or worlds. Provisionally, we can claim that while the animal *has* its habitat, humans *make* their habitats. They do this by imagining their habitat, by making images and representations of it, and then by possessing it, owning it, embracing it and claiming it as their world. These passages are also provocative, for they claim that what is world forming in man is something that determines its essence as human. The world-forming capacity of the human is prior to our humanity. It is inasmuch as we are world forming that we ascend to the height of our proper Dasein. There is another aspect to the world-forming capacity of Dasein that is profiled— inchoately yet effectively—in light of Heidegger's remarks on Americanism, Bolshevism, and the Jews, and that is that Dasein also appears as world destroying. In order to form worlds, Dasein may also have to destroy worlds. If truth is both unconcealment and concealment, the worldhood of Dasein is one that also pivots between creation and destruction. Dasein is world destroyer. In this sense the *polemos* that is epochal and disclosive takes on a bellicose, violent, overpowering character.[21] In fact, in *Introduction to Metaphysics* we find the following passage:

> But humanity is *deinon*, first, inasmuch as it remains exposed to this overwhelming sway, because it essentially belongs to Being. However, humanity is also *deinon* because it is violence-doing in the sense we have indicated [i.e., it gathers what holds sway and lets it enter into an openness]. Humanity is violence-doing not in addition to and aside from other qualities but solely in the sense that from the ground up and in its doing violence, it uses violence against the over-whelming. Because it is doubly *deinon* in an originally united sense, it is *to deinotaton*, the most violent: violence-doing in the midst of the overwhelming.

(*GA* 40:159/167)

Heidegger then ponders why *deinon* is not translated as "strange" (*unheim-lich*), as that which is not at home or is without home. The violent one is also the one who is without a proper place. In fact, in the reflections on *polis* that follow these etymologies of *deinon*, Heidegger turns to an analysis of polis, which is the wherein, the there, the being-in and the being-with of historical being-there. But, when the poets, thinkers, and priests truly are, in the being-historical sense of being-there, then they turn out to be the violent ones. They "*are*—but this says: [they] use violence as violence-doers and become those who rise high in historical Being as creators, as doers. Rising high in the site of history, they also become *apolis*, without city and site, lone-some, un-canny, with no way out amidst beings as a whole, and at the same time without ordinance and limit, without structure and fittingness [*Fug*], because they *as* creators must first ground all this in each case" (*GA* 40:162/170). The violent ones are the true founders and creators of historical worlds.

Similar thoughts are expressed in the seminar from winter 1933–1934, titled *Nature, History, State*, to which we have access through the procotols kept by his students. As the many contributions to the present volume document, these thoughts also resound through the *Black Notebooks*. In these notes, which we know are not from Heidegger's own hand, but which nonetheless were corrected and annotated by him, he claims: "The Now requires the We. For it is the we who says, 'Now it is seven o'clock.' The Now obliges us to decide both forwards and backwards. The animal does not stand under this obligation to decide, because otherwise it would have to be able to order things, as we know from the lecture course. *The animal has no time*" (NHS 67/33, em). And: "We do not understand time as a framework, but as the authentic fundamental constitution of human beings. And only an entity whose Being is time can have and make history. *An animal has no history*" (NHS 69/37, em).

From 1929 to 1934, we have in Heidegger's corpus a clarification of the worldhood of the world. The world is not simply spatiality, the *Da*, of Da-sein. The worldhood of the world is intricately related to time, to temporality, to temporalizing. The world is also a temporalizing of Dasein. The worldhood of the world is the Da—as the here and now of the Dasein. The world-forming essence of the human is related not simply to a projecting-appropriating image making but also a prospective-retrospective temporalizing of Dasein. The animal is world poor because it cannot temporalize. Its world is a habitat without time and thus without history.

Conversely, the Dasein that is world destroying is also the destroyer of history, i.e., is dehistoricizing and detemporalizing. This Dasein tears us out of history and plunges us into the time of flows and processes. We are returned to the natural time of the earth's geological time.

During the summer of 1934, after he has ceased to be *Rektor,* in the course originally announced as The State and Science but that appeared bearing the title *Logic as the Question Concerning the Essence of Language,* Heidegger again takes up the question of the relationship of temporality, history, and the animal. Now, however, Heidegger does acknowledge that there is something like a "history of nature." Fossils give us "instructive evidence" of the history of life on the planet. Heidegger acknowledges that there is indeed "history" outside the region of the human, but, at the same time, even within the region of the human, history can be missing, as is shown by Heidegger's comments on "Negroes" (*GA* 38:81–83/71–73). In order to get to the essence of the history that is proper to the being that is Dasein, Heidegger introduces a tripartite distinction within history or time. We can see time: as flow (as with the earth), as movement and process (the time of life), or as the event or happening that is proper to the human being. Heidegger claimed that "*history* [*Geschichte*] is an event [*Ereignis*], insofar as it *happens* [*geschieht*]. A happening [*Geschehen*] is *historiographical,* insofar as it stands in some *lore* [Kunde], is *explored* [Erkundet] and manifest [*bekundet*]" (*GA* 38:87/76). Then Heidegger's central thesis here is that "'history is the distinctive kind of being of the human being'" (*GA* 38:88/76). History as an event and as a happening is the result of a decision decided out of the resoluteness of a "we," which, in its decision, answers the question Who are "we"? We know that, in this course, history and decision are linked to language. Temporalizing takes place in language. Language is the temporalizing of Dasein. The animal, which does not have time and thus no history, cannot temporalize, and thus it cannot speak. The animal, then, is both speechless and unhistorical. And, we should add, the animal is also incapable of silence, the kind of willful reticence that silently lets *Seyn* speak its truth.

In this same course we also find Heidegger making the following claim: "Even nature, the animate as well as the inanimate, has its history. But, how do we come to say that Kaffirs are without history? They have history just as well as the apes and the birds. Or do earth, plants and animals possibly have after all no history? Admittedly, it seems indisputable that that which goes by, immediately belongs to the past; however, not everything that passes by and belongs to the past needs to enter into history" (*GA* 38:83/73). So the choice is not between nature having a history and Negroes not having one or between nature having no history and Negroes having one. The choice is between what enters properly into history, i.e., enters into it through language, resoluteness, and decision. In short, what is at stake is the affirmation/formation of a people who finds its historical being in its state. Thus Negroes are assimilated to the time of life as process and organic movement because of their lack of a properly metaphysical language and a world-historical state. The time of Kaffirs is the time of living organisms, but not the time that is proper to human Dasein. Interestingly, Heidegger's Negroes are no different than Kant's happy sheep on Tahiti—or his conception of the Tahitians themselves.

With these reconstructions on hand, we can perhaps begin to see how Heidegger's ontopoetic-geopolitical anti-Semitism can lead to the bestialization of the Jew. The Jew is the last human, and the one that plunges Dasein back into animality: the Jew is the beast that bestializes. If Jews are worldless, if they are deprived of a proper metaphysical language, and if they stand as personifications of a calculative attitude toward the being of beings then none of this is entirely different from the thought of an animal being guided by instinct. One can see how it is that Jews are thus also rendered ahistorical, speechless, and without world, even world destroying, without being apolis, in the positive sense discussed in the *Introduction to Metaphysics*. The Jew, the lonely wandering nomad of the desert, is outside history, is without world, but destroys worlds. The Jew is like the rock, worldless, and like the animal, world poor, but also like those who are apolis, the violent ones who are world destroying. The Jewish people may be a people, but they are no different than Kaffirs, Negroes, and Tahitians—the peoples, chimeras of Being, without history, who may as well be happy beasts stranded on the Jurassic Islands of political bestiaries.

4

"STERBEN SIE?"

The Problem of Dasein and "Animals" . . . of Various Kinds

BETTINA BERGO

Now, technology as secularization counts as a force: it is destructive of the pagan gods and their . . . cruel transcendence.

—EMMANUEL LEVINAS, "SECULARIZATION AND HUNGER"

This chapter grows out of three themes in Heidegger's philosophical anti-Semitism as explored by Peter Trawny: worldlessness, "machination," and the "*brutalitas* of being." I would like to expand a tension between Heidegger's critical stance toward racial thinking, caught as it is in the subjectivism of modernity, and his more "practical" attitudes toward *Rassenkunde* in Freiburg. Trawny's evenhanded arguments remind us that we should "consider how [Heidegger's] being-historical interpretation of race belongs in the context of the . . . narrative of the history of Being more generally."[1]

While for Heidegger the science of race that emerged in the nineteenth century belongs to the history of being, itself caught up in the world domination of machination and technology, racial sciences demanded policies in institutions such as the German universities and related research institutes. Trawny reminds us that, for Heidegger, the "'unconditionality' of machination includes the absoluteness of 'race thinking.'"[2] Yet it is one thing to believe that Heidegger's own fundamental ontology would escape such absoluteness by situating race thinking within the history of meta-physics as a perverse phenomenon of modernist subjectivism, and another to observe the impact of the explosion of sciences like *Rassenkunde, Rassenhygiene, Vererbungslehre* on philosophers and their projects in the 1930s. This concerns the relationship between hermeneutics, transcendental phi-losophy, on the one hand, and the legal, scientific, and political context on the other. How to think such complex interactions? More important, when scientific thinking unfolds as a radically critical project in service to the people and the nation—and thus at the level of what ultimately becomes collective delirium—how can we imagine that the absoluteness of race thinking does not entail an ontological claim about what is, about the reality of concrete existence? Moreover, can the new and intersecting sci-ences of bodies and worlds not lead to the introduction of levels or types of lives within our conception of existence itself? Can we imagine that an elaborate interest in the way beings inhabit their environments would have no implications for the question of being? Trawny has argued that "race thinking" in Heidegger receives a clear being-historical contextualization, and presumably this contextualization offers Heidegger the wherewithal by which to distance himself philosophically from race thinking. Yet biological questions, as broadly conceived as they were in the 1930s, surely proved dif-ficult to bracket, despite Heidegger's growing awareness of the limitations of National Socialist ideology. There is no question that relationships between environment, behavior, and the discourses of biology and life were philo-sophically fraught—no question either that the intuition of studying life within its lifeworld or criticizing concepts such as "the survival of the fit-test" or natural selection as *bourgeois* were sometimes quite profound. Indeed, Heidegger had recourse to such intuitions in the works of Jakob von Uexküll in his 1929 lecture course *The Fundamental Concepts of Metaphysics*. Perhaps one way to address the aforementioned relationship between organ-isms, environments, and something like the levels of being is to focus on Heidegger's approach to "life" in his philosophical works from 1927 to 1936.[3]

This focus is motivated by a surprising remark Trawny makes in his introduction to *Heidegger and the Myth of a Jewish World Conspiracy*. In light of Heidegger's defensive claim that the "arranging of racial breeding" should not be attributed to "life itself," Trawny adds that, "with this thought, Heidegger does not mean to meddle in matters of biology."[4]

But we are well founded to wonder whether a concern about life would not require meddling in the anti-Darwinian biology promulgated in the German schools of *Umwelts-* and *Erbbiologie* that proliferated in the 1920s and 1930s. I will argue that Heidegger's meddling moves from his extensive examination of von Uexküll's ethology (1929) toward a search for a new relationship to living beings and the question of a hierarchy of existents (1936).

This chapter is drawn from a longer study on Heidegger, embodiment, and *Angst*, which argues that *life* is central to a difficulty that Heidegger confronted from at least 1927 to at least 1936. This is a question he received, inter alia, from his long meditation on Nietzsche's hermeneutic of forces and bodies and his "idea of ideas," eternal recurrence, which concerns minimally the meaning of being-alive and the possibility of getting one's life into view.[5] Put succinctly, in the age of mechanism and vitalism, a question surreptitiously dogged *Being and Time*: in what way is the existent called Dasein alive, if it can be said to be so at all?

DASEIN AND LIFE

Perhaps Heidegger could not but meddle in biology. Let us begin pragmatically. How to resist the temptation to recall one "professional" act of meddling that occurred on April 13, 1934, shortly before Heidegger resigned from the rectorship at Freiburg. Emmanuel Faye observes that, though he was no longer obliged to make any display of activism, Heidegger wrote to the ministry at Karlsruhe, informing them that he had been demanding "for months" a "full professor's chair in racial doctrine and racial biology."[6] Faye's point is that Heidegger was not simply following orders; rather such studies were crucial to the work of the university. Ultimately, Theodor Pakheiser, member of the Association of National Socialist Physicians, who had been teaching at Freiburg as an adjunct, received the chair, and shortly thereafter, thanks to Heidegger's urging, Hans Riedel, former director of the Office of Race of the Freiburg SS, became full professor. Riedel was a gifted student of Eugen Fischer, a personal friend of Heidegger and the founder of the eugenicist Berlin Institute. The overarching goal was to promulgate "the National Socialist worldview and racial science."[7]

But what of the philosophical level? Here, we must be more prudent, as the thinking of being should not be reduced simply to a sort of metaphysics of German essence and action. Nevertheless, Heidegger did meddle there as well in biology—a biology elaborated on the findings of entomology and inspired by von Uexküll (who did not focus on higher primates), but also a biology shot through with metaphysics, albeit more sophisticated than works like that of Ludwig Clauß (*Die nordische Seele*, 1923) or Erich Rothhacker, whose *Geschichtsphilosophie* Heidegger appreciated.[8] Now, arguably, if a weakness of *Being and Time* was its proximity to philosophical anthropology, then works like the 1928 *Metaphysical Foundations of Logic* and the 1929 *Fundamental Concepts of Metaphysics* represented efforts to move past philosophical anthropology and address the question of being, as well as life, by strengthening the distinction between man and animals, exploring new *Stimmungen*, like boredom attuned to nothingness, and ultimately posing the redoubtable question of *Stufen* or levels within Being itself (*GA* 26:106–111/85–89).[9] This enumeration of themes is condensed, intending to suggest simply some of the difficulties Heidegger encountered as he moved toward a largely a-subjective approach to being as *Ereignis*.

The argument concerning Dasein and life, which I will take up momentarily, consists of three leitmotifs: *Benommenheit*, *Eigentlichkeit*, and *Nichtigkeit*. *Benommenheit* concerns the relationship between a being and its environment. *Eigentlichkeit* concerns selfhood or ipseity, the presence or absence of a self in beings able to pose the question of their being and in beings moved by drives. The third, *Nichtigkeit*, is about the experience of nothingness versus that of elimination in animals caught up in their environments. In order, then

1. *Benommenheit*, or being taken up, distracted, captivated: In contrast to Dasein (whether conceived as alive or not), the animal is captivated by its environment. The circuit of existence that it has therewith is so close and encompassing that the animal could never be conceived as deploying a world. It is fundamentally world poor. Yet we might forget that Dasein can also be *benommen*—and here the vast semantic network growing out of the verb *nehmen* shows its power in Heidegger's thought—Dasein is *benommen* when anxiety takes it "all the way back [*zurückgenommen*] to its naked uncanniness [such that it] becomes fascinated [*benommen*] by it.

This fascination [*Benommenheit*], however, not only *takes* Dasein back from its '*worldly*' possibilities, but at the same time *gives* it the possibility of an *authentic* potentiality-for-being."[10] While Dasein receives this potentiality from *Benommenheit*, the animal, a mere drive being, derives nothing from its version of captivation. Nevertheless, the term is the same.

2.   *Eigentlichkeit*, as opposed to *Eigentümlichkeit* or animal "ipseity": We recognize authenticity, attributed to Dasein from 1927, in *Eigentlichkeit*, but when read in light of *The Fundamental Concepts of Metaphysics* we are justifiably tempted to contrast *Eigentlichkeit* with animal *Eigentümlichkeit*. The merely living being is not *eigentlich*, because its behavior is said to be entirely instinctual. While Heidegger admits that life possesses "a wealth of openness" that may even be greater than that found in the human world (*GA* 29/30: 371–72/255), and although instinctual behavior brings about "*self*-proposing" and "*self*-production . . . *self*-regulation . . . *self*-renewal" (*GA* 29/30:339/232), it remains that the *eigen*- of *Eigentümlichkeit* has nothing to do with the *eigen*- of *Eigentlichkeit*. Dasein must never be reduced to the animal life studied by von Uexküll. Indeed, Heidegger never spoke of Dasein as a drive or instinctual being (although an exception may be found in infants' Dasein).[11] The hermeneutic level afforded no bridges to the biodynamic level, and this may be unavoidable once we have defined Dasein's existence as that of a communicative being-with others (*GA* 2/*SZ* §34)—though it did not keep Heidegger from being concerned about the sense of the livingness of Dasein. After all, a finite being is, by implication, one that dies. Only a living thing can die. But the *eigen* of the animal, although translated as "self," implies no "I," no "ego," and certainly no correlative deployment of a world. In an important sense, the animal *is* its Umwelt.

3.   *Nichtigkeit*, or negation and nothingness: If drive behavior, as found in bees, entails satiation, inhibition, and disinhibition, then we can qualify this behavior as a relating to "this *versus* that"; inhibition, disinhibition, and elimination characterize animal behavior. Caught in the "ring" of its drives (*GA* 29/30:367/252), the animal thus satiates one drive (eliminates it), only to pass into another. Elimination is the animal equivalent of negation. The praying mantis copulates with the male, and, once this drive is "satisfied," the male becomes her prey (copulation is eliminated). If elimination is a mode of negating, it is in no way that of the negating effectuated by anxiety. Indeed, the 1929 lecture "What Is Metaphysics?" deepens

Heidegger's heuristic of the semantic universe of nothing (*Nichts*) and negating. Using psychological and existential factors like the experience of "unyielding antagonism," "stinging rebuke," "galling failure"—experiences his audience would have found comprehensible and moving—Heidegger argues that these open onto the nihilating nothing (*Nichten des Nichts*) that robs us of speech (*GA* 9:117/92, 112/89). Here to be a Dasein means "being held out into the nothing" and out over beings (*GA* 9:115/91). This existential-hermeneutic transcendence, in which we become "aphasic," nevertheless has nothing to do with the *Be-seitigen* of animal behavioral elimination.

We thus see three fundamental dimensions thanks to which Heidegger distinguishes the hermeneutic existence of Dasein from animal life: fascination versus captivation, a hermeneutic self *versus* a drive self, and two senses of negation distinguished by transcendence *versus* pure immanence. That is the "transcendence" effectuated by anxiety, and, later, by being held out into the nothing, *versus* the immanent negation of mere elimination. One becomes hermeneutic, the other is purely behavioral; one implies having (and losing momentarily) a world, the other is poor in world or strictly driven by conditions in the environment.

I am admittedly proceeding quickly, because, beyond highlighting the cases of semantic parallels whose intersections are radically foreclosed, I want to come back to a few arguments from the 1936–38 *Beiträge*. I am guided in this by Heidegger's query in "The Danger" (1949), "hundreds of thousands die in masses. Do they die? They perish. They are put down [*Sterben Sie? Sie kommen um. Sie werden umgelegt*]" (*GA* 79:56/53). This is a well-known discussion of mechanization and the fabrication of corpses, followed immediately by an allusion to the starvation of millions in China.

Much depends on three things here: that Dasein remain autonomous with regard to its bodily drive existence (presumably through discourse); that Dasein alone (and perhaps not all Dasein) can and must take up its ownmost potentiality for being through the trial of anxiety, and, finally, that Dasein alone deploy and inhabit a world. These factors are interrelated. First, Dasein is a hermeneutic being, although even Husserl did not insist so vehemently on the distinction between the body as experienced and the body as a collection of drives and sensations.[12] Second, any Dasein confronts its ownmost possibility—of impossibility or death—although it is not clear that most human beings thereupon take up their existence as finite. Finally, any Dasein presumably deploys a world, although this again may be hindered by the impositions of technology. If it were the case that a Dasein failed to assume its mortality, or that it received rather than deployed a world, then it could hardly be said to have an authentic existence. This is why some humans merely perish (*kommen um*) rather than die (*sterben*). Could this be one implication of the putative worldlessness of "the Jews"– not to mention their abilities for calculation, which have allowed them to participate in the *Machenschaft* and gigantism that Heidegger argues is destroying the world? Be that as it may, the *Beiträge* hardens the world-deploying versus world-poor binarism of man and animals, correcting what Heidegger fears might have been a source of error, namely, that animals could ultimately have *some* kind of world. But no animal has a world; no animal deploys a world because it is captive to its environment, and humans themselves stand today under the threat of degenerating into *technisierte Tiere* (technicized animals). What the ontological implications of such a degeneration might be is not clear. I would suggest, however, that Heidegger's earlier qualification of animals as world poor may have been transferred, in 1936–38, to those humans who, as technisierte Tiere, are unable fully to assume their ownmost possibility and open themselves to the question of questions. Does Heidegger not write: "To die however means bearing death in its essence" (*GA* 79:56/53)? This issue becomes all the more pressing insofar as the *Beiträge* seem to be saturated with Heidegger's reading of Nietzsche, for whom, as I suggested earlier, the question of life is complex and unavoidable. Let us proceed then to 1936.

HEIDEGGER CLARIFIES HIS POSITION ON ANIMAL BEING (1936-1938)

One should object that "dying" for Heidegger is always already within the hermeneutic framework, which understands dying authentically as the possibility that alone happens to "me." But what, if not animal or bodily death, underlies the hermeneutical appropriation? What, if not death as the literal impossibility of possibility, as Levinas reformulated the expression, makes possible the challenge of appropriating my "end" as my eigentliche possibility? We cannot know our physical death. We know death only through the death of other beings, both Dasein and animal. Yet we can imagine why Heidegger refused to address a death that was corporeal, embodied: any turn to biological death—of whatever being—would require that he return to the question of biological *life*. He foreclosed such an approach at least as early as *Being and Time* (§10).

In 1936, at a time when he was writing his *Überlegungen* (*GA* 94) and pondering the work of "the last metaphysician," Nietzsche, Heidegger inserted notes on "life" into the section entitled "The Leap" in his *Contributions to Philosophy* (*GA* 65:227–92/177–227). There is not space enough here to go into an extensive discussion of those notes. We are here in what has been called the thought of Heidegger after the "turn," which is a turn toward the resonance of Being in the (poetic) Word.[13] The two sections explicitly on life (§§153 and 154) follow a reflection about the aforementioned *Stufen des Seyns*, the levels or layers of being, which seems to be implicit in the contrast Heidegger introduces between animals and Dasein, even between Dasein assuming its existence authentically and Dasein as *technisiertes Tier*. This question of levels is also found in the *Metaphysical Foundations of Logic*, but the problems it resolves (the nature of animal life, for example) are at least as significant as those it elicits. In the *Contributions*, after recapitulating the systems of thought in which being effectively unfolds at different levels (e.g., Platonism, Neoplatonism, Christian theology, Leibniz), Heidegger rejects such approaches. Arguing that Platonic-Idealistic systematics are impossible because they do not go far enough (*weil unzureichende*), Heidegger asks "how to rank what is living, 'nature' and what is non-living in it" (*GA* 65:274/215, tm). Presumably, a hierarchy in nature, beginning with what is not living and ascending through life forms (not unlike Ernst Haeckel's elaborate 1879 schema) would address the distinction between drive organisms whose behavior was strictly dependent on environmental activation *versus* organisms capable of ek-sisting relative to their environments (Dasein). However, even Leibniz's hierarchy of existents failed to provide criteria sufficient to account for the questioning being that is the human. Indirectly, the question was nevertheless settled, if provisionally, on the basis of world formation versus world poverty.

By 1936, Heidegger has radicalized the binarism of world formation *versus* world poverty, presumably setting himself in the position where the

Stufen des Seyns seems unavoidable. He states, in §§151 and 152, that the mere distinction between being and beings, in the new beginning he is proposing here, "says nothing and leads into error" (*ist jetzt nichtssagend und irreführend*). If the distinction of being and beings opens onto "the domain of the event of the originating essential occurrence of being"—in short, the *Ereignis* or event of subjectless being in truth—then levels of being are implicit but require new criteria. "If we consider the differentiation between beyng and beings as an appropriation of Da-sein and a sheltering of beings, and if we note that everything here is thoroughly historical and that a Platonic-idealistic system has become impossible on account of its insufficiency, then there remains the question of how to place in order what is living, "nature" and what is non-living in it . . . and their power of truth (primordiality of the sheltering of truth and thereby the originating essential occurrence of the event)" (*GA* 65:74/215). In the thinking of the event, which characterizes the project of the *Contributions*, the possibility arises of thinking about life in a new way—both in relation to the consequences of technology and apart from them, if possible. However, this implies situating the biology of his time and determining whether or not it affords a viable approach to beings, much less levels of being not limited to mere entities, that is, reaching all the way to the being, Da-sein, for whom being "events" or comes to pass as an event. "But must there be 'biology' as long as the fundamental relation to living beings is unclear, as long as the living being has not become the other resonance [*anderen Widerklang*] of Da-sein" (*GA* 65:275/217)? Under the sway of Machenschaft, the sciences of life serve the instrumentalization of beings, living and nonliving, and within the framework of technology biology has proved better able to destroy the living being than to bring out any relationship of truth and sheltering between Da-sein and other animals.

Heidegger does not have an answer to this problem. In *Contributions* §154, "Das Leben," he returns to the dilemmatic distinction between the authentic self and the self-absorbed by its environment, which returns him to the relationship between the being that is Dasein and those selfless beings in which species life predominates (*der Vorrang der "Gattung," die kein "Einzelnes" als selbstisches kennt*; *GA* 65:277/218). This leads him to a surprising conclusion. If we supposed that he would explore the relationship between living beings and Dasein in light of the truth of being and the event, then we are disappointed. The animal, any animal, undergoes an inevitable darkening (*Erdunkelung*) through the action of its instincts. It is darkened and worldless; almost a stone, whose sole difference from the animal is that it is not darkened by instincts. Both animal and stone, river and plant, belong to the earth.

It thus appears that, prior to 1936–1938, Heidegger had not thought through living things as nature (*GA* 65:275/216). Notably, he had not thought through the all-important relationship between "earth" (*Erde*) and "world" (*Welt*), separately or in their interpenetration. He had neglected the question of acceding somehow to earth apart from world.[14] We see these issues arise also in "The Origin of the Work of Art" (1935–36). Again, world is that which Dasein creatively deploys; it is made manifest in the long heritage of culture. Earth is not excluded from this so much as it appears difficult to access outside of world. "Earth, because it is related to history, is in one respect *more originary* than nature" (*GA* 65:275/216). World, on the other hand, is "higher than merely 'created' things, because it is *formative of history* and so lies closest to the event" (*Ereignis*) of the appropriation of Being (*GA* 65:275/216). Heidegger's concern in the *Beiträge* is thus with the relationship between two domains: nature and history. (By 1942, of course, German historicity will be threatened by "Americanism," but behind this lies the stateless, ahistorical "world Judaism").[15]

In 1936 Heidegger simply considers the question of how to reach a dimension of thinking deeper than these two domains, nature and history, conceived separately:

In accord with the types of "ontologies" proper to the different "realms" (nature, history), does there not yet remain at least a provisional way of creating a horizon for the projection according to being [*seinsmäßigen Entwurfs*], whereby those realms might be experienceable in a new manner? Something like that could become necessary as *transition* [*Übergang*]; but it is still precarious [*verfänglich*] inasmuch as it will be very tempting to slip from there into a systematics of the earlier style [of scientific or philosophical discourses or disciplines].

(*GA* 65:274/216)

Heidegger would avoid introducing layers or stages into beyng, even as he seeks a deeper, more obscure ground beneath the separated "domains" called nature and history. It is not that the logic of levels is wrongheaded; it is that it does not take sufficient account of the relationship between Da-sein as the site of the eventing revelation of being and Da-sein as a living being. How then to establish a hierarchy of beings that includes the transition to the event? Rather than solving this difficulty, Heidegger ventures: "Then does beyng itself possess levels? Properly speaking, no; but *neither do beings*" (GA 65:275/216, em).

The question thus shifts to the distinctions between earth and world, nature and history. The new criterion appears to be degrees of *openness* to the world or the ability to unfold a world. However, because Heidegger never considered the higher primates, and because technology has robbed humans of the possibility of deploying a world, it is now humans themselves, as technisierte Tiere, that are often world poor, and animals that are worldless. But is there really one being that creates a world *versus* an immense array of world-poor living things—especially now, in the age of technology and Machenschaft? In *Contributions* Heidegger seeks the ground hidden beneath nature and history, but, however we discern it, it must not be allowed to become a new "discipline" like biology or ethology. The task is made more difficult by the contemporary complexification of the world and destruction of nature, and Heidegger turns to these problems without further elaborating the ground in question. He asks: "Is technology [*Technik*] the historical path to the ending, to the reversion [*Rückfall*] of the last human being into the technicized animal [*technisierte Tier*], the one that thereby loses even the original animality [*Tierheit*] of the inserted [or configured] animal? If technology is taken up beforehand as a sheltering, can it be inserted into the grounding of Da-sein?" (GA 65:275/216).[16]

In his writings after the "turn," technology appears firstly to belong to the abandonment of being and the loss of any possible way back to nature, understood as *physis* or creative flourishing. Technology is not exclusively an abandonment though, because the Greeks (unlike "the Jews") first opened up being through the reciprocal relationship of *physis* and *technê*, which formed a (Greek) *world* (see GA 40:65/67). It is important to note that, in the Greek epoch, *physis* is a word for the process of being; "the basic word for the 'how' of this 'activity' of being."[17] In a move not unlike his approach to the world poverty of animals, Heidegger nevertheless wonders whether, given originary animality and in light of the massive changes brought about in nature as a whole by technology, *any science of beings could be possible*, especially if it opened a fundamental relationship to living being *as* living (not as mere standing reserve for machines)—and which, one way or another, would include ourselves (*GA* 65:276/216). It would seem that we are not ready for such a thing, as biology remains preoccupied not only with the domain of the present-at-hand but is in thrall to what Heidegger calls "contemporary machination" (*neuzeitlichen Machenschaft*). We divine who would benefit from this.[18] But could there be a relation or attitude toward the "living" outside of biology as science? As his discussion proceeds, we learn that this question amounts to knowing in what "space" (*Raum*) such a relationship could unfold. We must keep in mind that Heidegger's hermeneutics had foreclosed Husserl's phenomenological approach to living beings through empathy, not to mention Nietzsche's monism of forces, which unifies living beings without introducing layers or levels. The implications of this foreclosure were greater than the works of 1927–1929 seemed to suggest. In 1936 Heidegger stated them: "'Living beings,' like everything that can be objectified, will offer scientific progress endless possibilities and yet will also withdraw more and more, the more groundless becomes science itself at the same time" (*GA* 65:276/217).

As technology transforms living beings into tools and means, the legitimating *ground* of technology proves ever less probative (cf. "The Question Concerning Technology" [1953], *GA* 7:8–11/*QCT* 5–9). Curiously, like Dasein itself, the living being now withdraws before technology's attempts to instrumentalize it. Scientific progress is unrelenting and reduces living beings and the earth itself to the status of standing reserve (*Bestand*) (*GA* 7:15–17/*QCT* 14–17). Heidegger's observations here illuminate his search for a bridge between nature and history, as well as the question he continuously vacillated on concerning levels of being. No new probative ground had emerged from which to approach Dasein and living beings, history and nature, and, to all intents and purposes, the difficulty remained in the rift between the essence of Dasein as an opening and the essence of the animal as a creature of drives captivated by its environment. The other binaries, earth and world, history and nature, flowed from this obstinate difficulty.

As I suggested, the *Contributions* extends the discussion of drives and captivation begun in 1929 into a new concept of profound *darkening* vis-à-vis any opening to Being (defined now as *Lichtung* or clearing). In animals the Benommenheit of the instincts moves toward Erdunkelung, or the contrary of openness. "['Life' is] a 'mode' of beingness (beyng) of beings. The initial opening of a being toward itself in the preservation of the self. The first darkening in the preservation of the self grounds the numbness [*Benommenheit*] of the living being, and in this numbness all stimulation and stimulatability are carried out, and so are the *various levels* of darkening and of its development [*die verschiedene Stufen des Dunkels und seiner Entfaltung*]" (*GA* 65:276–77/217–18, tm, em). In these surprising lines Heidegger affirms that life is a "mode" of beyng, understood as processual (*Seyns*), thereby introducing a new series of levels—this time, of darkening! Can it be that a being is able to open itself to life, even if the same entities were argued to be incapable of opening to being? Here, the first opening to life, as a "mode of beingness," occurs through self-preservation, which belongs to drive activity. And the activation of the drives entails layers of darkening and thus a foreboding sense of animal Benommenheit. But this poses a terrible question: would *any* living being undergo a darkening in cases where the preservation of self is in question? Would Dasein experience darkening in cases where its preservation of self was at stake? Would it then still be Dasein? If so, then Dasein is both a living being and Dasein, and any living being, "experiences" or is seized by the darkening that grounds the captivation of drives in service to self-preservation. In this context, darken-*ing* as process (Erdunkelung) seems to stand in contrast to lighting; but to what lighting? It clearly cannot be the lighting "of the truth of being" although that too is understood as a process.

Given their imprisonment in their Umwelt, animals open precisely with the drive behavior called self-preservation. That means that opening and darkening neither exclude each other nor should be opposed, since in animals at least darkening already supposes some kind of opening. It is thus quite unclear what the distinction is between the open that is Da-sein and the opening occasioned by instinctual self-preservation. Heidegger had long argued that it was of the essence of instinctual drives to bring about the Benommenheit for which there could be no bona fide world. But does this have implications for Dasein? Again, have we not here an unforeseen reference to the *drive-existence* of *any* living being? Are we not obliged to admit that, in respect to their embodiment, animals are closer than ever before to Dasein as a living being? And, in that sense, how could we understand the difference between them? Why and in what sense is the opening in animals radically different from the opening that Dasein experiences through *Angst*? Did Heidegger not argue that in anxiety Dasein too is benommen, captivated by its sheer uncanniness?

Let me repeat, in 1936–38, Heidegger rejects the introduction of levels into being, which might have allowed him to distinguish between the hermeneutic Dasein and the living human being.[19] This means that humans are in a sense split between their hermeneutic communicative selves and their living animal selves—a disappointingly traditional move. By 1949, in "The Danger," Heidegger's rejection of levels doesn't seem so clear, some beings die while others only perish. *In fine,* how can the darkening of self-preservation be radically separated from the darkening of Benommenheit in *Angst,* that darkening precursive to encountering (the lighting of) being, especially when darkening is no longer diametrically opposed to the lighting of being for Dasein? The very least we can say is that anxiety as darkening suggests something like an "edge" between the two planes— that of hermeneutic existence and that of drive life.

I am less concerned to answer these questions here than to emphasize a certain slippage of meaning between Dasein and living beings that has occurred and will be clearer in 1949. In *Fundamental Concepts* the "self" (*Eigen*) that Heidegger denies to the animal, can nevertheless be observed in his 1929 characterization of it: "accomplishing *self*-proposing and self-*pro*-posing into its own wherefore, intrinsically into itself" (*GA* 29/30:338–39/232). The animal's "self-proposing" activity serves the finality of self-preservation. Seven years later, the preservation of self inaugurates "the first darkening" that is the Benommenheit of living beings. How could this not include humans? We have to take a further step before returning to this question.

We learn in this period that earth and world, brought into articulation by the work of art, are not simply separated, and the technisiertes Tier that we are, or that some have become, appears to have the same instincts of self-preservation as the "animal." Now, the articulation of nature and history (*GA* 65, §152) might permit us to find a path that reconciles Dasein as alive and Dasein as meaning forming. However, rather than pursuing that possibility in the *Contributions,* Heidegger reactively intensifies his separation of Dasein and animality. He writes: "The darkening and *worldlessness.* (Earlier as *world-poor!* Liable to be misunderstood . . .)"

(*GA* 65:277/218). A Dasein would thus be subject to darkening but not be worldless; the animal is now worldless and no longer world poor. There is no progress possible through a comparative approach to beings (Stufen des Seyns), and Heidegger's resolve to avoid systems thinking or to recur to anything like an Aristotelian hierarchy of souls (i.e., a ranking of beings) leaves him with the question: "How does the decision about 'life' rise and fall?" He answers—if this is an answer—"meditation on 'the biological'" (*GA* 65:277/218). Where does Dasein stand in regard to such meditation; where do living humans stand? It seems unavoidable to imagine two biologies here: first, that of *Rassenkunde* and *Erbbiologie* in the line of Eugen Fischer and Heinz Riedel; second, a biology in which there might be a place for the hermeneutic being—at least the one that grasps that "death is the highest refuge of the truth of beyng itself" (*GA* 79:56/53).

THE SOJOURN OF THE GODS

Heidegger's seminar of 1933–34 was entitled *On the Essence and the Concept of Nature, History, and the State* (*Über Wesen und Begriff von Natur, Geschichte und Staat*). It was published in its entirety in English in 2013 and moves in its sixth session from time as "*our* past" to the nature of the state itself.[20] The rest of the seminar entailed reflection on Hitler's state. The possibility of reflection on "the biological," or nature, emerged there only to give way to political considerations. Perhaps Heidegger felt that only a specialist could readily illuminate *das biologische*.[21] However that may be, within and without the university, reflection on the biological was opening onto questions about races and forms of life: if you will, *an applied Stufen des Seyns.*

Like some of the *Überlegungen* (1931–1938), the *Beiträge* were written between 1936 and 1938. In that period, the least we can say is that Heidegger retreated from anything like traditional biology, attempting to imagine what nature might have looked like without the intrusion and domination of machination. He was not really alone in this.[22] Critiques of technology and Darwinism could be found in the *Umweltsbiologie* of von Uexküll (1864–1944), the organicism of Hans Driesch (1867–1941),[23] and throughout the journal *Der Biologe* headed by the "holistic biologist" Ernst

Lehman, who joined the Nazi Party, bringing the journal under its aegis in 1935.[24] Heidegger was perfectly clear that technology—including "machination" and "Judaism"—was contributing to the destruction of nature.[25] He asked, "What was it once?" and answered that nature was the site of the moment (*des Augenblicks*) of the sojourn of the gods; it was creative *physis* for which the essencing of beyng took place (*GA* 65:277/218). His question about an erstwhile nature led Heidegger to several other questions that we also find in "The Origin of the Work of Art": notably, the terrible query of whether nature would ultimately have to be wholly abandoned—and most living things with it—or again, that of who or what could turn such an evolution around (*GA* 65:278/219). Such a turnabout required a return to the "Greek" conception of *physis* into which *technê* flowed harmoniously—most notably in the construction of the beautiful *polis*, the expression of the "genius of a [pure] people."[26]

The unavailability to the project of fundamental ontology of a thinking able to open onto the question of livingness (humans as living beings and animals, particularly "higher" animals, as having some manner of world) comes into a new light in the *Contributions*, which attempts to rethink the relationship between nature and history, earth and world—while deepening the concept of world poverty. An opening had been afforded early on by the embodied quality of that revelatory *Stimmung* called anxiety. After all, whether we approach it hermeneutically or from physiology, the embodied quality of anxiety is not only patent but led thinkers like Freud to argue, in 1920, that anxiety was the sign of the death drive, the drive whose telos was quiescence. This opening is lost definitively after the *Kehre*, or perhaps it was always already lost to hermeneutic phenomenology. (Of course the loss may be our loss too, as we have not solved the difficulties Heidegger pointed out, and some biologists have argued that our best path today may entail multiple, irreconcilable approaches to life: a new conception of the Stufen des Seyns?)[27]

CONCLUDING REMARKS

I argue elsewhere that Nietzsche's ordeal of eternal recurrence elicited profound anxiety, at least in its initial reception.[28] Nietzsche realized this, and he argued that to the one who could say "yes" to his past, the possibility arose of a freedom no longer bounded by the tyranny of that past. It was the dismantling of linear and sequential time, and the destruction of any Archimedean point outside it, that allowed Nietzsche to reach a profound existential sense of time from which Heidegger would work, qualifying it as "ecstatico-horizonal" (*GA* 2:523/*SZ* 396).

While for Heidegger the world is revealed as without significance through anxiety, in Nietzsche eternal recurrence confronts us with *life*, our life. Despite his criticism of the will in Nietzsche and his reticence toward the concept of life itself, Heidegger's 1927 emphasis on resoluteness was indebted to Nietzsche's willing; indeed, he says as much in his 1936 study of the great philologist (see *GA* 6.1 43/*N1* 46–47). From a discussion of Nietzsche, will, and will to power, I came to the question of living beings in light of drives and as compared to the hermeneutic existence of Dasein. This led me in the present essay to the question of "life" in Heidegger and the *impossibility of reconciling it with fundamental ontology's approach to existence.*[29]

The Fundamental Concepts of Metaphysics contains the most sustained discussion of animal life, drives, and world poverty in the Heideggerian corpus (*GA* 29/30:311–404/212–79). Following the biological investigations of von Uexküll, Heidegger defined life in terms of living organisms and organisms as syntheses of organs. This permitted him to distinguish organs from tools in light of the plasticity of organic capacities that phenomenalize as behaviors. Whereas a tool admits of universal use and may require instructions, its finality is determined. Capacities are, by contrast, adaptive; in the animal they are drive based, and this is clearly evinced by the ways in which an environment inhibits or disinhibits a given drive. Having foreclosed the possibility of examining anxiety as the complex "edge" at which embodied processes become simultaneously conscious ones, Heidegger will never address drives in light of human Dasein. Disposing, again, of a path toward life for the Dasein—which might have obliged him to rethink his question "Sterben sie?"—Heidegger further argued that behavior in animals is self-promotion, although the animal can never be said to share an authentic selfhood, or ipseity, with Dasein. Thus, what is proper or eigentlich to the Dasein can never be brought back to what is proper or eigentümlich to the animal. Yet, as I argued, the fact of anxiety itself points toward the ambiguity of Dasein's corporeal and hermeneutic dimensions, not to mention the fact that Eigentümlichkeit ought to be the "property" of the flesh of *any* living being.

Lacking "self" and world, the animal is also not a machine, given its organs; this despite the fact that, according to Heidegger, it enacts, or essentially *is*, its drives. The purposiveness of drives and their resemblance to functionality suggest that, for animals, the distinction between organs and tools needs reexamination. After all, when he addressed Medard Boss and his psychoanalyst colleagues in 1962, Heidegger repeated that it is absurd to speak about drives in terms of humans, because what drives explain is "not the human being at all *but rather mechanics*" (ZS 217/172). Does this too flow from Machenschaft? Even if organs are self-regulating systems whereas tools are not, it remains that the explanation of their operation requires a heuristic extrapolation from mechanics. But even if we acknowledge Heidegger's 1962 Zollikon argument that drives explain behaviors mechanically (by something that is neither conscious nor directly observable because it is purely material), it remains the case that anxiety's embodied roots are linked with more than events occurring in Dasein's world. What explains the trembling, vacillation, and exudation of this state? Psychology at least had long associated anxiety with drives; in Freud it will ultimately be linked to the infant's initial suffocation during separation from the mother's body, just as it was, before that, to what Freud called the death drive. Had Heidegger inquired, then, into the bodily roots of anxiety, he would have been compelled to explore his Dasein or Open in light of our animality, and the aforementioned degrees of openness, which might have attenuated the slippage in his arguments from world poverty in the animal to sheer worldlessness. And one cannot but wonder what that would have implied for his considerations of those who simply "perished" in the camps.

I have argued that the theme of Benommenheit originates in *Being and Time* where Dasein is captivated *not* by any *thing* in its world but by its own Unheimlichkeit, its radical homelessness and its being in a world without objects that is, consequently, nothing, the groundless. What, after all, can it mean that, in anxiety, "I" am confronted by my being-in-the-world when everything that had up until then defined my interest in and relation to that world has evaporated? Is it not the case that Dasein experiences "states" and moods in which its opening to the world is so transformed that it becomes difficult to say that, at all times, Dasein can really deploy a "world" around itself? Is it not, at such times, itself world poor, itself overtaken by a darkening? Or shall we say that there are different types of being poor-in-world? What would be the deciding criterion, above and beyond the dichotomous oppositions: meaning versus drives, world versus environment?

For a poetizing being as opposed to a calculating one, meaning attaches in a privileged way to what Dasein encounters in its world, whether this be what is present-at-hand, ready-to-hand, or other Daseins. To insist that meaning depends strictly on the being that is Dasein, or that drive behavior is proper only to those living beings called animals, is to do violence both to the possibility of "meaning" in animal existence *broadly* conceived and to the Dasein, which thereby finds itself cut off from its life and its embodiment. It is not the same thing to argue that Dasein goes looking for the physiological grounds of its anxiety because it is anxious through and through and to insist that its hermeneutic interest is not dependent on its embodiment or its being alive. To the contrary: inasmuch as Dasein is incarnate, and despite its privileged hermeneutic status, must it not also be a drive-being? Heidegger's distinction between the two Benommenheiten proceeds on the basis of a distinction already established, which only grows stronger in the 1930s. This is not an accident, but its implications are several.

Anxiety is tied to the process of nihilation in "What Is Metaphysics?", where it is at the root of Dasein's transcendence, understood now as "being held out into the nothing" (*GA* 9:118/93) or hovering over beings. This extended interpretation of anxiety does not bring us closer to life as such, though it is an "experience" that returns us to the prehermeneutic situation of speechlessness. Without directly impugning the particular status of Dasein as meaning forming (to adapt an expression from *The Fundamental Concepts of Metaphysics*), anxiety seems to leave Dasein briefly aphasic and unable to distance itself from its world, just like the animals. And this is certainly due to the *bodily* transformation that occurs in anxiety (sweating, trembling, suffocating). Discussing our being held-out-over-the-nothing, Heidegger emphasizes our finitude and our presumptive passivity: "We are so finite that we cannot even bring ourselves originally before the nothing through our own decision and will" (*GA* 9:118/93). Yet, even here, if this finitude implies death, then that death goes unacknowledged as *bodily*; either that is something obvious or it is not worth pondering. The separation between existence and life is worse than tenacious; it becomes insurmountable starting from the way Heidegger thought of biology in 1929 and afterward, first in line with von Uexküll's organicist biology and afterward in light of machination and technology.

The being-historical text entitled *Beiträge zur Philosophie* thus hardened the distinction between Dasein and animal life, largely dispensing with the attunements explored in his *Daseinsanalyse*. It is not without interest, however, to observe this hardening occurring around the time, 1933–1934, that Heidegger was teaching an advanced seminar on the people as the racial substance of the state.[30] Heidegger could have explored—if critically—degrees of openness, or something like Aristotle's types of *psuchai*, without necessarily recurring to the notion of the soul. However, in the *Contributions* §152, entitled "Die Stufen des Seyns" (the levels of beyng), he leaves this eventuality trailing. If he asked in 1936: "How to rank what is alive?" it seems he was also *allowing a certain ranking to occur* in the university, if only for the sake of the metaphysical people.

We have seen that, following the much discussed *Kehre*, Dasein's deployment of world will be elaborated in terms of the tension between earth and world, out of which arises truth. Here, it is art, the poetic word, that opens the clearing for being. But living beings, so far as they are animals (or "Jews"?), have neither culture nor world to deploy (are they just part of earth?). Beyond any question, now, of anxiety and its effectivity, what Heidegger calls "history," a distinctly human concern, is definitively segregated from "nature." This does not go without eliciting in Heidegger a certain malaise.

We can read this malaise in his musings about a biology apt to foster and respect the relationship between the living being in its world and being, albeit a being (*Sein*) that is anything but present-at-hand. "But must there be 'biology,' since it derives its justification and its necessity from the sovereignty of science within modern machination? Will not every biology necessarily destroy 'living beings' and thwart a fundamental relation to them? Must this relation not be sought completely outside 'science'?" he asks (*GA* 65:275–76/217). To be sure, science, framed by "modern machination," itself received as the heritage of Platonic metaphysics, and, in a degenerate way, of "world Judaism," cannot approach living beings in this new way. But, for Heidegger, contemporary science was increasingly proving to be groundless, in perpetual search of itself. Thus the problem of anxiety and embodiment gives way to the vaster problem that preoccupied Heidegger (notably, in light of his renewed attention to Oswald Spengler as "political educator" in 1939): the problem of being, its epochs and the highest values of the West (*GA* 94:420–21; see also *GA* 94:209).[31] In the *Contributions* Heidegger ventures, within the complex context of the *Zukommende* (those to come), whose champion he identifies with Hölderlin, that our ability to withstand the trial of being, understood as the event that takes place in strife, may help us to get out of the current situation, characterized by the abandonment of being, the loss of any ground for life and body, and the reign of utility and technology.

Beyond the *Zukommende*, another possibility also remains, such that "the falling back into the mere life of *world*-poor beings" continues and with it the dominance of those same beings who held the earth as "only something to be exploited" (*GA* 65:399/317).[32] In this alternative an enlarged, virtually apocalyptic vision of those who are to come, as well as the coming god who will help Dasein abide poetically in the tension between earth and world, displaces the meaning of world-poor animals onto the "last men," which recalls Nietzsche's expression. We see now why the animal can no longer be deemed "world poor." Those who cannot abide the struggle unfolding between a world subjugated by technology and those silent, reticent ones who endure now frame the distinction between *weltarmer Wesen* (world-poor entities) and *die wenigen Zukünftigen* (the few who are to come). Both are, presumably, human, and Heidegger adds that a few of them may already be present among us (*GA* 65:400/317). *Their* mood is an enduring, stolid anxiety, an *Unruhe* . . . but they are not world poor like their brethren.

Rather than seeing the living humanity of Dasein, Heidegger looked increasingly, if hesitatingly in the *Überlegungen*, toward the *Zukünftigen*, whose initial appearance seems to take him beyond Hölderlin, penning eschatological musings in a spirit disturbingly close to Spengler.[33] "Yet who is able to adopt that resolution within the self-forming site of the sheltering of truth, and before this, who could even perceive that resolution completely and sacrifice all they have learned for the sake of acquiring the Wholly-other [*für das Übernahme des Ganz Anderen*]?" (*GA* 94:498). We hear in Heidegger's musing an echo of Spengler's devastating remark in *Der Mensch und die Technik* (1931): "We are born into this time and must bravely go to the end that is determined for us. There is no other. To persist at lost posts without hope, without salvation, is duty. To persist like that Roman soldier, whose legs were found before a gate in Pompeii, and who died because one forgot to take him away when Vesuvius erupted. *That* is greatness, that is called 'having a *race*.' This honest end is the only one that one cannot take away from human beings."[34] For Heidegger, only being-historical thought could offer a solution to such a pessimism, but at the cost of an insuperable diremption between Dasein and other living beings, and then Dasein and the "last men," poor in world and unable to assume their ownmost possibility—among them perhaps those who perished in the camps.

5

INCEPTION, DOWNFALL, AND THE BROKEN WORLD

Heidegger Above the Sea of Fog

RICHARD POLT

Heidegger's *Black Notebooks* were kept secret for decades, and now that they have been published they still harbor mysteries. In fact, they often speak of the need "to write from a great silence" (*GA* 94:28). For Heidegger, the most important matters *cannot* be said, at least not in a way that is accessible to common sense; "when philosophy makes itself understandable, it commits suicide" (*GA* 65:435/344, tm). He sees publicness as a threat to genuine experience and insight: in the public sphere, everything is subject to ambiguity, hearsay, and mere curiosity. With publication comes publicity, and with publicity come superficiality and sensationalism—as is evident in some of the initial discussions of the notebooks. Heidegger would be indignant at this reception, but he would also take it as proof of his point that "yanking everything into the public sphere means destroying all genuine Dasein" (*GA* 94:158).

But it was Heidegger's own choice to deliver lectures, to publish books, to preserve these notebooks, and to provide for their eventual publication in the *Gesamtausgabe*. So the spirit of Martin Heidegger has no grounds for complaint. The best way to combat any flaws in the public discourse is to present better public discourse: to develop interpretations of these texts that are not ready-made takeaways, but invitations to focus more intensely and think again.

The anti-Semitic passages in the notebooks have received a great deal of attention, and they deserve it; they raise deep and troubling questions about Heidegger's character and the character of his thought. But some of the more irresponsible discussions have created the impression that the *Black Notebooks* as a whole are an anti-Semitic screed. This is simply a distortion. The first four volumes (*GA* 94–97) comprise 1,753 pages by Heidegger. By my count, twenty-seven passages refer to Jews or Judaism, and these references along with their context easily fit on ten pages. I consider about ten of these twenty-seven passages to be overtly anti-Semitic: that is, they express hostility to Jews as a group or to supposedly Jewish traits, drawing on anti-Jewish stereotypes and conspiracy theories.[1] Some of these passages are arguably ambiguous, and some of the other passages can be read as indicating an implicit hostility.[2] But however we may interpret these texts, it is clear that Jews are not the main focus of Heidegger's notes; they are treated almost incidentally, mostly in passing comments, and Heidegger did not even list Jews as a topic in the indexes he prepared for his own notebooks. What we find for the most part is indifference to the destiny of the Jews, an indifference communicated in that most Heideggerian of forms—silence. Evidently, such indifference can be very culpable. But it is fair to say that, although he had persistent anti-Jewish attitudes, Heidegger was not obsessed with the topic.

AN OVERVIEW

How, then, should we characterize the texts as a whole, and what are their most important topics? I will start with a bird's-eye view and then focus on three themes—inception, downfall, and the broken world—that can go some way toward illuminating Heidegger's troubling attitudes toward both Jews and Nazis.

First, are these texts philosophical? Philosophy (or "thinking") is certainly one of their main themes: what is demanded of thinking, how the contemporary world is failing to meet these demands, and how to prepare for the thinking of the future. These reflections presuppose the experience of engaging in thought. But, in general, Heidegger is not working out philosophical questions and problems or breaking new philosophical ground;

he is reflecting on philosophy as part of a more general meditation on his times and on his own position in the world. (The first-person singular appears far more often in these pages than in nearly any other volumes of the *Gesamtausgabe*.) Heidegger certainly refers to and uses concepts that are developed in his lecture courses and in other nonpublic texts, but he rarely extends them here.

It is another distortion, then, to present the *Black Notebooks* as the capstone of Heidegger's philosophical system. First of all, there is no such system. "I 'have' no 'philosophy'" (*GA* 96:193). Philosophy, for Heidegger, is an adventure one undertakes, not a doctrine one possesses. And even in these terms the notebooks are less philosophical than most of the other volumes. But what they do provide is a valuable glimpse of Heidegger's moods, attitudes, and motives—none of which is irrelevant to philosophy, but primarily illuminate Heidegger as a thinking human being with his own passions and prejudices.

If I had to choose one word to describe the predominant mood of the notebooks, I would say *sour*. These journals were a place where Heidegger went to vent his spleen—characterizing everything from Bolshevism to Americanism, from the movies to hostile readings of his own work, as manifestations of an age utterly lacking in meaning and thought. The sourness sometimes becomes misanthropy, especially once the war has broken out and Heidegger feels overwhelmed by blind and destructive forces that are sweeping across the planet. He then makes extreme statements such as this one: "The last act [of technology] will be that it blows up the Earth itself, and today's humanity will vanish. Which is no misfortune, but the first purification *of being* from its deepest deformation by the predominance of beings" (*GA* 96:238).

"Machination" (*Machenschaft*), i.e., technology, is the predominance of a calculative, manipulative relation to beings that is oblivious to the question of being. (In German, the word echoes *machen* or "making.") Heidegger sees machination as the culmination of the combined subjectivism and objectivism of the modern age: we represent ourselves as self-conscious and willful subjects who stand against objects to be overpowered: "the power of machination . . . must cast down beings, in all their domains, into planned calculation" (*GA* 96:56).

The concept of machination fits all too neatly with anti-Semitic stereotypes that Nazism took to a new extreme. Jews are represented in the *Black*

Notebooks as scheming and rootless; Heidegger refers to their "tenacious skillfulness in calculating, hustling, and intermingling" (*GA* 95:97) and to their "empty rationality" (*GA* 95:46, cf. *GA* 95:56). Jewry has adopted "the uprooting of all beings from being as its world-historical 'task'" (*GA* 96:243).

The Jews are hardly alone in embodying machination, according to Heidegger. America, England, Catholicism, Bolshevism, fascism, and National Socialism all come in for similar criticisms. In fact, Heidegger emphasizes that the Nazis show the same mentality as their supposed enemies, the Jews; they are metaphysically equivalent (*GA* 95:161, 258, 326, *GA* 96:56, 218). There are some glimmers of skepticism here about Nazi representations of Jews, and one almost gets the feeling that Heidegger is about to break through the stereotypes. But I do not think he does, and certainly the negative imagery about Jews is not balanced by any positive images.

Only two groups emerge in the notebooks as having the potential for something other than machination: the Germans, who Heidegger hopes will someday recognize their true vocation as the people of poets and thinkers, and the Russians, whom he distinguishes from Bolshevism, a mere Western import (*GA* 96:47–8, 56–57, 109–10, 124, 134, 139, 148, 235, 237, 241). Some of these thoughts on Russia may have been inspired by the Hitler-Stalin pact, but Heidegger takes care to note that his interest in Russia goes back to 1908 (*GA* 96:148).

It is fairly easy to tally up the many things Heidegger is "against," and the few that he favors. But there are two caveats here. First, he denies that his criticisms are simply negative. "Whoever encounters the distorted essence [*Un-wesen*] by merely negating it is not yet ready for the essence either" (*GA* 95:1). A thinker's "no-saying" should not be taken as "mere opposition and turning away" or simply as an "expression of anger and surliness"; "in truth it is the struggle for the most essential yes" (*GA* 95:20–21). So although Heidegger may be horrified by the so-called distorted essence, this is not a simple matter of yes versus no.

The second caveat is that we must be very clear that Heidegger's standard for judgment is not a moral one. Morality, he insists, is a superficial criterion, based on a bankrupt metaphysics (*GA* 95:13). The Christianity that sustained it for so long is now a pathetic remnant, "screaming as loud as possible about the long-dead God" (*GA* 95:396). Nonreligious but suprahistorical moral ideals of a Platonic or Kantian sort are also obviously dead for a thinker who insists on the historicity of being itself (cf. *GA* 36/37:165–66/129). As for the moral pretension of Anglo-American democracies, Heidegger sees it as a hypocritical ideology, a veneer for the profit motive (*GA* 96:114–15).

It may be true that Americans are prone to self-righteously scolding other nations for their injustice while turning a blind eye to their own misdeeds. But to point this out is usually a moral act, whereas Heidegger refers to American hypocrisy as part of his rejection of the moral stance in general. He attempts to think beyond supposedly childish categories such as moral good and evil or optimism and pessimism. For him, such categories are myopic: they focus on the benefit or harm of one, a few, or many without reflecting on the deeper currents of the history of being, developments that occur on such a vast scale that they reduce all such incidents to epiphenomena, to "the outermost gray scum of a concealed history" (*GA* 95:96).

Although Heidegger is avowedly nonmoral in his judgments, he does have a standard of goodness in a nonmoral sense: "The '*good*' is not the 'pleasant' and not 'happiness,' not the agreeable and not utility, not what ought to be and no mere value, but Dasein's insistence in freedom on the basis of belonging to beyng. But because beyng becomes what is most worthy of questioning for the future ones, freedom is [the] poverty of the stillness of holding out" (*GA* 96:159). The future ones hold out for "beyng." This archaic English spelling has become the most common rendition of Heidegger's somewhat less archaic *Seyn*—a spelling still used by Hölderlin. There is no strict definition of *Seyn*, but it gestures toward an alternative to traditional metaphysical understandings of being as the most universal feature(s) of beings. "Beyng" could be glossed as the granting of the meaningfulness of what is.[3]

What does it mean to hold out for beyng? Heidegger's first caution would be to avoid a *historisch* way of thinking here—chronological calculation based on the science of history, which comes in for surprisingly vehement attacks in the notebooks. The future we must await is not some point on a timeline when things within the world will be altered and rearranged, but a new configuration of worldhood itself; and its coming will not be announced in the news, but will be an inconspicuous event, intimated by the few who are qualified.[4]

INCEPTION

An event that reconfigures the world itself is an inception (*Anfang*). Heidegger distinguishes it from a beginning (*Beginn*), which is just the starting point or the first phase in a process. A beginning is chronologically specifiable; an inception is far more elusive. "The inceptions withdraw from all will to capture them; in the withdrawal, they leave only the beginning behind as their mask" (*GA* 94:283). "We never grasp the *inceptive*; so that it not become a bygone given [*ein vorhandenes Gewordenes*] and thus lose itself, it must constantly withdraw. This is why the inception can never be represented, but only carried out—that is, in the downfall of stepping back, so that the withdrawal may truly *remain*" (*GA* 94:334). An inception is the nonreproducible, nonrepresentable founding of an entire order of meaning.

According to Heidegger, the history of beyng needs to be understood in terms of "the first inception" and "the other inception" (*GA* 65:5). The first, Greek inception asked the question: What are beings as such? The answer was *physis*, the burgeoning and enduring presence of things. This experience degenerated into the categorizing of various sorts of presence and ultimately into the scientific and technological description and manipulation of what is taken as present.

The other inception would "inwardly remember" physis yet no longer take physis as its point of departure (*GA* 94:241). It would turn from *what is*, or beings, to *beyng itself* and ask how it essentially happens. The first inception was "an immediate Yes that took a stand for endurance and permanence" (*GA* 94:49)—it affirmed presence as the central sense of being. In contrast, Heidegger writes in the early 1930s, the other inception is open to "the full essence of being—in which presence (the 'is') is positively incorporated. . . . Not the 'it is,' but the 'so be it' (thrown projection)" is the primary clue (*GA* 94:51). In other words: no longer can we stand before the given as what *is*; that stance has long degenerated from awe and wonder to mere objectification. Instead, we have to become alive to history, to the way in which any givenness of entities presupposes "thrown projection," which draws on a heritage for the sake of a destiny.

What difference would that make? Another entry from this period is cryptic but suggestive: "Here is the original limit of history—not empty, supratemporal eternity, but the stability of rootedness. *Time becomes space*"

(*GA* 94:38). The passage seems to express the desire to belong, to stand, to inhabit a meaningful place—a *there*. Such a place would be founded in a transformative, transfiguring event: "the event of world" (*GA* 94:93, 94), the event of the grounding of the there, the appropriating event—*das Ereignis*.

During his rectorate, Heidegger thinks of this founding in terms that are racial, even if they are not grossly biological: "The projection of being as time . . . opens and binds blood and soil to readiness for action and to the *capacity* for effective *work*" (*GA* 94:127). (Against biologism see, e.g., *GA* 94:143.) This would be a kind of liberation, but not negative freedom as the dissolution of bonds; to the contrary, it would be a kind of binding (*GA* 94:126–27, 140).

As the notebooks continue, Heidegger loses his faith that the new inception can be provoked by a nationalist revolution; it becomes a more elusive possibility to be explored by poets and thinkers. But the relation between the first and the other inception continues to serve as a potent organizing scheme. We stand before a decision between these two, for which "the future ones" can perhaps prepare the way. Only a very few can be admitted to the "domain of essential decisions," and many are excluded. In particular, "The more original and inceptive the coming decisions and questions become, the more inaccessible will they remain to [the Jewish] 'race'" (*GA* 96:46).

DOWNFALL

If the first inception is to be superseded by the other inception, then the first must, somehow, come to an end. This brings us to the theme of *Untergang*. Literally the term means "going under"; it is often translated as "decline." Both translations fail to capture the enormity of the event as Heidegger thinks of it. I will translate *Untergang* as "downfall" and the verb *untergehen* as "collapse."

The first point to note is that an inception, if it is great, ends in a great downfall. "The great collapses, the small remains forever" (*GA* 95:427). "Only those who can never know the inception are afraid of the downfall"

(*GA* 97:17). Or as Heidegger puts it in *Introduction to Metaphysics*, "The great begins great, sustains itself only through the free recurrence of greatness, and if it is great, also comes to an end in greatness. . . . Only the everyday understanding and the small man imagine that the great must endure forever, a duration which he then goes on to equate with the eternal" (*GA* 40:18/17).

Inception and downfall are linked in "the *storm* that blows in beyng itself"; downfall is a sign of beyng (*GA* 94:429). Again, I take "beyng" as the granting of the meaningfulness of what is; Heidegger is claiming that such granting is a powerful upheaval that lasts only until its eventual collapse. Thus, "*beyng* itself is 'tragic'—that is, it has its inception in downfall as an abyssal ground" (*GA* 95:417). "Beyng itself brings itself into the 'catastrophic' course of its history, it becomes revealed in and through it; and 'metaphysics' proves to be the prelude to it" (*GA* 95:50). What we need is "a καταστροφή into the abyss of beyng" (*GA* 95:417).

If beyng is essentially "catastrophic" or "tragic," then we should not fear the collapse of modernity but leap into it. "The *abyssal refusal*—is already the essential happening of beyng! But for the metaphysical gaze, everything looks like a 'downfall,' and downfall appears as no longer standing above in the light and in the security of the ordered above and below of the metaphysically conceived world" (*GA* 96:93). Instead of a decline, downfall might be the highest manifestation of destiny and might become a "transition" to the other inception (*GA* 94:277).[5] Heidegger links this idea to the fate of Germany in a troubling question: "If a truth lies in the power of the 'race' (the innate), will and should the Germans then lose—give up—[and/or] organize away their historical essence, or instead will they not have to bring it to the highest tragic outcome?" (*GA* 94:168).

But what if the greatness of an inception fails to eventuate in a great downfall? Then "there remain two possibilities for the age of the completion of modernity: either the violent and sudden ending (which looks like a 'catastrophe' but in its already decided distorted essence is too low to be able to *be* one), or the degeneration of the current condition of unconditional machination into the endless" (*GA* 96:138–39). For Heidegger, the latter is the more insidious: "The great doom that everywhere threatens modern humanity and its history is this: that a *downfall* remains forbidden to it, for only the inceptive can collapse. The rest comes to an end, and does so in the endlessness offered by the possibilities of a special kind of 'infinities'" (*GA* 96:251). That is, we can continue indefinitely increasing the stock of information we possess about beings, developing ourselves as "the masters and possessors of nature," without questioning the understanding of being that underlies this condition. In one of his more misanthropic versions of this thought, Heidegger writes: "The more gigantic man becomes, the smaller must his essence become, until, no longer seeing himself, he confuses himself with his machinations and thus 'survives' even his own end. What does this mean, that the human mass is no longer worthy of being annihilated at a *single* blow? Is there any more stringent proof of the abandonment of being?" (*GA* 94:282). What Heidegger fears is the indefinite continuation of a tradition whose essential possibilities have been played out. "The sequence of generations can be propagated for centuries, and thus perhaps bring forth examples of human beings in ever greater masses—but there need be no history here, and no people [*Volk*]— for the innermost, formative law of a historical people is itself temporally limited to a span of ages" (*GA* 94:286–87).

A long, well-populated pseudofuture can mask the absence of destiny.[6]

THE BROKEN WORLD

We stand, then, between the first inception and the possibility of the other inception, awaiting a decision that may bring a great downfall, or a sudden destruction that fails to attain the rank of a downfall, or—the worst—a dreary, indefinite prolongation of machination. How does the world look now to Heidegger in this period suspended between inceptions?

Being, he writes, was once "the suddenly arising *lightning* that drew all things . . . into its light," but is "now a tired semblance . . . a used-up possession, prattle, boredom, a name" (*GA* 94:89). "The 'world' is out of joint; it is no world anymore, or more truly said: it has never yet been a world. We are still preparing for it" (*GA* 94:210). Whether the brilliance and integrity of worldhood in the full Heideggerian sense is behind us or ahead of us, today it is absent.

Instead, we live in a time of "criminality" (*Verbrechen*). In a line that Peter Trawny reports from the manuscript of *Die Geschichte des Seyns*

(1938–40), which was omitted from the published version, Heidegger says: "The question remains . . . what is the basis for the peculiar predetermination of Jewry for planetary criminality."[7] In the same text he speaks of a handful of unnamed "planetary criminals" (*GA* 69:77–78/66).

But what sense can this make in Heideggerian terms? Criminality would seem to be a legal and moral concept. However, an important passage in the *Black Notebooks* gives it a "being-historical" interpretation:

> The authentic experience that has been allotted to today's generation, but which it was not able to take over, see through, and lay back into its essential inception, is the unrestricted outbreak of the unconditioned criminality of the modern human essence, in accordance with its role in the empowerment of power into machination. Criminality [*Verbrechen*]: that is no mere breaking up [*Zerbrechen*], but the devastation of everything into what is broken. What is broken is broken off from the inception and dispersed into the realm of the fragmentary. Here, there remains only one possibility of being—in the mode of order. Ordering is only the reverse of criminality, understood in terms of the history of beyng (not in a juridical-moral way).
>
> (*GA* 96:266)

So when Heidegger refers to Jews and others as "criminal," he means that they are contributing to a devastated world, a broken world. Brokenness is not the obvious shattering of things and bodies in "the catastrophes of war" (*GA* 96:45) but an insidious senselessness, a desertification of meaning. Heidegger is more concerned about this "invisible devastation" than about "visible destructions" (*GA* 96:147, 159). Destruction could even be "the herald of a hidden inception," whereas "devastation is the aftereffect of an already decided end" (*GA* 95:3).

In the broken world, ordering is merely "the reverse of criminality." In a narrow sense, lawbreaking and policing are the two sides of crime. In a broader sense, what has been smashed into pieces can be picked up and artificially stuck back together. In a broken world, a world without meaningful connections among beings, the only solution seems to be a forced consolidation or arrangement, a willed and planned order. When worldhood in the Heideggerian sense has faded away—when there is no organic, felt, meaningful coherence to life—it remains possible, and even urgent, to coordinate the remnants. We thus seem to be faced with the choice between "complete destruction and disorder" or "the enforcement of a complete coercion" (*GA* 95:70). Modern man thus becomes the "organizer of nihilism" (*GA* 94:452).

What would heal a broken world? What would count as a whole world? Sometimes Heidegger looks to the Greek *polis* as the pole of a people (*GA* 40:161–62/169–70). Or, in his 1933–34 seminar, he shows a certain nostalgia for the Middle Ages—not in their doctrines or their specific social arrangements, but in the unity that he imagines obtained before modern dualisms broke it apart. According to this seminar (as recorded by Heidegger's students):

> Three great disintegrations . . . have occurred many times since the dissolution of the universal commitments and obligations of the Middle Ages: 1) The collapse of dogmatic-ecclesiastical faith . . . occurred [when] man became a self-legislating being that wills to, and must, found his own Being himself . . . based on reason, that is, mathematical *ratio*, which is elevated to the decisive power of the world. 2) The second disintegration consists in the disintegration of the community—the fact that the individual in himself is the final court of appeal. 3) Descartes carries out the sharp separation between mind and body.
>
> (NHS 88/63–64)

At this time, Heidegger believed that Nazism could overcome these disintegrations and establish a new unity: "Like the medieval order of life, the order of the state today is sustained by the free, pure will to following and leadership, that is, to struggle and loyalty" (NHS 77/49). This attitude was to be replaced by a much more critical one—but, as we will see, Heidegger still declares a certain "affirmation" of Nazism.

NATIONAL SOCIALISM AS THE COMPLETION OF MODERNITY

Heidegger tells us that he saw positive potential in Nazism as early as 1930: "Thinking purely 'metaphysically' (that is, in terms of the history of beyng), in the years 1930–1934 I took National Socialism for the possibility of a transition into another inception, and gave it that interpretation" (*GA* 95:408). This passage is consistent with his statement in 1966 that "I believed at the time that, in engagement [*Auseinandersetzung*] with National Socialism, a new path could open itself up—one that was the only remaining possibility of a renewal."[8] Nazism might reestablish a quasi-medieval or polislike harmony that would unify the modern broken world and maybe even disclose new possibilities for an inception. Near the beginning of his rectorate he writes, "If the German Dasein that is now breaking out is great, then it carries millennia ahead of it—and we are obliged to think correspondingly far out in advance—that is, to anticipate the arising of a wholly different being" (*GA* 94:119–20).

After this initial period of enthusiasm, which is not devoid of apprehension and disagreements, Heidegger increasingly sees that the only unity Nazis can provide is a coerced, calculated order, a totality held together by the exploitation and "mobilization" of the populace and resources of the territory—rather than a deeper gathering in terms of the people's belonging to being. He increasingly attacks particular facets of the new regime and then—in conjunction with an intense study of Nietzsche and Jünger— tries to identify its metaphysical underpinnings. Here Heidegger's views are more philosophical and original than in his scattered remarks on other groups and ideologies. I suspect that if there is something of lasting philosophical value in the *Black Notebooks*, it may well be Heidegger's critique of Nazi metaphysics.

Even in 1933, Heidegger was eager to distinguish his own conception of the potential of the National Socialist movement from its stupider forms. These baser, cruder versions of the ideology, for Heidegger, always included biological racism, which he increasingly sees as a form of subjectivism and will to power. To quote one example: "all glorification of 'blood' is just a surface and pretext, which is necessary to hide from the many what really and solely *is*: the unconditional domination of the machination [*Mach-schaft*] of destruction" (*GA* 95:381–82).

Commentators have rightly observed that Heidegger himself sometimes adopts the language of race and that race does not have to be understood in reductive biological terms.[9] There is a certain concern for the ethnic in his reflections, a concern for the rootedness of the *Volk* in its soil.

The following passage, which dates from around 1939, clarifies the matter to some extent:

> The Jews, *with their marked gift for calculation*, have already been "living" for the longest time according to the principle of race, which is why they also defend themselves as vigorously as they can against its unrestricted application. The establishment of racial breeding does not stem from "life" itself, but from the overpowering of life by machination. What machination is bringing about with such planning is a *complete deracialization* [*Entrassung*] of peoples, by fastening them into the uniformly constructed, uniformly sliced arrangement of all beings. Deracialization goes hand in hand with a self-alienation of peoples—the loss of history—that is, of the domains of decision for beyng.
>
> (GA 96:56)

Here Heidegger returns to his favorite trope of finding sameness in apparent opposites: both Nazi eugenics and Jewish attention to who counts as a member of the chosen people reflect a calculative management of genetic resources. This rationalist perspective prevents one from digging deeper into a people's heritage to discover its distinctive destiny. Thus the Nazi persecution of the Jews is itself " 'Jewish' in the metaphysical sense" and constitutes a "self-annihilation" (GA 97:20).[10]

We must also note that Heidegger gives some credit to concern with "race" as a necessary though not sufficient condition for a people, as in this passage from around 1938: "What is the use—if use is the deciding factor at all—of the best race if it is only a race of dogs, and if one avoids the decision of *who* the ones are for whom—and rightly so—a good race must be demanded?" (GA 94:465). The question "Who are we?" always exceeds race, but that does not necessarily mean that racial cultivation is not needed at all.

Nonetheless, the question "Who are we?" should provoke a people to look for its destiny beyond its merely given facts. Thus Heidegger fights against crude nationalism (GA 95:31)—the idea that a people is an object that can simply be found and fostered as an end in itself. This is a main theme in the first course on Hölderlin that he delivers after stepping down as rector, where he emphasizes the difficulty of finding "the free use of the national," and the rarity of the moments when a thinker or poet can discover such a "use" (GA 39:294/267). This is a retort to reductive notions of a people simply as a mass of millions of genetically related human beings.

Many more aspects of Nazi ideology come in for critique in the notebooks. For one, the Nazis' anti-intellectualism leaves no room for genuine philosophy. Heidegger sums up this mentality as "ego *non* cogito, ergo sum" (*GA* 95:300).

The Nazis' extreme hostility to their designated enemies is another flaw. For Heidegger, the surface enmity of modern states and peoples is based on a fundamental sameness in their goals and means (*GA* 95:39), a shared subjectivist machination. There can be no creative confrontation as long as one is unfreely fighting for a political dogma (*GA* 95:83) and making oneself dependent on one's opponent (*GA* 95:326). "When the opponent is immediately turned into the enemy, and the enemy is turned into the 'devil' in advance, then all opposition loses not only creativity, but any room for a struggle" (*GA* 95:56). In the following passage, Heidegger distinguishes greatness from domination: "The small betrays its smallness most keenly through its choice of an opponent, for it chooses as its opponents only what it thinks it can surmount because it can count on getting applause for making it an object of contempt. But whoever feels contempt always makes himself smaller by what he despises. Only one who can still overcome contempt no longer needs superiority in order to be great, that is, in order to *be* and to let the other lie where and how it lies" (*GA* 94:507). For the Nazis, enmity was of course a matter of potential and actual violence—a power struggle. But as the notebooks unfold, Heidegger increasingly associates this point of view with the Nietzschean will to power as the last stage of modern metaphysics and insists that beyng lies beyond both power and powerlessness (cf. *GA* 66:101/84, 187–88/165–66). "The stupid obstinacy of mere violence-doing becomes the tool of inner destruction" (*GA* 96:176). "Futureless violence-doing" is an example of "*complete lack of questioning*" (*GA* 94:455). Heidegger even speaks of the "mildness" of the thinking of being (*GA* 96:22, 24).

This is a significant shift from *Introduction to Metaphysics*, which seemed to celebrate violence as a fundamental way of being in the world. As the world around him becomes more violent and brutal, Heidegger draws back.[11] He distinguishes heroism from "purely corporeal masculinity in its brutality" (*GA* 94:183) or "the sheer brutality of a street brawl" (*GA* 95:438).

Heidegger even develops a concept of *brutalitas* as the counterpart of *rationalitas* (*GA* 95:402; *GA* 96:18). As the "rational animal," modern man is split in two: he develops logical calculation to its extreme while indulging the bestial impulses. "The *capacity for brutality* is the sign of the actuality of everything actual at the end of metaphysics. In this consists the 'mastering' of technology" (*GA* 96:253–54). Violence and brutality are summed up in the figure of the predator (*Raubtier*). "It is no accident . . . that in the completion of Occidental metaphysics . . . animality comes forth in its completion as the predatory animality of the roving beast; the predator, lusting after victory and power . . . becomes the 'ideal' of humanity" (*GA* 95:422–23; cf. *GA* 96:14, 21–22). True thought and action are replaced by the logistics of bestiality. This striking analysis does seem to capture something of the horror of Nazism—what Heidegger was to call after the war "the production of corpses" in annihilation camps (*GA* 79:27/27).

Other aspects of Heidegger's critique of Nazism include attacks on the quest for *Lebensraum* (*GA* 96:131) and on propaganda as "the art of lying" (*GA* 96:229, cf. 274).

All these thoughts make for gratifying reading. It is hard to avoid taking pleasure in seeing Heidegger, even before the war, condemning feature after feature of the Nazi worldview. It seems safe to say that by the late 1930s he was no National Socialist anymore.

But is the kind of pleasure we take in these passages appropriate? Is it not a *moral* relief of a sort that Heidegger would in fact denounce? We should not fool ourselves into thinking that Heidegger was an anti-Nazi in the way that we take ourselves to be or imagine that we would have been. He does not criticize Nazism as morally inferior to any other contemporary political movement. His criticism is not ethical at all, but purely *seynsgeschichtlich*. His refrain is that Nazism is machination—but so is all else. There is no nonmachinational alternative.

Even worse: despite the fact that Heidegger sees Nazism as profoundly nihilistic, he asserts in 1939 that it must be "affirmed." Let us read further in the important passage that speaks of his early enthusiasm:

Thinking purely "metaphysically" (that is, in terms of the history of beyng), in the years 1930–1934 I took National Socialism for the possibility of a transition into another inception, and gave it that interpretation. With this, I misunderstood and underestimated this "movement" in its authentic forces and inner necessities as well as in the kind of greatness and granting of greatness that is proper to it. Instead, what begins here is the completion of modernity—in a much deeper, that is, more encompassing and gripping way than in fascism. [The] completion [of modernity] required . . . the complete "mobilization" of all capacities of a humanity that has based itself upon itself. . . . On the basis of the full insight into the earlier deception about the essence and historical essential force of National Socialism, there results the necessity of its affirmation, and indeed on *thoughtful* grounds. This also means that this "movement" remains independent of its contemporary shape in each case, and of the duration of these particular visible forms. But how does it come about that such an essential affirmation is appreciated less, or not at all, in contrast to mere agreement, which is mostly superficial, clueless, or just blind?

(*GA* 95:408)

Heidegger "affirms" Nazism even after recognizing that it is no new inception but the ultimate manifestation of modern machination. Why? Let us remember that the great first inception needs to eventuate in a correspondingly "great" downfall. Modernity needs to end tragically—with a bang, not a whimper.

Here we see to what extent the mythos of inception and downfall led Heidegger to abandon all prudential judgments and think apocalyptically. He wavers on which modern movement is the worst, but at no point does he wish Nazism to be defeated by a rival, such as liberal democracy. The moderation and moralism of Anglo-American liberalism only forestall the total catastrophe that is necessary to clear the way for the other inception. All that liberal democracy promises is a half-hearted, prolonged diminution. Democracy lacks "the strength for the step into the completion . . . no decisions come from there." Democracy is "a barrier to the transition into the completion of modernity"; it is "modern, but without the courage for the developed essence and the utmost essential consequences" (*GA* 95:406). These consequences must be brought out in order for modernity to collapse, and totalitarianism is a necessary part of this process: "The supposed 'dictatorships' are not a *dictans*, but are in themselves the *dictatum* of that essence of being from which modern man cannot withdraw, because in order to be himself he must affirm it in all its essential consequences" (*GA* 95:431).[12]

What does Heidegger mean by "affirmation" (*Bejahung*)? As we noted early on, he is trying to think beyond the simple duality of yes and no. The "distorted essence" of beyng should not just be an object of negation (*GA* 95:1, 7), and a thinker's "no-saying . . . is the struggle for the most essential yes to the full essence of beyng" (*GA* 95:20–21). Rather than simply criticizing current conditions, the notebooks attempt to think beyond them "into beyng itself and its simple basic movement" (*GA* 95:24), by experiencing what seems to be merely deficient and senseless as the "refusal" that is an event in beyng itself (*GA* 95:37).

To "affirm" National Socialism then means to view it as a sign of the self-concealment of beyng. It is a sort of *amor fati*: "*The new politics is an inner essential consequence of 'technology'* . . . 'technology' can never be mastered by the ethno-political [*völkisch-politische*] world view. What is already essentially a servant can never be a master. Nevertheless, this birth of the new politics from the essence of technology . . . is *necessary*, and thus is not the possible object of a shortsighted 'opposition'" (*GA* 94:472). Does this assent to "necessity" imply material support for particular Nazi goals? Not necessarily—but it certainly does not imply any resistance, either.[13]

The passage on "affirmation" sheds light on the notion of the "inner truth and greatness" of National Socialism, which infamously appears in *Introduction to Metaphysics* but is echoed in other texts as well.[14] We can now understand that Heidegger was not only distinguishing this "inner truth" from external, superficial manifestations of the "movement" but was also developing a peculiar conception of greatness. In 1953, in a letter to *Die Zeit*, he endorsed Christian Lewalter's interpretation of the phrase as "accurate in every respect."[15] In Lewalter's reading, "the Nazi movement is a symptom for the tragic collision of man and technology, and as such a symptom it has its 'greatness,' because it affects the entirety of the West and threatens to pull it into destruction."[16] This has always had the ring of a dubious exercise in apologetics, but the *Black Notebooks* support the claim that it was precisely the global destructiveness of Nazi "machination" that made it "great" and "true," in a sense: it was the unvarnished expression of modern metaphysics. However, what is misleading in Lewalter's reading is the unspoken assumption that the West should *not* be destroyed—whereas, at least in the increasingly desperate times of the 1930s and 1940s, Heidegger often seems to have wished for a complete collapse.

Under these circumstances, the brutality of National Socialism can appear as its advantage (*GA* 94:194). "The greatest danger is not barbarism and decline, for these conditions can drive [us] forward into an extreme and thus into an emergency. The greatest danger is averageness and the equal control of everything" (*GA* 94:330).[17]

Now we need to ask whether Heidegger would have "affirmed" the most barbaric Nazi acts, including the so-called Final Solution to the Jewish question. A horrifying passage from 1934 appears to justify rooting out the internal enemy—or even first *making* the enemy, so that the people's "Dasein may not lose its edge"—and then pursuing that enemy "with the goal of total annihilation" (*GA* 36/37:91/73). This is why Emmanuel Faye considers Heidegger an annihilationist—a murderer in spirit. We should dwell on the point about "making" the enemy. Here Heidegger seems to recognize that anti-Semitic propaganda may be a pack of lies—but he endorses scapegoating anyway. This is, arguably, more evil than if he had actually believed the lies. But at least it does leave open the door for the truth.

When we look to the late 1930s and early 1940s, we find Heidegger dealing in some crude and thoughtless anti-Semitic stereotypes. Now he seems to be swallowing the propaganda. But does he endorse the annihilation?

Again, the answer cannot be either a simple yes or a simple no. As we have seen, he says Nazism must be "affirmed" precisely because it is the most uncompromising form of machination—the form most likely to bring the West to its tragic fate. So there is no resistance here to any concrete Nazi policies, certainly not to the anti-Jewish measures. At the same time, though, Heidegger does not accept any of the Nazi justifications for such actions: he condemns (not morally but in being-historical terms) racism, domination, brutality, violence, and the demonization of opponents. So although he is no pacifist or moralist, he did move beyond his early endorsement of the "annihilation" of invented enemies and he could not have agreed that the Holocaust was a solution, final or otherwise, to any problem that made any real difference. If both war and peace are merely ontic affairs (*GA* 95:189, 192, 235), the same would be true of mass murder.[18] "Neither annihilation nor ordering nor reordering essentially satisfies a historical vocation, but only poetizing the essence of being" (*GA* 95:260).

By the late 1930s, it is clear that Heidegger does not expect Nazism to heal the broken world. The gathering he hopes for would not be a human act at all, but would be centered on a god whose coming can never be brought about or calculated in advance. Heidegger craves a theophany.

THE SEA OF FOG

Heidegger denounces "the age of the world picture" and is often at pains to distinguish world views from philosophy. But it is obvious that in the *Black Notebooks* he is a man with a worldview. He is enmeshed in his narrative of the Greek inception that must be played out to its end before another inception can dawn. Under these terms he sketches his images of nationalities and ideologies—images that are almost constantly at work in the notebooks, shifting places but always playing menacing roles in the drama.

There are moments of lucidity when Heidegger sees through the crudity and hypocrisy of Nazi propaganda. He is also relentless in his criticisms of journalism and history—that is, *Historie* as the investigation of supposed facts about present or bygone states of affairs. But these criticisms come with a glaring blindness: for where is he getting his opinions about foreign countries and ethnicities except from historians, journalists, and propagandists? There is little evidence of firsthand observation of these groups. His comments are often appalling, but also philosophically disappointing in that, for the most part, they are nothing but thoughtless clichés.

Not only are Heidegger's views simplistic, but he shows no sign of concern for the victims of dictatorship and war. It makes no difference, he writes, who will apparently win the war and who will be "pulverized" by it (*GA* 96:133)—because all this takes place on the level of beings and power, not on the level of beyng. In one of the more embarrassing entries, Heidegger says that the G's in his name stand for the goals of *Güte und Geduld*, goodness and patience. After "goodness" he adds: "(not sympathy)" (*GA* 94:273). That is a notable understatement in three volumes packed with overstatements. Heidegger comes across as a wholly unempathetic individual.

In the postwar entries this narrowness and coldness lead to a grotesque indifference to the victims of the Nazi regime. He does refer to Nazism as a "reign of terror" (*GA* 97:84) under Hitler's "criminal madness"

(*GA* 97:444). But, at the same time, he rejects the victors' claims to morality and justice, which he sees as mere masks for the spirit of revenge (*GA* 97:50, 64, 117, 134–35). In a typical passage, Heidegger almost contemptuously refers to "the broadly visible devastation and the horrors that can be graphically portrayed on posters" (which showed photographs of concentration camps) (*GA* 97:84–85); these crude, ontic facts pale in comparison to the "self-annihilation that now threatens Dasein in the form of a betrayal of thinking" (*GA* 97:83; cf. *GA* 97:59, 63, 99–100). What is the prime example of this betrayal? Heidegger's own forced retirement after the war.

Of course, Heidegger's scorn for morality, his lack of empathy, and his egocentrism should not simply be condemned from a moral point of view. He challenges us to ask ourselves: Is our moral indignation based on a rotten philosophy, religion, or political ideology? Is it myopic and hypocritical? In response I would suggest that the readiness to respect and care about other individuals is always something deeper than the fumbling, simplistic words and concepts in which we may try to express and justify it; ultimately, openness to the other goes deeper than any metaphysics or worldview or any narrative about the fate of the globe. This openness has something in common with the phenomenological attentiveness that Heidegger showed in his writings of the 1920s, which faded away in the 1930s, along with signs of concern for individual human beings.

One of the notebooks' little surprises is Heidegger's praise for the painter Caspar David Friedrich, whom he calls "a peak towering into the godforsaken spaces of the divinity of the past gods," a figure on a par with Hölderlin (*GA* 95:364). Heidegger must have known what is today Friedrich's most famous painting, *The Wanderer Above the Sea of Fog*. A man adopts a bold stance on a craggy peak, and we look out with him over a breathtaking landscape where the lower elevations are shrouded in mist. Heidegger must have felt that exhilaration when thinking of himself as one of the rare dwellers on mountaintops. But did he reflect on the mist? The wanderer in the painting has a magnificent view, but he does not see all: the clouds obscure the valleys below. Maybe he does not care—maybe that is part of his triumphant mood. So be it. But at least he should realize that he does not know what lies under the mist. The heights are heights of both knowledge and ignorance.

This is one reason why Zarathustra goes down in the beginning of Nietzsche's book, and one reason why the philosopher-kings must return to the cave in the *Republic*—where they will initially see nothing, because their eyes are too used to the bright sunlight of the outer world. Heidegger's interpretations of the allegory of the cave exemplify this blindness instead of recognizing it: he takes the returning philosopher simply as a victim of the masses' stupidity and resentment rather than understanding that the philosopher himself needs to relearn to see in the dimness (*GA* 34:80–94/58–68, *GA* 36/37:180–85/138–42).

It is a mark of Heidegger's untruth that he not only has no sympathy for real, suffering individuals but also thinks that he knows them when he does not. The dismissive statements in the notebooks—such as the repeated claim that he is living in the age of the total lack of questioning and thought—are themselves thoughtless, because the fact is that he does not know whether others are questioning.

Heidegger's "being-historical thinking" brings with it an attitude of dismissive superiority to all that lies beneath the fog. "All references [in the notebooks] to what can be grasped historiologically and to incidents and to the contemporary are made only in passing, leaving behind all this stuff devoid of history [*all dieses Geschichtslosen*]. But these frayed threads of the fluttering semblance of the hidden history must at times be named" (*GA* 96:250). But isn't Heidegger flying too fast into abstractions? He dismisses this objection: "Being-historical thinking has no 'content' and creates the appearance of the 'abstract' and empty. But what looks like emptiness is only the falling away of beings in the determination of beyng" (*GA* 96:26). "Genuine experiencing has no need of the 'empirical.' It consists in being thoroughly attuned by being. . . . There is a phantasy of concepts that draws all beings together into what is essential in being, and precisely does not 'abstract'" (*GA* 96:253, cf. *GA* 96:225, *GA* 95:118).

Attuned by being or not, Heideggerian "phantasy" certainly runs the risk of falling into the purely fantastic and losing all perspective on everyday reality. Consider his statement that the Antichrist "would be just a harmless boy in the face of what is 'happening.'" What merits this statement in the year 1940? The fact that the world looks like an American humor magazine (*GA* 96:194).

What brought on such distortions?

In the 1920s Heidegger scrutinized not just texts but experience and was able to show that the usual metaphysical concepts were inadequate to that experience. He was able to build new, subtle concepts that were flexible enough to point to the richness of human life. Now Heidegger sees life itself as determined by metaphysics; the alternative is not to be found in experience but in a wholly other beginning, a new inception that would establish a relation to being itself. He falls into the illusion, then, that his ability to critique the metaphysical concepts is also the ability to grasp human existence, what is happening on the ground. He not only fails to see through the mist but fails to see the mist itself.

We know that it was in 1930, by Heidegger's own account, that he began to believe that National Socialism could represent a new inception for the West (*GA* 95:408). Before this, he may very well have had predilections and opinions about politics, but they stayed out of his philosophy, which was focused on describing what seemed to be universal human conditions. Perhaps we can pinpoint the moment when he allows himself to take a fateful step into the political in a lecture course. Halfway through his 1929–1930 lectures, he shifts from a phenomenological account of boredom (based on experiences such as waiting for a train) to a question about "*our* Dasein," "*the Dasein in man today*" (*GA* 29/30:242), and claims that we are suffering from profound boredom and a lack of distress. This is a shift into cultural critique, into the divination of a shared orientation. And, interesting though it is, it obviously rests on flimsy grounds. After all, Heidegger does not know what "we" are all feeling, thinking, or experiencing.

This passage is the start of what soon becomes a political-metaphysical worldview that gets woven into a narrative about Western history. This narrative becomes increasingly difficult to disentangle from the question of being itself, and "Dasein" is no longer the human condition but a possible transformation of the human (e.g., *GA* 65:3, 9, 248, 294, 300).

What provoked this change in Heidegger's thought? We could speculate about his new professional circumstances: he had a chair in philosophy and no longer needed to pay attention to academic conventions. We could point out the desperation that so many were feeling after what looked like a failed experiment in liberalism.

But Heidegger himself might prefer to think of the change in his thought in terms of the requirements of philosophy itself as a risky adventure. Thinkers must learn "long, useless errancy"; "The history of philosophy is in itself an errant voyage" (*GA* 95:227). Heidegger says that he *must* venture upon errancy—as if he knows, on some level, that he is about to go down a very dark and problematic path. He writes in 1931 or 1932, "Only if we truly err—*go* into errancy—can we run up against 'truth.'" The philosopher is an essentially "errant" figure (an *Irrgänger*, GA 94:13), but he must steel himself for his straying and go "*unflinchingly* [*unbeirrbar*] *into the ineluctable!*" (GA 94:34). The authentic, historical "so be it" (GA 94:51) requires one to choose a particular option that is necessarily limited and partially opaque; it must be chosen with bold daring, τόλμα (GA 94:3, 95, 96, 323).

When Heidegger becomes rector, he writes that he is "acting for the first time *against* my innermost voice" (GA 94:110). But once in the position he steels himself, reminds himself of his determination, and fights all the harder—as if he is determined to plunge into the opacity of errancy, into what he calls "the difficult becoming of a dark future" (GA 36/37:3/3).

Although Heidegger did leave his position as rector and eventually—as the notebooks prove—left Nazi ideology behind, he did not leave unscathed. He left wounded, poisoned, embittered—and never managed to get in the clear. He was not fully clear with himself or with others, nor was he clear in 1930 about the world that he had chosen to see from a particular, befogged point of view.

THE CONFRONTATION

What should our stance be toward the anti-Semitic and other disturbing elements in the *Black Notebooks*?

It would be a mistake to minimize them—to emphasize their ambiguities, their relative mildness for the times, and to be left finally with a handful of assertions we can dismiss as part of a personal journal that has nothing to do with Heidegger's "real philosophy." This would be a mistake because the remarks on Jews (and Americans and Englishmen and Christians) are part of a whole. It is not a mathematically deductive system, but more like an ecosystem: it may well survive if one element is removed, but only in a changed form. In Heidegger's thinking, suspicion of rootless, calculating, nomadic, cosmopolitan ways of life goes hand in hand with his emphasis on thrownness, which is to say rootedness and historicity. His hostility to rationalism, universalism, and all things global fits with his attempt to think of Dasein and being as radically finite.

But it would also be a mistake to maximize the anti-Semitic remarks by representing them as the capstone or cornerstone of a Heideggerian edifice or by assuming that it is impossible from the start to find fruitful insights in his thinking that can contribute to our own philosophical ecosystems.

The time for childlike admiration of Heidegger has passed. For a mature appropriation of Heidegger's thought, we need a different kind of maximization of the troubling elements in the notebooks. We must take them as gifts, as opportunities to think as hard as we can about Heidegger's limitations and our own: about errancy, finitude, and responsibility. If we find them morally unacceptable, let us take this as an invitation to reflect on Heidegger's hostility to moral points of view and on the basis of our own moral positions. If we find his remarks politically obtuse, let us take this as a chance to rethink politics in a productive struggle with Heidegger, the kind of struggle that he called an *Auseinandersetzung*—a confrontation that sets the opponents apart and clarifies their positions as they learn from each other.

This is exactly what Heidegger, at his best, would have us do. He wants a fight—not followers. So let us take these statements from the *Black Notebooks* to heart:

I still do not have enough enemies.

(*GA* 94:9)

Tell me *which* thinker you have chosen as your "opponent" and *how*, and I'll tell you how far you yourself have entered the realm of thought.

(*GA* 94:377)

Perhaps even my *errors* still have a power to provoke in a time overloaded with correctnesses that have long lacked truth.

(*GA* 94:404)

6

THE OTHER "JEWISH QUESTION"

MICHAEL MARDER

As you will have surmised, my title alludes to Marx's 1843 essay "On the Jewish Question." Before I align that text with the comments Heidegger made about the Jews in the already published volumes of the *Black Notebooks,* separated from this essay by roughly one century, I'd like to highlight a word that, despite being uttered, is typically not heard at all in this context, namely the *question.* In what sense can the existence of a certain group or a people become a question? For whom are they a question; to whom is it addressed? What of self-questioning, putting oneself into question, still prior to making a fateful decision about one's own being, which presumably defines the human? And, above all, how does it stand with what Heidegger himself reveres as "the question-worthy": "the question that first opens the worthiness of what is most question-worthy, the question of the truth of being" (*GA* 65:52/42)?

My hunch is that the root of the problem with Heidegger's anti-Semitism is his failure 1. to turn the figure of the Jew, let alone "international Jewry," which he parades on the pages of the *Black Notebooks,* into a question and, worse still, 2. to interrogate the very logic and necessity of coming up with a concrete figuration, a clandestine "agency," if you will, for the nihilistic completion of metaphysics. Much more than a temporary lapse of critical vigilance is at issue in this dual failure: by slotting a raw, determinate figure into his grand history of being (particularly when the latter comes detached from beings), Heidegger conjugates the most question-worthy and what he treats as the least question-worthy. The term *being-historical anti-Semitism,* coined by Peter Trawny, condenses in itself this very a- or prelogical contradiction, this hidden clash of the least and what is the most worthy of questioning in Heidegger's philosophy.[1] For no matter how "world Jewry" is metaphysically deployed and loaded with the dirty work of world destruction, absent the questioning impulse, its insertion within the "being-historical" narrative will not rise to the thought of being.

To be sure, there are different ways of refusing the question. *On the one hand,* this refusal may be attributed to a deficit of reflection and critique. In *Überlegungen (Considerations)* 9 of the *Notebooks,* Heidegger appeals to the courage (*der Mut*) necessary for fundamental reflections, "the courage to track one's own presuppositions back to their ground and to interrogate the necessity of the goals one has set." This, for him, is the essential task of self-reflection (*Selbst-besinnung*), understood not in a crass "psychological," "characterological," or "biological-typological" sense but ontologically, as asking about "being and its truth and its grounding and lack of grounds [*das Sein und seine Wahrheit und deren Gründung und Grundlosigkeit*]" (*GA* 95:258).[2] Needless to say, Heidegger did not track his own presuppositions about the Jews "to their ground" (did he lack the courage to do so?), but fell back on characterological and typological crudities surrounded by a mere facade of ontological significance.

On the other hand, the refusal of the question may resort to *ultraquestioning,* as it does in Derrida's *Of Spirit.* Although Heidegger "*almost* never stops identifying what is highest and best in thought with the question, with the decision, the call or guarding of the question," the possibility or the privilege of the question is, itself, unquestioned.[3] Questioning the question is, in turn, subverting the sovereignty of critique and of the subject who launches it. More than that, it is a precondition for radical hospitality, whereby the other is not put to the question, in the inquisitorial or Inquisitional mode, but maintains the right to interrogate the I.

Far from contemplating a conscious refusal of the question, Heidegger forges out of it a polemical weapon, an implement in an "attack" (*Angriff*) that is meant to outstrip the power of critique: "The attack on Descartes, that is, the counterquestioning [*Entgegenfragen*] that is *appropriate* to his basic metaphysical position on the basis of a fundamental overcoming of metaphysics, can be carried out only by *asking the question of being*" (*GA* 95:168). Along the same lines, he confesses: "My 'attack' [*Angriff*] on

Husserl is not directed against him alone, and in general is inessential—the attack is against the neglect of the question of being" (*GA* 96:47). For all its phenomenological insight, its "rejection of psychological explanations and historiological reckoning of opinions," Husserl's philosophy "never reaches into the domain of essential decisions [*die Bezirke wesentlicher Entscheidungen*]." Why?—Because, as Heidegger declares in the same paragraph of the *Black Notebooks*, "the power of Jewry" (*Machtsteigerung des Judentums*), which hinges on "the spread of an otherwise empty rationality and calculative skills," is powerless insofar as essential decisions are concerned. The strong implication here is that, despite coming closer to the ontological domain than "the Jew 'Freud'" did, the Jew Husserl could not free himself from the power that blocked his access to the question of being. Right before he opens the brackets, where he discusses his attack on Husserl, Heidegger notes emphatically: "The more original and inceptive the coming decisions and questions [*die künftigen Entscheidungen und Fragen*] become, the more inaccessible will they remain to this 'race' ['*Rasse*': i.e., the Jews]." The limits of Husserl's philosophy, to which these decisions and questions remain opaque, are thus, presumably, demarcated by his Jewishness.

In this regard, I am reminded of a bitterly ironic episode from my biography. While I was still attending primary school in Moscow during the 1980s, my mother inquired during parents' night as to the reasons why, among all the other subjects, "Russian Language" was the only one that did not merit the maximum grade of 5 on my transcript. The teacher's response was brutally honest: "Well, of course, because a Jew cannot master Russian for a 5!" On the surface of it, Heidegger seems to say the same about Husserl's philosophy: "Well, of course, it fell short of the highest ontological question, the phenomenological rejection of psychologism, biologism, and historicism notwithstanding! How could it not, seeing that Husserl belongs to the 'race,' to which fundamental decisions and questions are foreclosed?" The point, however, is that Heidegger does not isolate the Jews from other groups that are similarly oblivious to being, notably the Cartesians, but also the Bolsheviks, the English, the Americans . . . He showcases them as though they were different specimens of an indifferent metaphysical nihilism. Still, in and of itself, this nondifferentiation among political orientations, nationalities, philosophical positions, and so forth—the nondifferentiation that mirrors the at times oversimplified story about the

forgetting of being in the West, within which wildly dissimilar philoso-
phies appear to be interchangeable—is indicative of the persistence of the
unquestioned in the thick of the essential question and of the thoughtless
(to be distinguished from the unthought) in the midst of rigorous thought.

In light of the two ways of rebuffing the question—the unreflecting and
the hospitable—the *Jewish question* can be finally reframed. If a certain
critical deficit needs to be remedied, then we must intensify the questioning impulse, keeping fast to the ground rules of fundamental ontology.
Instead of spawning caricature-like avatars of Western metaphysics, we
would then allow the *who* of the questioner or the self-questioner to flour-
ish. The existential freedom of this flourishing dovetails with the other
method for dealing with the Jewish question: resolving it as a question not
with a view to providing a definitive answer or a solution (we are all too
familiar with the horror of "final solutions") but with an eye to the emancipation of the questioned and questioning subject(s).

"Emancipation" (*Emanzipation*), is one of the first words in Marx's "On the
Jewish Question." Everything then revolves around the meanings of this
word, taken in the political, civic, religious, or humanist senses. To this list,
we should add the patently Heideggerian existential emancipation, which
requires one to ask who, rather than what, a human being is. What does
one free oneself from when one is liberated from the what-modality of the
question? Among other things, from the "predetermination" of humanity
by animality (*Tierheit, animalitas*), "the modern *anthropological* determination [*Bestimmung*] of man, and with it, all previous anthropology—
Christian, Hellenistic-Jewish and Socratic-Platonic" (*GA* 95:322). Like
Bruno Bauer, with whose insights Marx engages in his text, Heidegger
thinks that the Jew cannot be emancipated as Jew, any more than a Christian can be emancipated as Christian or a Platonist as Platonist; on the terms
of Judaic, Christian, Hellenistic, and modern metaphysics, existential emancipation is impossible unless it goes beyond the confines of these systems
of thought. The anthropological posing of the Jewish question, within and
beyond Judaism, is bound to be: "*What* is a Jew?"

Oppositions, such as Jew/Christian or Jew/Greek, are insignificant
because epiphenomenal in relation to the all-encompassing animalization

of the human. Now Marx suggests that the opposition Jew/Christian, for example, will be resolved or dissolved not thanks to finding a deeper ideational ground uniting the two, subsequently discounting it as a vestige of the same anthropological prejudice, but through meticulous historico-political work. The first stage in this work involves a critique of religion *as such*, rather than of Judaism, unable or unwilling to drop the attitude of "a foreigner [*Fremdling*] towards the state": "The most stubborn form of the opposition between Jew and Christian is the *religious* opposition. How is an opposition resolved? By making it impossible. And how is *religious* opposition made impossible? By abolishing religion [*Dadurch, daß man die Religion aufhebt*]."[4] The second stage elaborates a critique of the state *as such*, rather than of the Christian state, unable or unwilling to extend recognition to the Jews: "We criticize the religious failings of the political state by criticizing the political state in its secular form, disregarding its religious failings. [. . . But p]olitical emancipation is not the final and absolute form of *human* emancipation."[5] In other words, as is the case in Heidegger, albeit for different reasons entirely, Marx's "Jewish question" is neither a question, nor one about the Jews *proper*, but the pretext for a meditation about modernity.

A third stage of emancipation, silently coded as communism, will be announced at the end of Marx's influential essay. But how do the first two resonate with what Heidegger has to say about the Jews in the *Black Notebooks*? Marx's question is formulated more or less conventionally with regard to Jewish particularity, nonparticipation in and subtraction from the universality of the political sphere, be it filled with Christian content or rendered formal and abstract in a secular state. Heidegger turns this formulation upside-down, so that "empty rationality," which I have already mentioned, as well as "the tenacious skillfulness of calculating [*die zähe Geschicklichkeit des Rechnens*]," disseminating the "worldlessness," *Weltlosigkeit*, of abstraction worldwide, are all embodied in the Jews (*GA* 95:97). For Marx, the Jewish question rests upon the stubborn exceptionalism of the Jews combined with the dream of a universal emancipation from religious differentiations and the bourgeois political form alike. For Heidegger, "Jewry" (*Judentum*) is not the exception but the rule, which, in his peculiar vernacular, is given the designation "the *gigantic* [*Riesige*]," seeing that its worldlessness spreads around the world, transforming itself into the default state of modern humanity (*GA* 95:97). Deplorable as this accusation might be, his reformulation of the question does not leave much space for genocidal fantasies of purification that, in one way or another, proceed along the lines of wishing, "*if only* the exception were eliminated . . . " Evidently, where the prevailing rule is defective, nothing short of a total overhaul of nihilistic worldlessness would do; hence the stress on the need for a new inception (*Anfang*) of the West.

From Heidegger's perspective, Marx's proposal—to abolish religion altogether and to promote scientific principles in its stead—is actually the core of the problem, guilty of fostering the growing worldnessness of the world, disembedded from its autochthonous formation. An appropriate discipline for studying leveled-down social phenomena in such a world would be sociology, which, as Heidegger remarks, is "gladly pursued by Jews and Catholics [*mit Vorliebe von Juden und Katholiken betrieben*]" (*GA* 95:161). Most likely, the remark itself is a jab at Marx, among others. Be this as it may, in the list of disciplines or paradigms to which Heidegger voices his aversion (anthropology, psychoanalysis, biologism, psychologism, historicism, and so forth), sociology occupies a special place because it systematizes the breakdown of the world and gives it a scientific expression.

At bottom, Heidegger would consider the opposition between religious and secular outlooks (subject to overcoming in the initial project of Marxist emancipation) meaningless against the backdrop of the metaphysical heritage of which both partake. Anticipating the thesis of secularization as a movement *within* Christianity, Marx himself admits that pitting the one outlook against the other does not ring entirely true. He argues that "the perfected Christian state is not the so-called *Christian* state that acknowledges Christianity as its basis, as the state religion, and thus adopts an exclusive attitude toward other religions; it is, rather, the *atheistic* state, the democratic state, the state which relegates religion among the other elements of civil society."[6] For Marx, the atheistic state is the "perfected" fulfillment of a doctrinal Christian state; for Heidegger, the uprooted cosmopolitan Jewry is the purest culmination of Judaism. On the heights of metaphysics, the difference between religious and secular Jews (but also, in a certain sense, between Jews and non-Jews) vanishes: "The question of the role of *world Jewry* [*Weltjudentum*] is not a racial [*keine rassische*] question, but the metaphysical question about the kind of humanity that, *utterly unattached* [*die* schlechthin ungebunden], can take over the uprooting [*Entwuzelung*] of all beings from being as its world-historical task"

(*GA* 96:243). This phrase, however, demands a scrupulous analysis, going beyond the scope of the *Black Notebooks* to Heidegger's predecessors and to his other texts from the fateful period of the 1930s.

Heidegger's 1933–34 seminar *On the Essence and Concepts of Nature, History, and State* refers to the Jews as "Semitic nomads" who are not privy to the German experience of space (as a fixed place of shared existence): "We heard that people and space mutually belong to each other. . . . For a Slavic people the nature of German space would definitely be revealed differently from the way it is revealed to us; to Semitic nomads, it will perhaps never be revealed at all [*den semitischen Nomaden wird sie vielleicht überhaupt nie offenbar*]" (NHS: 82/56). And what is the nomad's experience of space, according to Heidegger? "History teaches us that nomads have not only been made nomadic by the desolation of wastelands and steppes, but they have also often left wastelands behind them where they found fruitful and cultivated land—and that humans who are rooted in the soil have known how to make a home for themselves even in the wilderness" (NHS: 81/55). It follows that the difference between the original "Semitic nomads," i.e., religious Jews, and their modern counterparts, i.e., secular cosmopolitan Jews, is one of scale. With modern uprootedness, nomadism ceased to be an exception and has come to affect the whole planet, with deserts expanding and forests diminishing at an alarming rate. The lack of "attachment" in the "world-historical task" of "world Jewry" is conditioned by the Jews' not being bound to any determinate lived space. Moreover, Heidegger implies that the nomads' ruthless exploitation of and destructive passage through places they encounter on their errant itinerary parallels the unrestrained "uprooting of all beings from being." The ontic displacement of traditional Jews, sublimated into the secular version of Jewish cosmopolitanism, has been translated into the ontological deracination of the world and of being itself. The "world-historical task" of "world Jewry" is, therefore, the denial to the world of its worldhood, of its placeness irreducible to the grid of geometrical spatiality, and finally of its habitability.

I have no doubts concerning the correctness of Heidegger's environmental views on world destruction or on our planet becoming a dump, something that is reaching truly cosmic proportions given the increasing orbital debris rotating around the Earth. What is obnoxious is the attribution of blame for this situation to "Semitic nomads." Having said that, Heidegger's argument, including its ontological dimension, is not original.

In "The Spirit of Christianity and Its Fate" Hegel foregrounds the revolt of Jewish law, a force of deadly ideality, against life itself:

> And since life was so maltreated in them [i.e., in the Jews; *das Leben in ihnen mißhandelt*], since nothing in them was left un-dominated, nothing sacrosanct, their action [*ihr Handeln*] became the most impious fury, the wildest fanaticism. . . . The great tragedy of the Jewish people is no Greek tragedy; it can rouse neither terror nor pity. . . . It can rouse horror alone. The fate of the Jewish people is the fate of Macbeth who *stepped out of nature itself* [*aus der Natur sebst trat*], clung to alien Beings, and so in their service had to trample and slay everything holy in human nature, had at last to be forsaken by his gods (since these were objects and he their slave) and be dashed to pieces on his faith itself.[7]

How can one fail to see the connection between this passage and Heidegger's idea of uprooting as a rebellion against nature and, in the last instance, against being, wherein beings are primordially rooted? Doesn't the qualification "*utterly unattached*" apply to that uprooting which is stamped with the lethal force of the ideal set over and against nature and life?

If I have shifted, for the time being, from Marx back to Hegel, that is because the emancipation from religion required by the author of "On the Jewish Question" does not accomplish anything within the Heideggerian scheme. The only effect it might have is that of generalizing the destructiveness of pure ideality, with which Judaism is charged, initially to the entire planet and then to being as such. What, in the eyes of the young Hegel, appears as the "maltreatment" (*Mißhandlung*) of life within and outside the Jewish people, under Heidegger's pen becomes "the overpowering [*Übermächtigung*] of life" in "machination" (*Machenschaft*) (*GA* 96:56). Alleged Jewish nihilism percolates from its religious core to the secular domain where it assumes a properly metaphysical character, that is, continues to unfold in the guise of a scientific ontotheology. But how is it possible to square nihilistic hostility to life with the anthropological determination of the human as an animal, which, according to Heidegger, Judaism shares with Hellenism and with Christianity?

Despite vehemently disowning the racial nature of the Jewish question, it is in living "according to the principle of race [*Rasseprinzip*]" that Heidegger locates the power of overpowering life itself:

Through the concept of race, "life" is brought into the form of what can be bred, which constitutes a kind of calculation. The Jews, *with their marked gift for calculation*, have already been "living" for the longest time according to the principle of race. . . . The establishment of racial breeding does not stem from "life" itself, but from the overpowering of life by machination. What machination is bringing about with such planning is a *complete deracialization* [*vollständige Entrassung*] of peoples, by fastening them into the equally constructed, equally divided arrangement of all beings.

(GA 96:56)

The formalization of life in the principle of race—the act of making life breedable—at the same time animalizes it and drains its vitality. Bred like the animals that they are in keeping with their anthropological predetermination, humans entrust their lives to a contentless calculative rationality. Nihilism and animality merge in the form of racial breeding, and Heidegger again places the Jews at the center of this strange fusion, based on the characterological conjecture of "*their marked gift for calculation*."

Regardless of all the intellectual contortions inherent in this argument, it is glaringly obvious that, having neglected the call of thinking, Heidegger indulges in extreme stereotyping, insofar as he imputes mutually contradictory traits to the same stereotyped subject—the subhuman and the superhuman, an animal and a calculating machine, a racializing and a deracializing agent . . . (This list will only keep growing in what is to come next.)

Perhaps without realizing it, we have stepped over the threshold of the second stage of Marxist emancipation, namely the political. Marx made this kind of emancipation contingent on a critical appraisal of the state form and, in particular, on a critique of the bourgeois state. In a nutshell, the modern state "solves" the Jewish question, along with every other problem of the sort, by driving a wedge between the abstract equality of political citizenship and universal participation, on the one hand, and the pursuit of private interests and protection of "basic liberties," such as the freedom of religion in civil society, on the other. As Marx puts this, the "consummation [*Vollendung*] of the idealism of the state was at the same time the consummation of the materialism of civil society. The bonds, which had restrained the egoistic spirit of civil society, were removed along with the political yoke. Political emancipation was at the same time an emancipation of civil society from politics and from even the *semblance* of a general content."[8]

Just as Heidegger would regard as irrelevant the distinction between the religious and the secular manifestations of "Semitic nomadism," so he would dismiss the difference between political idealism and the materialism of civil society. Both essentially pertain, as two sides of the same coin, to the completion (*Vollendung*) of Western metaphysics, above and beyond the efforts Marx pours into their dialectical reconciliation in communism. The political evil, as far as Heidegger is concerned, lies in the common foundation of abstract state and concrete civil society: "the equally constructed, equally divided arrangement of all beings" (*die gleichgebaute und gleichschnittige Einrichtung alles Seienden*) (GA 96: 56). Whether separated by private, egoistic interests or united on the grounds of shared abstract citizenship, we have no other choice but to enter such an arrangement, which is as much ontological as political. How is this order constructed? Through rampant calculation, deracialization, and the untethering of beings from being: the three powers of "machination" Heidegger identifies with the Jews. Unlike Marx, then, he does not discern in the Jewish question one of many analogous emancipatory projects of modernity, but views it as the synecdoche of the end of metaphysics. He does not deny, to be sure, that the Jewish people existed well before the latest phase in the history of being has commenced; instead, he insinuates that the three powers of "machinations" he associates with them have gained extraordinary prominence in this epoch.

While Heidegger's philosophy insists on a more or less straightforward inversion of the first and the third of these powers, things get complicated when it comes to deracialization. It would be fairly uncontroversial to say that Heidegger wishes to recover thinking beyond planning and calculation and that he wants to reaffirm the bond between being and beings in the shape of ontological difference. Both this difference and noncalculative thinking resist the abstract equality of "the arrangement of all beings," reminiscent of the abstract equality of the bourgeois state criticized by Marx. But the race principle is by no means a panacea from the sameness that installs itself in the heart of a deracialized humanity. Clumsily and objectionably, Heidegger presents the thesis of race and its antithesis with reference to the figure of the Jews: they overpower life by planning its form, breeding it, and, by the same token, dissolving its qualitative differences by forcing it into an indifferent calculative mold. So, if not the race principle, then what is meant to supplant the second "power of machination"? Curtly stated, the response would have to be: a lived sense of history.

Immediately after he registers his ontopolitical complaint about the creation of a leveled, homogeneous arrangement for all beings, Heidegger writes: "Deracialization goes hand-in-hand with a self-alienation of peoples [*eine Selbstentfremdung der Völker*]—the loss of history [*der Verlust der Geschichte*]—that is, of the domains of decision for be-ing" (*GA* 96:56). Between the lines of this diagnosis, one can read another charge against "Semitic nomads": the Jews have been the most self-alienated of peoples because their history has not unfolded in a specific "Jewish space," in the manner that German history has taken place in a "German space." For Heidegger, only in the unity of the place and time of a people's existence can a "decision for being" be made. Without such unity, history can only appear as an abstraction, as World History, which is, ultimately, historyless. The uprooting from a place entails uprooting from history, marking the end of metaphysics as much as the nature of Jewish experience, as Heidegger construes or misconstrues it. Thus, in an earlier notebook he writes: "*What is happening now* is the *end* of history [Was jetzt geschieht ist das Ende der Geschichte] of the great inception. . . . To know what is now happening as this end hence remains denied, from start to finish, to *those* who are appointed to begin this end in its most final forms (i.e., the gigantic [*das Riesigen*]) and to put forward the historyless in the mask of the historiological as "History" itself [*und das Geschichtlose in der Maske des Historischen als die Geschichte auszugeben*]" (*GA* 95:96). We have already seen how Heidegger deemed Jewry with its presumed "worldlessness" to be "the gigantic," thanks to generalizing its condition to the modern state of uprooting. The historyless is the temporal supplement to spatial deracination so that, jointly, these two factors amount to worldlessness.

As I pointed out in an article published in the *New York Times* in July 2014, Heidegger has—willfully, most likely—overlooked the uniqueness of Jewish attachment to tradition. I wrote then that the "Jewish mode of rootedness was temporal, rather than spatial; before the Zionist project undertook to change this state of affairs, the Jews were grounded only in the tradition, instead of a national territory. Such grounding is anathema to modern uprooting, with which Heidegger hurriedly identified Jewish life and thought and which is expressed, precisely, in the destruction of tradition."[9] Were he to have paid attention to this lived sense of history unbound from physical space, he would have thought twice before lumping together religious and secular Jews under the same heading of "Semitic nomads." Granted: cosmopolitan, secular, and largely assimilated Jewry might have still corresponded to aspects of the unflattering portrait of uprooting painted by Heidegger, but so would, also, other atheists, be they from Christian or other backgrounds.

Regarding Marx's view of history, Heidegger acknowledges that it "is superior to that of other historical accounts," insofar as it recognizes the estrangement indicative of "the homelessness of modern human beings" (*GA* 9:340/258–59). Likewise, in the conclusion of "On the Jewish Question" the fulfillment of history in a truly human emancipation (communism is still unnamed here) might resemble Heidegger's expectations for the other inception germinating in the completion of Western metaphysics. "*Every* emancipation," Marx writes, "is a *restoration* of the human world and of human relationships to *man himself.*"[10] It is possible, for instance, to hear the words "the human world" (*menschliche Welt*) with a Heideggerian ear in terms of a decisive victory in the struggle against worldlessness, historylessness, and the powers of machination. What speaks against such an interpretation is the kind of reconciliation that Marx envisions for emancipatory world restoration.

In the narrative structure of his essay, "feudal society was dissolved into its basic element, *men*; but into *egoistic* men who were its real foundation" (45, tm). These utility-maximizing members of civil society are the passive, apolitical, sensuous subjects of need who have nothing to do with the "*political* man," the "abstract, artificial man, man as an *allegorical, moral* person" (46). Only with the advent of communism, or "human emancipation," will the confrontation of the actually existing member of civil society and the abstract political agent be sublated, "when the real, individual man has absorbed into himself the abstract citizen; when as an individual man, in his everyday life, in his work, and in his relationships, be has become a *species-being*; and when he has recognized and organized his own powers (*forces propres*) as social powers so that he no longer separates this social power from himself as *political* power" (46).

Heidegger's assertions in the *Black Notebooks* would make of Marx's reconciliation nothing more than a Jewish solution to the Jewish question. Whereas Marx detects an intense contradiction between the political and the economic, Heidegger pinpoints diverse manifestations of the Jewish "powers of machination" on both sides of the divide. The private egoistic member of civil society represents the power of calculation; abstract citizenship and public, artificial, allegorical personhood stand for deracializing homogenization and the divorce of beings from being. If anything, the "absorption" of the one in the other, of the ideal political actor in the real egoistic individual, would betoken, for Heidegger, the consolidation and the coming into its own of the Jewish essence, the gathering of its three "powers" into a unity.

Indications of Heidegger's proclivity for converting the figure of the Jew into a *complexio oppositorum* (i.e., the complex of opposites, where the otherwise antithetical traits coexist without the work of dialectical mediation) continue to abound. Besides the religious and the secular, the private and the public, racialization and deracialization, the pair pacifism/militarism is made applicable to "international Jewry": "The imperialistic-warlike way of thinking and the humanistic-pacifist way of thinking are only 'dispositions' that belong to each other . . . because they are just offshoots of 'metaphysics.' Thus, 'international Jewry' [*das "internationale Judentum"*] can also make use of both, can proclaim and bring about one as the means for the other—this machinational concocting of 'history' catches all players equally in its nets" (*GA* 96:133). There is more than a grain of truth in saying that war and peace are more and more indistinguishable, from "the war to end all wars"—which is probably the implied background for this insight—to the permanent states of exception (Agamben) and humanitarian wars (Zolo) of the late twentieth and early twenty-first centuries. But, since Heidegger allots to the Jews the role of the vanguard in the age of the completion of metaphysics, he concentrates this tendency in their hands. Insofar as "all players are equally" caught in the nets of this machination, "the equally constructed, equally divided arrangement of all beings" at the social level of deracialization is replicated at the political level of meaningless divisions between the right and the left as well as war and peace. The nonseparation of social and political powers, lauded by Marx, shows itself here in the form of a metaphysical cobelonging of different parts in the same homogenized order.

It is time to take stock of this exegetical exercise. First, however, I cannot neglect to mention that Marx is in a better position to relate to the "Jewish question" because he is more attuned to the singular situations in which it is raised: "The Jewish question presents itself differently according to the state in which the Jew resides. In Germany, where there is no political state, no state as such, the Jewish question is purely theological. . . . In France, which is a *constitutional* state, the Jewish question is a question of constitutionalism, of the incompleteness of *political emancipation*. . . . It is only in the free states of North America, or at least in some of them, that the Jewish question loses its *theological* significance and becomes a truly *secular* question" (30). Heidegger, on the contrary, focuses on "international Jewry," a theoretical fiction and an abstraction that is on the par with the "intangible" (*unfaßbar*) power he invests in it (*GA* 96:262). He does not feel that he ought to qualify his statements depending on the distinct national contexts of the Jewish people, because, for him, the "historyless" and landless existence of "Semitic nomads"—in a word, their worldlessness—exceeds all such contexts and justifies a sweepingly generalizing approach. Where are phenomenological method, fundamental ontology, the hermeneutics of facticity, and the question vis-à-vis this "intangible" presence, accompanied by a barrage of other negations (of the world, of history, of the decision, and so forth)? What kind of logos makes it tangible and visible? Is thought absolved of *its* limits, responsibilities, and fidelity to being when it deals with an object it perceives to be devoid of inherent limits, responsibilities, and ontological bonds?

To reiterate, Heidegger's failure to pose the Jewish question as question bespeaks a lapse in his thinking about the figuration of metaphysics at the time of its completion. However valid, the rejoinder that the Jew is the wrong figure for this epoch in the history of being is insufficient, unless we add that, perhaps, no figuration at all suits the age of impersonal technologism and technocracy *per definitionem*. At the same time, the reasons behind the choice of the Jewish figuration in the *Black Notebooks* are clear, though certainly indefensible: in the Jew, Heidegger discovers a figureless figure, rid of racial connotations and referring, above all, to the cosmopolitan Jewish diaspora, positioned at the leading edge of globalizing uprootedness. In other words, he comes as close as possible to the notion of an absent presence or a representation without presentation, matching the current stage of metaphysics. To put it differently still, he describes the Jews in terms of what we now call "a trace."

In a slim but important volume, *Heidegger and "the jews,"* Lyotard repeats Heidegger's gesture of dissociating "the jews," spelled with a lower case *j* and placed between quotation marks, from prefabricated identitarian categories. "I write 'the jews' this way," Lyotard explains, "neither out of prudence nor lack of something better. I use lower case to indicate that I am not thinking of a nation. I make it plural to signify that it is neither a figure nor a political (Zionism), religious (Judaism), or philosophical (Jewish philosophy) subject. . . . I use quotation marks to avoid confusing these 'jews' with the real Jews. . . . 'The jews' are the object of a dismissal with which Jews, in particular, are afflicted in reality."[11] He, too, writes "the jews" as a trace; at this point, the other "Jewish question," as the question of the other, effectively commences. Outside the strictures of biologist, nationalist, religious, and other impositions, the singular-universal question "*Who* are the Jews or 'the jews'?" is finally raised, spearheading their existential emancipation. Unwittingly, Heidegger has contributed to the enunciation of this question insofar as he 1. refused to reduce it to the issue of race, 2. outlined the placeless place of the Jews or "the jews" in the history of being, and 3. distinguished anthropological whatness from existential whoness. But he also churned up a careless answer when he suggested that the Jews or "the jews" were the faceless face, the obscure and distended figuration, if not the "intangible" incarnation, of the end of metaphysics.

In Lyotard's book and in the thought of Levinas, the Jews or "the jews" are, in sharp contrast to Heidegger, the others of metaphysics who do not fit within its totalizing contours. As such, they cannot be understood as the representatives of calculation or computation, which is the metaphysical framework for the age of technological rationality, even though ontological homelessness remains crucial to the thinking of their nonidentity. " 'The jews,' never at home wherever they are," writes Lyotard, "cannot be integrated, converted, or expelled. They are also always away from home when they are at home, in their so-called own tradition, because it includes exodus as its beginning, excision, impropriety, and respect for the forgotten."[12] This, then, is a perfect illustration of how one can think with and against Heidegger, thinking "further on his path, despite, against, or with his past," as Marcia Sá Cavalcante Schuback and I suggest in our commentary on the 1934–35 Hegel seminar.[13] Lyotard's examplary strategy is one of inversion and intensification: the inversion of the meaning and value of homelessness and the intensification of the process whereby identity is denaturalized, first, by being stripped of its biologicist trappings derived primarily from the traditional concept of race and, second, by shedding all stable ontic markers and flipping into a nonidentity. Not by accident, this move looks almost identical to the repetition of metaphysics after its completion. After all, underlying the Jewish question is the question of metaphysics itself—of its current state or status, possible representation, and figuration. It would be ineffective to negate "metaphysical prejudices" directly, since they would be replicated in every such negation. And it would be futile simply to reject Heidegger's own prejudices or, worse yet, his entire philosophy as "tainted" by them. If the *Black Notebooks* have anything to teach us, it is the art of saying "yes-no" to Heidegger and, by implication, to the legacy of metaphysics.

7

HEIDEGGER AND NATIONAL SOCIALISM

He Meant What He Said

MARTIN GESSMANN

National Socialism is a barbarous principle. That is its essence and its potential greatness.

—HEIDEGGER, *ÜBERLEGUNGEN UND WINKE III*

For decades Heidegger has been defended against questions concerning his entanglement with National Socialism. His philosophy was held to be no Nazi philosophy, in spite of whatever pertinent passages Victor Farías, Emmanuel Faye, and others unearthed. Heidegger's choice of words supposedly conformed to Nazi standards and the Nazi idiom temporarily, but in the end there was never a real match between his philosophy and their ideology. Heidegger as a person has been seen as a failure, his philosophy not so. This was the commonly accepted position across the philosophical spectrum from Jürgen Habermas to Peter Sloterdijk.

Alas, that was before the publication of the *Black Notebooks*. After reading them, we face a new situation. It is necessary to admit—contrary to all attempts at a charitable reading—that Heidegger himself viewed his philosophy in a different light than that in which many scholars had long perceived it. It is necessary to admit that he himself did not wish to uphold the distance between thinking and dictatorial politics during the 1930s. One also has to concede that he pressed for an "empowerment of being"

(*Ermächtigung des Seins*) (*GA* 94:101) and almost wanted to "enforce" a new philosophical beginning in strict parallel to Hitler's "empowerment" in politics. The caesura in history was supposed to be accompanied by an equally epochal caesura in thought lasting for "millennia" (*GA* 94:119). And Hitler's takeover ought to have been a major step in this process.

Does this mean that all the voices were right in claiming a close proximity between Heideggerian thought and National Socialism from the start? My short answer is: it is much worse than that. For the *Black Notebooks* do not just validate the views of those who have always suspected a dark ideological backdrop behind Heidegger's rhetoric. They also invalidate the idea that any philosophy following Heidegger in any way could be conducted without the danger of ideological entanglement. In retrospect, the fairness that even Habermas or Sloterdijk showed toward Heidegger (in spite of personal or moral disdain) appears to be less than completely disinterested. The defense of Heideggerian philosophy against its fascist usurpation was ever a form of self-defense, however morally or aesthetically impeccable the Frankfurt School or the deconstructive movement held themselves to be, something I will try to explain and justify in the following pages. In the end, we will have to ask what we can draw from reading the *Black Notebooks;* more to the point, we will have to ask how philosophy in the twenty-first century should deal with Heidegger and even make use of Heidegger's own thought to avoid repeating the old mistakes of the last century.

A PRINCIPLE OF CAUTION

Until now the construal of Heidegger's involvement with National Socialism was based on a simple thesis. It was human weakness that led the philosopher politically astray.[1] As Rüdiger Safranski suggests, from a biographer's point of view, Heidegger never managed to escape the native limits of Meßkirch, his high-flying thought notwithstanding. All too human *ressentiments* plagued the academic upstart and outsider—a role he himself cultivated. In his latest book, Peter Trawny has pointed out Heidegger's special reservation toward Jewish colleagues. Generally Heidegger found it difficult to see himself as a part of the establishment. The anecdotes about anarchic activities within academic proceedings are legion. For example, it was always especially amusing for Heidegger to draw the perturbed or irritated looks of his colleagues when he taught his students skiing before taking them to his Black Forest hut for a seminar. Yet he certainly was always clever enough to let his distrust of the academic upper class appear in the guise of theory. His lashing of the professorial attitude was always couched within a general attack on the modern, businesslike conditions of the university and therefore on the failure of publicly commissioned intellectuals to further the cause of true thought.

If one accepts this basic approach of human weakness, Heidegger's connection to National Socialism was nothing more than the biographical culmination of his rage against the system. His endorsement of Hitler's regime would have served only the aim of becoming the head of the University of Freiburg in order to realize his fantasies of revenge. Finally he could have banned his colleagues from doing what they liked to do best, i.e., from his point of view, the conflating of that which is with being. "All science is philosophy, whether it knows and wills it—or not" as he put it in the rectoral address (*GA* 16:109/MHNS 7). Those who did not know or did not know better could be educated. The university would have been turned into a college for professors, a *Dozentenhochschule* and a "work camp" (*Arbeitslager*) for students (*GA* 16:168, 125). "Teachers and students" would have been molded into a fateful "battle community" (*Kampfgemeinschaft*) (*GA* 16:116/MHNS 12)—to leave such a community would have constituted treason toward the higher good.

THE "SITUATION" OF PHILOSOPHY

After reading the *Black Notebooks,* no interpretation based on merely personal motives, however morally dubious they might have been, will suffice. Instead it has become clear that the connection between political commitment and philosophy is very tight indeed and of a thoroughly systematic, not personal nature. It is systematic because Heidegger's political activities obviously need to be understood as an answer to a problem arising from a turn in his philosophy at the beginning of the 1930s. To return to a merely personal perspective one more time, it seems that Heidegger's mood (as disclosed in the *Hefte*) has been struck by two insults. First, he was aggravated by the fact that his philosophy brought about no epochal change whatsoever and was repeatedly misunderstood by everyone but himself. Second, he became impatient, since his message was now in danger of losing any historical force and traction.

Instead we might also take a more philosophical approach and start off with Heidegger's dissatisfaction about his own *Being and Time*. His basic criticism concerns its failure to achieve what he aimed for—a failure he now perceives to have been necessary: "So it was a mistake of *Being and Time* to try to overcome 'ontology' directly. Its ghastly 'success' is just more and even more abysmal babble about being" (*GA* 94:10). While it is possible to find a certain amount of vanity in such a claim about the public's misunderstanding, Heidegger's insight into his own error appears to be honest as well as fitting. The problem as such is now named and it can be reconstructed thusly.–

Ontology is the name of that classic philosophical discipline concerned with the being of objects, or being qua being, as Aristotle puts it. Heidegger uses quotation marks around *ontology*, indicating that the discipline misses its own goals. Originally Heidegger viewed ontology as an open horizon wherein the essence of things discloses itself to us almost on its own. The world offers itself to our understanding without any theoretical activity on our side. Contemporary ontology, however, is nothing more than the product of ideology or a *Weltbild* we form of the world. The world therefore appears to us only as a philosophical construct or artifact. We have become readers and interpreters imbuing the world with our own completely subjective meaning.

Three factors are to blame for this strange warping of our worldview. The first culprits are the sciences, subscribing to reductionism since the nineteenth century: all issues concerning the world could now be treated only within the (terminological) framework of natural and causal laws. The groundbreaking results in the 1920s and 1930s in particular led to the total dominance of physics in all matters of *Weltanschauung*.

The effects of technology (*Technik*) constitute the second factor. They are the deep reason for the obstinacy of modern science and the idea that science might be the exclusive agency of academia. Technology in Heidegger's sense equals technical thinking, and technical thinking is, in turn, identical to technical problem-solving. To solve a problem "technically" means to look for a solution that is rationally comprehensible and therefore impossible to surpass. Technical solutions appear to be without alternative and final. For Heidegger, modern science is as blinkered as it is because it sees everything in the world as a problem with exactly one optimal technical solution. In terms of propaganda, this brand of thinking draws its successes from the sensational technical achievements of the 1920s and 1930s as well as from the aestheticization of technology in the wake of the *Neue Sachlichkeit* and Bauhaus movements.

However these effects of technology are not yet the deepest cause for the warping of our worldview. Behind science and technology Heidegger finds at work the essence of computing and calculating. Every calculation takes place within a general ethos of utility or exploitation; in the end this means that every scientific or technological advance needs to be profitable. Here we are then faced with a Marxist motive, insofar as in this line of reasoning three ideas become relevant: 1. every theory is grounded in some praxis— put critically: every discovery is motivated by some interest; 2. technological progress does not happen for its own sake or for the betterment of mankind, but in the name of profit; 3. the urge to exploit science and technology is in itself as meaningless as technology itself, yet it becomes an end—but a necessarily meaningless end. As the accumulation of capital only ever serves the goal of accumulating more capital, utilitarian calculations only ever aim at bringing forth more calculating utilization. And so it seems to Heidegger (as it did to Marx before him) that the calamity and fate of modernity is to get caught in this circle of self-motivating self-maximization. Science, technology, and calculation are now merely mutually supportive elements of universal doom. A persistent apocalyptic mood combined with radicalized "socialist" promises fosters this general undertone that even colors everyday life, particularly since the close of the 1920s. Heidegger sums it up as "We stand before the nothing" (*Wir stehen vor dem Nichts*) (*GA* 94:7).

A FIRST SOLUTION

This is, in short form, the point of departure for Heidegger's systematic self-critique starting in the *Black Notebooks* of 1931. Regarding his 1927 book, *Being and Time,* Heidegger sees himself faced with the difficulty that he wanted to surpass ontology "directly," as quoted earlier. This means he wanted to overcome the impending doom he had diagnosed philosophically with the help of a counterprogram; he wanted to show how a mental as well as an existential reorientation would have to be thought and implemented.

To achieve this, *Being and Time* operates on all three levels we have discussed: in regard to science, the things now exclusively understood as present-at-hand need to be thought of as practical and originally ready-to-hand. In regard to technology, all artifacts need to be understood in light of the ends truly inherent to them. Heidegger calls this the "what-for" of their "relevance." And finally, regarding the excesses of utilitarian thinking, Heidegger brings a notion of existence into play based on "care" and a meaningful connection to the world.

This juxtaposition of modernity and existentialism, pitting the modern (inauthentic) spirit and its consequences against (authentic) individual existence, fits perfectly with the general mood of the 1920s. In his *The Decline of the West*, Spengler had already argued that all so-called powers of modernity were waning and had brought the world close to the abyss—and that individual existence alone was still human enough to be relied upon to bestow meaning to the world anew.

Basically this mood was nothing but a stylization of what the soldiers returning from the trenches experienced: their home and hearth gone, no job to be found or livelihood to earn, no family or fatherland to return to, just the hardships of survival. The dramatic experience of the finitude of all things manifest in the consequences of the war, along with the sudden loss of meaning, lent a welcome pathos to Heidegger's talk of carving out an existence. "Care" or—as we should now translate *Sorge*—"sorrow" became an easily understandable byword of these times since it not only referred to everyday issues but invoked the menace to one's complete existence; "sorrow" is existential sorrow.[2]

As well as this new concept of existence and care/sorrow fit the mood of the interwar years, in retrospect it reveals a fatal conceptual flaw. For Heidegger's existentialism only partly fulfills the role of a counterconception to modernity. He manages to reductively shift existence from its modern context to a setting in which things appear simple and therefore manageable. Unlike the objects of relativistic astrophysics, they are not light-years away, merely present-at-hand and only to be marveled at, but still within reach and ready for use. They cannot be randomly recombined like the atoms of stardust, but they appear as familiar everyday items, predetermined in their use. Finally we are unable to utilize them to unleash uncontrollable chain reactions with unimaginable and destructive consequences. Whatever we produce using Heideggerian tools (such as hammer and nail) will only ever be the same few items we need to exist.

Yet even these existential surroundings of the craftsman's workshop and the artisan's studio just reproduce the same old type of ontology—as Heidegger comes to understand in hindsight. Even though there are no natural laws ruling this lifeworld and no need to reduce everything to the merely present-at-hand, it is governed by an almost primordial order of meaning emanating from the readiness-to-hand of equipment. There might not be any technical problem solvers in this world, but it is inhabited by artisans and repairmen. The unleashed fury of capitalism might be absent, but we are still faced with a sort of self-proliferation of life wherever existence frees itself from its state of *Geworfenheit* and sets forth to realize its own project. However one looks at the situation, in the end there emerges only a copy of modern ontology in premodern guise. We are still looking at a closed picture of the world, whose presence diminishes every notion that things could be fundamentally different from our current conception. The horizon of our worldview remains limited, even closed.

"*Being and Time*," Heidegger states accordingly in the *Black Notebooks*, did not "resist three ambient temptations . . . on its way," namely:

the ethos of "groundwork" stemming from Neo-Kantianism
the "existential"—Kierkegaard—Dilthey;
the "scientificity"—phenomenology (*GA* 94:75).

Heidegger offers us an academic version of our own error analysis. First, he sees the reentry of reductionism—this was his critique of Neo-Kantianism. Second, the lifeworld is still treated as a technical construct—this was supposed to be the mistake of Husserlian phenomenology. And thirdly the existential still looks like a technical problem in the form of either/or, like a flip switch—with this he targets Kierkegaard and Dilthey. Both engaged with the issue from a literary and historical point of view but did not reach a deeper philosophical understanding.

A SECOND SOLUTION TO THE PROBLEM

Heidegger's next idea is easily understood against this backdrop. Up until now his philosophy had only managed to set one ontology against another. Put more succinctly, romanticism was now in opposition to modernity.

The new task was to avoid the mistake of *Being and Time*. All philosophical projects up to and including *Being and Time* need to be illuminated in such a way that their shortcomings become clearly visible. The preferred means for this task is now the history of being. In it worldviews succeed ever older worldviews, and it becomes apparent that in truth there is no progress. Each new take on the world tries to outdo the one just overtaken by claiming sole validity and forcing its successors into oblivion. In the grander scheme of things, it turns out to be arbitrary which *Weltbild* currently holds sway, since it is barred from reaching the truth by the fact that it is a "picture of the world" in the first place. So far so good, one is tempted to say. Heidegger sees his "'idea (principle?) of destruction' determined" by this context of continuous discrediting (*GA* 94:75). In the *Black Notebooks* Heidegger turns it into an historical imperative: "To chase man through the otherness and strangeness of the essence of being" (*GA* 94:43). Poststructuralism aligned with this process of destruction in the history of Being and called it "deconstruction."

The real problems set in once Heidegger stops operating anarcho-critically and becomes affirmative insofar as he now wants to determine the position in the history of Being from which such a destruction of metaphysical claims is launched. But this means to turn a reflexive stance into a proper point of view or, to use Luhmann's vernacular, to move the observer who has to stand outside any dogmatic machinations into the history of Being. Using Kantian terminology, we might generally say Heidegger's move means to revert the modern transcendental approach back into a premodern metaphysical one. Heidegger does this by turning the perspective of the observer into a beginning of the history of Being. Since he still wants to hold his distance from the metaphysical positions he attacks, he makes this new beginning into a "grand beginning [*großen Anfang*]" to which "we have to revert" (*GA* 94:53). It is grand apparently because it not only happens within time but outside time as well, with temporality somehow emanating from it. All later pictures of the world react to this, although they never understand it in its essence—so says Heidegger.

A THIRD SOLUTION

It gets scary once this still transcendental conception of the history of Being is transformed into a "world-event [*Weltereignis*]" (*GA* 94:96). For some time Heidegger tried to cope with this in a classical way. He starts— like Kant—on a reflexive level and attempts to find a change of heart in the general mood.[3] Again and again he thinks he can perceive such a shift: "Finally: set firmly in the creative co-responsibility of the truth of national existence" (*GA* 94:112). Soon after this upswing follows disenchantment. Heidegger talks about the "economic affliction of the world," "(unemployment)," the "historical affliction of the state," "(Versailles)," and the "chain of these afflictions—but," he notes, "we do not yet feel the spiritual affliction of existence" (*GA* 94:148), and this is supposed to be "the worst affliction" (*GA* 94:149).

Another Kantian motive could be seen in the effort to find an external historical sign for the inner change of mood; it is an option Heidegger resorts to sporadically in the *Black Notebooks*. He speaks about the "world-moment of our history and its resolve," for example, claiming this world moment needs to be met with the "order and readiness for 'revolution'" (*GA* 94:112). The autumn of 1932 sees him commemorating the "incomparability of the world-hour that will make German philosophy resound," only to interrupt himself in finding that the "'philosophy' that is not" could "never ever be engaged in 'the political'" (*GA* 94:109).

On closer consideration, no change of mood takes place, the spiritual affliction of existence remains hidden, and we are granted no reliable historical sign that the "world-hour" is at hand. But for Heidegger, apparently, something needs to happen now; enter Nietzsche and the most worrying shift in Heidegger's thinking during the 1930s. As he summarized his experiences later: "Nietzsche destroyed me."[4]

But in 1932 Nietzsche still appears to offer the solution for his problem regarding the history of Being, since he alone supposedly saw the "'current situation'" and "could see it because he foresaw something different." (*GA* 94:49). This foreseeing of something different means Nietzsche "created a totally different ethos for man—a looking-and-demanding directed ahead" (*GA* 94:49). What initially reads as another rhetorical gesture of hope in hopeless times yields consequences of systematically staggering importance: The former caution modeled on transcendental philosophy is discarded; gone too is the stance of the neutral observer of possible mood swings. The task of philosophy is now to actively bring about this shift in mood.

Nietzsche (and now Heidegger along with him) conceives of this process on the model of the artist in times of decadence. If a time is deprived of meaning and conviction, a great work of art is needed to alleviate the misery. A (real) work of art shapes a time by not only interpreting it but by forming it spiritually. The great work of art sets the direction that understanding has to follow. It opens up a horizon wherein everyone finds themselves after having congregated there. Such an event of the constitution of meaning initiates an immediate admiration, a powerful amazement and an irresistible absorption. "*Being* once the suddenly flaring *lightning* that draws all things into its light according to their measure and law. . . . Being—a gift, a rejoicing and a thrill, a question—the beginning" (*GA* 94:89). Dionysian rapture and Apollonian form merge once more into a work, a work Nietzsche himself could not finish. "Nietzsche," says Heidegger, "did not succeed in changing being and creating the new horizon; not least because he himself did not understand the ancient problem of being" (*GA* 94:50). Since Heidegger is well equipped with this understanding, his philosophy is destined to become the driving force of a new era. This basically means that Heidegger continues the project of *Being and Time*, not in the form of another philosophical treatise, but as a great work in the sense of a great work of art: "It is necessary to eclipse *Being and Time* as a book by bringing about the goals it missed in a true 'work.' This would be the right refutation" (*GA* 94:37). Refutation is now effected not by word but by deed. Heidegger's new aim is to enforce the correct understanding of the original goals of *Being and Time* instead of leaving it open to interpretation and continuous misinterpretation by critics (or followers). To this end, Heidegger borrows Nietzsche's terminology of spiritual chastisement and cultivation (or breeding): "The cultivation" namely "of higher and highest kinds of thinking is primordial—before all mere communication of information. . . . How is a high kind of thinking bred? Through the constant pressure of a determined questioning bound to a mission; firm features!" (*GA* 94:124).

THE FINAL SOLUTION (OR *ENDLÖSUNG*)

From here on, disaster runs its philosophical course. Following Nietzsche, Heidegger adopts a metaphysics of the will, i.e., he assumes that his audience (now the *Volk*) is driven by a force to be molded and directed. He demands: "A far-reaching spiritual-historical will for the future must be awakened, must consolidate itself, and incrementally prepare at least the next half century in its spiritual constitution" (*GA* 94: 121). It is necessary to "enforce" and "cement" the new "way of seeing" in the "establishment of will" (*GA* 94: 118). It is enforced through "education," where education means "guidance—control—steering of Being-knowledgeable" (*GA* 94: 123). The place of "education to knowledge" (*Wissenserziehung*) is academia, which needs to be reformed in accordance with the standards of National Socialism. In this Heidegger employs a distinctly Platonic notion of Socialism. After stating what a socialism freely based on Nietzsche should not be (i.e., a "joy of leveling down," the "supremacy of those who solely degrade," or the "mere pursuit of the common good"), Heidegger states his goals for academia in keeping with the Platonic formula of "each his own," now understood as a "progressively ordering obligation of everyone to fulfill their own task according to their capacity and character within the whole of the nation" (*GA* 94:124). "Education," in a nutshell, is the "awakening and binding establishment of the state power as the will of a people to itself" (*GA* 94:121). What the will of the people truly is and what it strives for will thus be imparted or revealed to it only here.

In accordance with the new task of reeducating the people in a National Socialist fashion, the nature of philosophy changes as well. "Metaphysics" is now conceived of as "meta-politics" (*GA* 94:116). The totality of the world and Being is still the subject matter, but now the world is supposed to undergo a world "conversion" (*GA* 94:120). This is the work to be performed. In the words of Geibel: "The essence of Germany shall heal the world."[5] For Heidegger, the only remaining question concerns "what privilege fate has measured out for our people" (*GA* 94:97). His answer: "The erection of the world-greatness of man" (*GA* 94:95).

In its final step this approach becomes completely disastrous, first, because this work requires a creator and, second—following the artists' competition between Wagner and Nietzsche—because the creative process requires the overcoming of an adversary.

Heidegger was never naive enough to believe that Adolf Hitler was really the artist capable of accomplishing the world conversion that Heidegger envisioned. Only one entry, made early during Heidegger's time as rector, trusts him with this kind of positive role. There Heidegger speaks of the "great experience and delight that the *Führer* awakened a new reality, gifting our thinking the right path and power" (*GA* 94:111). Shortly afterward Heidegger doubts that actual National Socialism is a "real emergent power" (*GA* 94:114). Or rather that it could be under only one condition: That it be led and guided by philosophy. National Socialism was lacking any real future prospect. It needed to "become becoming" (*GA* 94:115), as Heidegger puts it cryptically. More specifically this means that the "mood" National Socialism generates needs to be complemented by a spiritual "image." The kind of biologism endorsed by the Nazis is of no help in this regard; to the contrary—Heidegger just calls it "murky" (*GA* 94:143). It is an "insane idea to think the spiritual-historical world ('culture') grows like a weed from the 'people'" (*GA* 94:143). Such a notion only leads to a "gradual worsening of civil intellect" and to the people giving in to "a dark urge towards the dullest philistine way of life" (*GA* 94:143). On the whole, the formula Otto Pöggeler invented still holds: Heidegger wanted to lead the leader (*Führer*).[6]

Finally, and under the darkest of historical auspices, we need to consider the antagonism resulting from the new artistry of the history of being. Looking back at *Being and Time*, Heidegger remarked early in the *Black Notebooks*: "Objection to the book: I'm still lacking enemies today— it did not bring me a great enemy" (*GA* 94:9). In the sense of Carl Schmitt, such a great enemy should be conceived of as the agent who makes our own questioning gain form. With *Being and Time* now dwarfed by a grander undertaking that includes the rebuilding of the world and the history of being, things have changed. Just as Heidegger has now become the agent making primordial questioning a reality, the Jews have turned into the enemies, the artists of the opposite, so to speak. He thinks of them as advocates of pure calculation and agents of the forgottenness of being. They operate from the shadows of the history of being, as Heidegger puts it perfidiously; a form of agency that makes their activities impalpable and unassailable. Right at the end of the *Black Notebooks*, Heidegger writes: "The Judaism of the world, spurred on by those who were allowed to emigrate from Germany, is intangible everywhere and does not need to engage in warlike acts in spite of their display of power,

whereas we are left to sacrifice the best blood of the best of our nation"
(*GA* 96:262).

Peter Trawny has already said everything of import on this matter. The
systematic absurdity in this context consists in the mistake of causally
combining a purely reflexive and therefore ahistoric point of view with a
historic subject. This can only be wrong, unless one follows Nietzsche in
discounting the whole of Western metaphysics as the invention of a philosophically minded priestly caste. In that case, the history of being would be
a rhapsody of personal *ressentiments*, completely devoid of anything coming close to a true understanding of being according to the precepts of
Being and Time.

AFTER THE FINAL SOLUTION (OR *ENDLÖSUNG*)

Only much later did Heidegger himself come to understand the insights
just stated: first, that his own attempt at a philosophical reeducation of the
people (or at least the Führer) was doomed from the outset and, second,
that philosophy is inherently incapable of bringing about a reconfiguration
of the world. This late admission is well recorded in the now famous *Spiegel* interview of 1966. Speaking after "long contemplation," Heidegger says:
"Philosophy will not be able to bring about a direct change of the present
state of the world. This is true not only of philosophy but of all merely
human meditations and endeavors. Only a god can still save us. I think
the only possibility of salvation left to us is to prepare readiness, through
thinking and poetry, for the appearance of the god or for the absence of the
god during the decline; so that we do not, simply put, die meaningless
deaths, but that when we decline, we decline in the face of the absent god"
(*GA* 16:671/*MHNS* 56–57).

The phrase about a god who alone is still trusted to save us might sound
humble in this context. From a systematic point of view, however, it
becomes apparent that this is not the case; because, far from abandoning
the notion of the subject (the artist), Heidegger merely moved it to the
realm of the transcendent. Even the accompanying formula of "thought
and poetry" does not constitute a deviation from the role of the philosophical prophet in this context. It just means that Heidegger has stopped

speaking in his own name but now speaks instead in remembrance and as an admonisher of the truth of a distant god. This god only communicates through gestures—Heidegger says it "beckons"—not through concepts or words. Poetry, interpreted by the philosopher in light of these new conditions, just turns out to be the reflection of a higher (or deeper) order—again. It reaches a new level of reflection and it suffers a conceptual refraction, but in the end it still displays the same old imperative character and all the traits of an annunciation.

In conclusion, it becomes apparent that what Heidegger says in the *Black Notebooks* was no subjective fancy, but a (seemingly) sober and objective analysis. He meant what he said. In a 1948 letter to Herbert Marcuse he confirms it again: "I expected from National Socialism a spiritual renewal of life in its entirety, a reconciliation of social antagonisms and the salvation [*Rettung*] of western Dasein from the perils of communism" (*GA* 16:430/*EL* 30, tm). The history of being and our real history suddenly seemed to run parallel for Heidegger; especially where his older existential analysis of *Being and Time* could be transformed into the project of renewing existence—a renewal his philosophy was supposed to supply with major "contributions," as he made known in the 1930s through the title of his second magnum opus.

If Heidegger was really going to actively contribute to this process, then a complete reorientation of the basic understanding of his philosophy was called for. He no longer cared to interpret the world; he sensed the time had come to change it. This Marxist-socialist maxim was combined with a more national-romantic notion. The "planetary movement of modern technology" (*GA* 16:668/*MHNS* 54) was to be opposed by a common reflection of the German people upon its premodern spiritual roots. This reflection was supposed to be enforced in a Nietzschean vein by breeding a new spiritual nobility. From that moment on, Heidegger conceived of his philosophy as an essential contribution to the National Socialist *Gesamt-kunstwerk*. Again following Nietzsche, Heidegger saw this as the grand Western cultural drama: awakening, going astray, catharsis, return. The task of the thinker was now the same as that of a great poet or even a god: "guidance—control—steering of being-knowledgeable" (*GA* 94:123).

Finally, our spiritually advanced leader was, of course, in need of a Manichaean enemy to complete himself and the drama he had designed. The Jews and their supposed spiritual world-political conspiracy fit the bill perfectly.

Where do we go from here?

If this is indeed the bottom line of our perusal of the *Black Notebooks* regarding Heidegger's connection to National Socialism, what follows for dealing with his oeuvre? Two things. First, those who previously defended Heideggerian philosophy must acquiesce to dealing with questions of a new kind: e.g., whether the attempt to save Heidegger after *Being and Time* forces us to retain the conception of philosophy as a kind of artistic modification of reality and whether retaining such an artistic paradigm in itself brings something fatal to philosophy. Michel Foucault, for example, feared as much when he accused Jürgen Habermas of adhering to a conception of humanizing discourse that depends upon the philosophical policing of all discourse. The same doubts were harbored by those critics of Peter Sloterdijk who, like Kurt Flasch, believe that Sloterdijk's references to Heidegger lead not only to a postmodern conception of life as a work of art but also to the post-postmodern reality of terrorism as a work of art. Moreover, as a consequence of what has come to light, we are obliged to start from a different point in Heidegger's oeuvre. Instead of building on the late Heidegger—as was common in postwar philosophy—we should take our departure from the Heidegger of *Being and Time*.

From the perspective of *Being and Time,* Heidegger had two strategic options at his disposal. The first one expected technology to turn into a force of doom, gradually ruining mankind. Technology becomes the *Ge-stell* (positionality) wherein man appears to be trapped as in an ontological cage. Philosophy is forced to react to this hardening by hardening itself, countering technology with technology, for in Heidegger's eyes the great work of art is nothing more than the expression of technology imbued with spiritual meaning.

The other option takes the completely opposite theoretical path. Instead of hardening and becoming less and less human, we expect technology to approach humanity—without external force or artificial artistic help. Heidegger expressed a vision of this phenomenon in his primordial scenario of the craftsman's workshop or the artisan's studio and conceived of it as at least a marginal possibility of existence. In the artisan's studio the

equipment seemingly offers itself to the hand of the craftsman and is nothing more sinister than a technological aid through which human praxis is
enabled.[7] Hannah Arendt transposed this option of unobtrusive technology into the realm of the political and the practical, although still at the
price of marginalizing it into a small existential niche in which this kind
of academic reflection is still possible in modernity.

The new approach I would like to utilize from now on assumes what
was unthinkable for the late Heidegger as well as for Hannah Arendt,
namely that the "planetary motion of technology" itself turns back and
submits itself to forms of a genuinely human praxis. The Ge-stell dissolves
into more elastic structures, no longer encircling mankind like the bars of
a cage or mapping our world for us. Metaphorically the Ge-stell transforms
into a web that turns out to be surprisingly flexible in regard to coping with
our daily businesses and errands. The fact that the culture of technology is
now a Web culture implies a second major change in the meaning of technology in accord with Heideggerian ideas: technology again is to be understood as a precondition of praxis. As soon as we manage to convince
ourselves that the nature of our new Web culture is not so much communication and control but interaction, we have taken this step at least theoret-
ically. In this light, the shift from Web 1.0 to Web 2.0 should be thought as
the turn of eras regarding technology.

I believe a new Web policy is the cue for both understanding Heidegger's critique of technology as well as for writing it anew. Obviously, all the
interactive proceedings of the Internet are not more than a prominent
example of what I mean; they are but one phenomenon instantiating the
structure of the Web. Our analysis needs to work with far deeper and wider
notions of Web and linking. I believe the decisive fundamental structure
of our new ontology will turn out to be what Bruno Latour called a parlia-
ment of things. But that is another topic for another essay.

8

"THE SUPREME WILL OF THE PEOPLE"

What Do Heidegger's *Black Notebooks* Reveal?

HANS ULRICH GUMBRECHT

TRANSLATED BY RODRIGO THEREZO

Apparently just a few days after the Nazi seizure of power (*Machtergreifung*) on January 30, 1933, Martin Heidegger, for his part quite seized (*ergriffen*), noted: "The Supreme will of the people [*volklich*] is trapped within an enormous world darkness" (*GA* 94:109). Heidegger identifies the critical reactions still possible within the German public sphere as part and parcel of a past, the present of which reminds him of a sewer: "The filthiness of our flushed-away era is attested by the fact that the only oppositional movement it can produce is the chit-chat of dilettantes and the hullabaloo of 'political science'" (*GA* 94:109). Heidegger obviously took for granted that this "incomparable" moment was meant to assign German philosophy—and thus Heidegger himself—a historical role to play: "The incomparability of the world hours, the reverberant space [*Schlagraum*] of which German philosophy is to set ringing" (*GA* 94:109; *Schlagraum* could no doubt be translated into today's German by the word *Resonanz*, "resonance").

Heidegger, at any rate, saw in the events of early 1933 the first answers to a question he had asked with rhetorical pomp. This was not really the question whether "we are able to experience and ask which priority does destiny allot to our people" (*GA* 94:97), the answer for which he always kept prepared as a succinct, schematic formula of his own philosophical position: the task assigned to the German people by destiny of "inceptually taking up their exposure to beings (thrownness) and in its severe individuation and lucidity of questioning to be transfigured!!" (*GA* 94:97). Rather, the real question for Heidegger was ipso facto open, concerned with the "destinal readiness" (an expression he was happy to use back then) of this people and its philosophers, specifically with whether they would find the "strength to step back into the readiness and preparedness for the formative recognition of this dignity of the people and for the further advancement of its rank, into which it should march" (*GA* 94:98). In other shorter and less confusing words, allowing Heidegger's pretentiousness to come to the fore: the whole destiny of the nation is supposed to hinge on its readiness and ability to take up Heidegger's own trajectory of thought and to work toward the greatness supposedly reserved for it.

As a short meditation from around those weeks on "the Germans" shows, Heidegger's reasons for being skeptical of the destinal readiness of his nation had to do with its "groundless impatience with any attempt at finding its way back into an essential growing power" (*GA* 94:95). This is why Heidegger saw in Adolf Hitler the seat of all hope, as his notes—actually only those during these few weeks—lead us to believe: "A momentous experience and joy: the *Führer* has brought to daylight a new reality which gives our thinking its correct course and impetus. Otherwise this thinking fundamentally would have remained lost in itself, barely able to take effect" (*GA* 94:111). A few days prior to joining the NSDAP on May 1, 1933, Heidegger had accepted the post of rector of Freiburg University in spite of an inner resistance to doing so—which was genuine, though probably overcome by Hitler's charisma: "Forced to accept the rectorship, I act for the first time *against* the innermost voice. At any rate, this position will enable me, in the best-case scenario, to *prevent* a thing or two from happening. For the task—assuming it is even still possible—the people are lacking" (*GA* 94:110).

All these Heidegger quotations are from the thirty-four so-called *Black Notebooks,* published for the first time last year in three *Gesamtausgabe* volumes and stirring a great deal of commotion among experts and the educated public alike of many countries. They contain notes, begun in 1930 though not individually dated, from a good forty years, notes that Heidegger apparently revised with a view toward book publication. In the middle of the 1970s, he presented them to the German Literary Archive in Marbach as part of his estate. In the murmuring tones typical of him,

Heidegger often characterizes these entries as "attempts at a simple nam-ing" (*GA* 94:1) and, first and foremost, as a testament to how he had come to philosophical inquiry. Be that as it may, there can be no doubt whatso-ever that Heidegger held these notebooks to be intellectually significant—something which, considering their thoroughgoing banality, is for me not merely surprising but actually horrifying.

After what is by now an almost rhythmic sequence of Heidegger scan-dals, it is shocking to find reactions that would newly discover his fascina-tion for National Socialism. But the *Black Notebooks* now make it possible to reconstruct the history of this fascination in all its microscopic detail. And yet, since 1933, there was never any doubt as to Heidegger's affinity with the National Socialist movement, it being then only predictable that he would partake of its ideology and motives. It was thus always possible, as it still is today—and on quite reasonable grounds—to respond to these historical facts by either deciding to ignore Heidegger's philosophical work or by being open to a revised appreciation of its significance.

The *Black Notebooks* confirm just about everything we could have antic-ipated and feared regarding that part of Martin Heidegger's intellectual biography. The only thing really surprising here is the absolutely devastat-ing intellectual quality of these notes. Over the course of the Nazi years—after a short period of enthusiasm and hope, in which the "renewal of Germany" plays a decisive role—Heidegger's growing disappointment with a National Socialism gone astray from his expectations raises itself to the personal level, to what an American commentator aptly described as a "rhapsody in resentment" along with the shrillest tones of academic condescension. To begin with, a predictable repertoire of positive con-cepts and themes assume prominence: the hierarchical complementarity between "leading [*führen*] and following," "destinal readiness," "resolute-ness," "hardness," "the joy of work," the dynamic of a move "forward," and, above all, the ever-returning insistence on a suitable "attunement." But this directly gives way both to a crescendo of condescension toward the colleagues receiving more attention from the NSDAP and to a noisy com-plaining—under the aegis of the omnipresent word *machination*—over a number of tendencies and phenomena that Heidegger held to be the symp-toms of a general decadence, among which we could cite "Americanism," "pacifism," and of course "liberalism"—but also "boxing," "the movies," and the "radio," which Heidegger called "idiotic" so as to honor it with one more of his etymological escapades in their typical philological shakiness (*GA* 96:265).

Similarly pitched remarks about "Judaism" appear rather seldom in the *Black Notebooks,* and when they do they correspond to the anti-Semitic standard of protofascist intellectual circles from the first third of the twentieth century, as sketched most succinctly by Oswald Spengler in his historico-speculative work *The Decline of the West.* For both Spengler and Heidegger, "the underlying reason for Judaism's temporary empowerment lies in the fact that western metaphysics, especially in its modern form, provided the starting point for the ensconcement of an otherwise empty rationality and calculability, which thus managed to find a home in 'spirit'" (*GA* 96:46). Heidegger is on a roll here and also relegates the "phenomenological investigation" of his teacher Edmund Husserl to that same vulgar "empty rationality" so as to preclude Husserl's philosophy from ever being able "to attain the realms of essential decisions" (*GA* 96:46). In the midst of this motley ocean of *ressentiment*-laden banalities without argument, intuition, or variation, the reader is nearly surprised to find that Heidegger typically puts the word *race* in quotation marks. Alluding to the "race-theory" propagated by the German state and party, Heidegger actually criticizes positing this as an absolute (which clearly does not require any special courage in the confines of a private notebook entry). But at the same time he was eager to stress the fundamental importance of this ideological horizon: "*Race*—which makes up *one* necessary condition of historical Dasein (thrownness), not only attains the fake status of being the one and only sufficient pre-requisite—but rather, at the same time, as that which gets talked *about* [sic!]. The 'intellectualism' of this approach: not being able to differentiate between racial indoctrination and actual racial theories. *One* condition is elevated to the status of the unconditional" (*GA* 94:189).

We readers of Heidegger have long ago accepted the bitter realization that neither all of his critical remarks on the "nationalistic movement" and its ideologico-political decisions nor his increasing resentment over the same ever allowed him to take a decisive distance or even a self-critical stance toward the movement—not even once in the thirty-one years between the end of World War II and his death. Despite all the internal disappointments and the "denigrations" he experienced during the years between 1933 and 1945, Heidegger's assurance of himself and of his mission remained unshaken: "For years now I know myself to be working down the right path toward the cultivating of knowledge and I cannot be taught by raw youth with their foolish idle talk of a 'new' concept of science" (GA 94:158). As this lasting self-consciousness races to hyperbolic amplitudes and heights, it frequently peaks in unintentionally humorous ways. Such is the case in a thought just as ceremoniously as auspiciously entitled "The Play and Uncanniness of Historical Calendar Dates at the Forefront of the Abyssal German History" (GA 94:523). Here Heidegger wishes to single out what he takes to be the decisive moments of German history during the nineteenth century. He starts out with the year 1806 and the beginning of Hölderlin's madness ("Hölderlin departs") and of a national romanticism ("the German gathering"), next comes 1813 ("the German commencement [*Anlauf*] reaches its summit and Richard Wagner is born"), Hölderlin's death and Nietzsche's birth (1843/1844), several works from Nietzsche and the death of Richard Wagner (1883), "Nietzsche's 'euphoria' before the collapse" (1883), finally landing right at his own birthday, inserted after two dashes and between parentheses: "(9/26/1889)" (GA 94:523).

But what is revealed—in the midst of such unfortunately unforgettable passages—in the many hundred pages of Heidegger's *Black Notebooks*, I mean in terms of its content, "values," and prejudices? Precisely what we could have anticipated from our previous knowledge of Heidegger's biography. Anyone who would still entertain the illusion that Heidegger was not really seduced or permeated by National Socialism must now be quiet. On the other hand, what is surprising and painful since the publication of the *Black Notebooks*—to everyone who believes themselves to have philosophically profited from reading Heidegger—is the hopelessly irremediable banality of its entries (especially when we know—as already mentioned—just how much importance he placed in their publication). Must this disappointment turn into the beginning of a devaluation of all other Heidegger texts? I think this question remains structurally similar to the question dealing with the consequences one should draw from the facts of Heidegger's life between 1933 and 1945. Taking a distance is a plausible response—even though the banality of the *Black Notebooks* does not fundamentally cancel out the significance of texts such as *Being and Time*, *Fundamental Concepts of Metaphysics*, or the "Letter on 'Humanism.'" Their inspirational force has stood the test of time and is fundamentally even independent of the quality of the thoughts in Heidegger's head that must have both preceded and attended the genesis of these texts.

⸺ ❧ ⸺

The question still remains as to how we should account for the conspicuous difference in quality between the *Black Notebooks* and other texts written and revised by Heidegger around 1930 (when the notebooks begin) up until his death in 1976. Most of the significant texts are underpinned by lectures or courses given by Heidegger—which were always nicely prepared and focused on a theme, yet with a peculiar and almost always justified faith in momentary intuitions. This lecture style entailed a particularly dramatizing gesture, which, in his philosophizing, relentlessly pointed out the possibility of a breakthrough in thinking and the "dangers" this brings with it. I often have the feeling, when reading post-1930 Heidegger texts, that precisely this self-staging, lecturing gesture could have been a structural predecessor for the motif of the "appropriative event of truth" as the "self-revealing of being" (according to which this self-revelation is, first, supposed to be impossible to control, and, second, destructive for human existence [*Dasein*]).

At any rate, this gesture of his self-staging, directed to a public (as a "reverberant space [*Schlagraum*]"?) seemed to have inspired Heidegger and brought a new agility to his thinking. This framing condition of thinking, which was apparently so important for Heidegger, drops out of the picture with the writing of personal notes, letting his intuitions drown in the endlessly repetitive and reactionary banality of seasonal calendar slogans. Writing polished sentences and aphorisms in the solitude of a writing desk—in the only way this can happen—this was never the sort of author Heidegger was.

9

PROLEGOMENA TO ANY FUTURE DESTRUCTION OF METAPHYSICS

Heidegger and the *Schwarze Hefte*

PETER E. GORDON

A t this late date, so much ink has been spilt on the question of Heidegger and Nazism that one feels reluctant to contribute additional remarks. That Heidegger was a Nazi by conviction well after the end of his service as Freiburg rector is widely known. That he harbored anti-Semitic opinions is also accepted as incontrovertible fact by all but his most recalcitrant apologists. We should all be grateful to Peter Trawny for his scrupulous work in editing the first volumes of the *schwarze Hefte* and for his own excellent and searching philosophical interpretation of their content in his book, *Heidegger and the Myth of a World Jewish Conspiracy.* Yet I am perhaps not alone when I say that much of the anti-Semitic material found in the *schwarze Hefte* did not strike me as terribly surprising, since it largely confirmed, though it gave a certain added philosophical depth to, the evidence that was already available in disparate sources, such as correspondence and memoirs, and also in the recently published seminars of 1933 and '34, especially the winter 1933–34 seminar *Nature, History, and the State.* That some of the most intemperate critics such as Emmanuel Faye have marshaled such evidence to declare Heidegger anathema to the philosophical canon, as if all his insights were thereby beyond consideration, strikes me as a hyperbolic response unbefitting our usual habits of philosophical interpretation. Still, given the extent of his political compromises and the mutual entanglement of his philosophy and his politics, I have much sympathy for those who simply wish to be done with Heidegger altogether.

Although I will not address the substantive material in the *schwarze Hefte*, I feel it would be irresponsible to avoid briefly mentioning some of their more extraordinary contents. The general complaint against *Machenschaft* (machination) that runs through the notebooks strikes me as remarkable chiefly because it demonstrates that, by the later 1930s, Heidegger had fallen prey to a virtually apocalyptic mood. In one passage he broods over "the unconditional power of machination" and "the complete groundlessness of things" (*GA* 96:30). In reading such lines, one has the sense that Machenschaft has assumed a quasi-mythic stature like that of a Gnostic god who reigns supreme over the fallen world. It is certainly true that the critique of Machenschaft and technology is a major preoccupation of the notebooks. In purely quantitative terms, one can even grant that this critique far exceeds the passages where Heidegger descends into anti-Semitism, antiliberalism, or indulges in other assorted chauvinisms. But it would be ironic to pursue a *quantitative* content analysis, as if anti-Semitism were less momentous and a mere distraction from Heidegger's critique of modernity. Clearly the two were intertwined. For me, the worst passages in the book are those that associate Machenschaft, technology, and "the gigantic" with the ascendant power of the Jews. Heidegger ascribes their ascendency to "the metaphysics of the West," which reinforces both a calculative disposition and an "empty rationality" (*GA* 96:46). Elsewhere Heidegger writes that "one of the most hidden forms of the gigantic and perhaps the oldest is the tenacious aptitude for calculating and profiteering and intermingling, upon which the worldlessness of Jewry is founded" (*GA* 95:97).

Regarding such passages two points should be made. First, they are clearly instances of anti-Semitism (and at first glance rather banal). The allusion to the Jews' "worldlessness" taps into an old belief that, having rejected Christ's divinity, the Jews are condemned to homeless wandering. Heidegger also recycled the rather more modern myth that that the Jews are gifted in finance (itself a refurbished meme from the medieval imaginary linking Jews to usury). But we would be wrong to dismiss this stuff as the unthinking echoes of past chauvinism. For it was Heidegger's singular genius to interlace these *idées reçues* with themes from his own philosophy. Even the idea of Jewish "worldlessness" evokes the argument from *Being and Time* where the disruption of skillful labor brings a loss of existential communion with things and (in Heidegger's phrase) "the deworlding of the world." The complaint against reason and calculation recapitulates themes from works such as *Kant and the Problem of Metaphysics* in 1929, and, from the same year, in the famous encounter in Davos with the philosopher Ernst Cassirer, where Heidegger insisted that a viable philosophy would demand the "destruction of the former foundation of Western metaphysics" in "spirit, logos, [and] reason" (*GA* 3:273/192).

The entanglement of Heidegger's anti-Semitism with his philosophical critique of Western metaphysics should give us pause. At the very least, it suggests that wherever Heidegger philosophized in a minor key about the modern age and the "abandonment of being" he was also thinking of the Jews as symptoms of this misfortune. Their reputed capacity for calculation was yet another sign, though it was not a cause, of the technological nihilism that he came to see as the metaphysical fate of the West. That Heidegger does not actually *blame* the Jews for the afflictions of the modern world invites the saving thought that his chauvinism was incidental, not intrinsic to his philosophy. But on the final page of a notebook from 1941 Heidegger writes that "the question concerning the role of *world Jewry* is not a racial but a metaphysical question" (*GA* 96:121). According to Peter Trawny, such passages show that Heidegger subscribed to a highly unusual species of "being-historical" (*seinsgeschichtliche*) anti-Semitism.[1]

I believe this is entirely correct. Now what is truly distressing in the allusion to Jewish *Weltlosigkeit* is the intimate association with Heidegger's overall critique of Western metaphysics. At issue is a specific and, one might argue, systematic feature of Heideggerian doctrine. In division 1 of *Being and Time* (specifically, in §§14 to 24 of the existential analytic) we are treated to a powerful description of the *Weltlichkeit der Welt*, the worldhood of the world, and this is the sort of worldhood that belongs to Dasein as constitutive of its own existential involvement, its practical engagement in the mode of *Zuhandenheit* with the *pragmata*, the items of equipment, of its surrounding world or *Umwelt*. Much of what Heidegger characterizes as the constitutive world for Dasein is precisely this Umwelt or environment, translated by Macquarrie and Robinson as the "surrounding world." This Umwelt exhibits a certain artisanal holism, where all tools refer to each other and, ultimately, refer back to the governing care structure of Dasein itself. To this surrounding world there is accordingly a certain spatiality—*existenziale Räumlichkeit*—that is deeper than the metric space associated with the modern natural sciences. It follows that Heidegger characterizes the emergence of natural-scientific space as a breakdown or "deworlding" of the surrounding world. In one of the more important passages, he writes as follows:

> When space is discovered non-circumspectively by just looking at it, the environmental regions get neutralized to pure dimensions. Places—and indeed the whole circumspectively oriented totality of places belonging to equipment ready-to-hand, get reduced to a multiplicity of positions for random Things. The spatiality of what is ready-to-hand within-the-world *loses its involvement-character*, and so does the ready-to-hand. The world loses its specific aroundness; the environment becomes the world of Nature. The "world" as a totality of equipment ready-to-hand becomes spatialized to a context of extended Things that are *just present at hand and no more*. The homogeneous space of Nature shows itself only when the entities we encounter are discovered in such a way that it has the character of a specific *Deworlding* (*Entweltlichung*) of the worldliness (*Weltlichkeit*) of the ready-to-hand.
>
> (*GA* 2:150/*SZ* 112)

I have analyzed this passage elsewhere, here I only want to draw out the most crucial point: it belongs to the cardinal principles of the existential analytic that the existential involvement of being-in-the-world is deeper than, and prior to, the distanced position of Cartesian analysis associated with mathematical reasoning and natural-scientific objectivity.[2] Against the metaphysical and epistemological tradition that describes the world as an independent reality disclosed in the mode of *Vorhandenheit*, Heidegger characterizes the world first and foremost in its mode of existential involvement or *Zuhandenheit*. As we know, from the priority of the *zuhanden*, it follows that the *vorhanden* world becomes available for analysis only if there is a breakdown of existential worldhood or what Heidegger calls the "deworlding of the world" (*die Entweltlichung der Welt*). Much of the language Heidegger uses in this argument suggests that he sees deworlding as a process of impoverishment, neutralization, and loss. We are not far here, I would suggest, from the theory of rational world alienation or disenchantment consequent upon the rise of the natural sciences, a historical process that Max Weber called *die Entzauberung der Welt*.

Now, what I find especially disturbing in Heidegger's *Black Notebooks* is the suggestion that the Jews, with their apparent gift for calculation, are themselves afflicted with worldlessness, as if they are agents of or signs of the very same process of world impoverishment that Heidegger associated with mathematics, with the natural sciences, with technology, and with modernity overall. It is a commonplace of European anti-Semitic discourse that the Jews are neither aristocrats nor artisans, that they lack the gift of authentic and skillful handicraft handed down as practical knowledge through the carefully guarded institution of the feudal guild. That the Jews lack "worldhood," however, strikes me as more than an anti-Semitic canard: it is a philosophical observation closely allied with the specific theory of deworlding developed in *Being and Time*. Because they apparently lack "worldhood" and all the various skills associated with existential involvement, the Jews become a virtual antitype in Heidegger's thought to the artisanal innocence of being-in-the-world.

I would find all of this less distressing were it not for the fact that the anti-Semitic complaint about Jewish unworldliness belongs to a whole syndrome of philosophical arguments that eventually inform Heidegger's critique of metaphysics itself. Remember, on the very last page of a notebook from 1941, Heidegger says: "The question concerning the role of *world Jewry* is not a racial but a *metaphysical* question" (*GA* 96:121). I take this claim seriously because the specific argument about deworlding prepares the terrain for Heidegger's larger suggestion that the history of metaphysics has fallen into a path of error where it misunderstands being itself as a deworlded and atemporal ground. The Heideggerian project of working out a so-called destruction of the history of metaphysics is therefore associated (at least in Heidegger's mind) with the antipathy to world Jewry as agents of the metaphysical tradition itself. In the notes written between 1936 and 1946, later published under the title "Overcoming Metaphysics" ("Überwindung der Metaphysik"), Heidegger writes that the modern world has become nothing less than an "unworld [*Unwelt*]" (*GA* 7:91/*EP* 104). The technological culmination of metaphysics manifests itself in this unworld as the reign of Machenschaft, or machination, with all of its various afflictions: subjectivism, calculation, technology, and—most of all, as the fate of the West—our general condition of *Seinsverlassenheit*. It is therefore hardly an exaggeration if we conclude that for Heidegger the metaphysical question of world Jewry unfolds within the larger question of *Seinsverlassenheit*. One cannot help but entertain the unpleasant thought that the task of overcoming metaphysics would therefore require an over-coming of the Jews. We do not know what form such an overcoming might have assumed in Heidegger's philosophical imagination. But we know only too well the form it assumed in the Third Reich.

I do not wish to develop these points further here. Instead, I am more con-cerned with the methodological question of how one might best proceed when reading Heidegger today in light of these associations and in the aftermath of the damaging evidence revealed in the 1933–34 seminars, in the *schwarze Hefte*, and in the interpretations so helpfully developed by Peter Trawny. We are all familiar with the passage from the B preface of Kant's *Critique of Pure Reason* where he entertains the thought that, like Copernicus, it will require a revolution in thought, recognizing that objects conform to the mind rather than the mind's conforming to objects, if there is to be any further progress in metaphysics.[3] In 1783 Kant wrote the *Pro-legomena to Any Future Metaphysics* so as to lay out, independent of the systematic critique, the basic claims that would guide such a revolution. It seems to me that with Heidegger we now stand before a question of simi-lar methodological importance: can we continue as we have been before in our reading of Heidegger's attempt at a "destruction" of the history of metaphysics, or do we require some introductory guidance or "prolegom-ena" for our work?

I cannot claim to have developed any definitive answers to this ques-tion. No doubt they are the urgent themes that will preoccupy us from this point forward. As readers of conscience, the burden will fall to each of us as individuals and to all of us as an interpretive community to remain alert to the manifold ways in which anti-Semitism is interwoven into the fabric of Heidegger's argumentation. The historian David Niren-berg has recently argued that Heidegger occupies a seat in the grand tradi-tion of anti-Judaism—a tradition that stretches from the ancients through the Church Fathers and from Islam through the Enlightenment. I do not know if this is wrong. Nirenberg shows convincingly that certain fantasies about Judaism have endured in the Western imagination because of the "work" they have done, the metaphors and concepts they have proffered.

But for the philosophical reader there are considerable disadvantage in Nirenberg's approach. It is a survey and, as such, it exhibits all the liabilities of an encyclopedic method that stresses commonality over difference, center over periphery, yielding the implicit (even if untended) message that all instances of anti-Judaism do "work" of equal significance. The unfortunate passage where Kant recommends the "euthanasia" of Judaism appears in the same rogues' gallery of anti-Jewish thinking as Shakespeare's portrait of Shylock and the lethal prejudices of the Spanish Inquisition. If we look only at the philosophical chapters, a great many of the instances of anti-Jewish commentary are quite well known, and they have long been the object of debate in specialists' literature. In fixing our attention once again on these (often quite unsettling) instances of anti-Jewish commentary in the canons of the great philosophers, the book takes insufficient care to explain whether these examples belong to the deep structure of philosophical reflection or whether they are merely extrinsic, that is, whether they are metaphors and images that we could cast aside without damaging the integrity of their arguments. Nor does it help that Nirenberg, a brilliant historian but less knowledgeable in philosophy, makes an occasional misstep in his philosophical exposition, as when he writes that for Kant sensible intuition, space, and time belong to "the pure forms of understanding."[4] To establish, for example, how deeply a given philosopher may have *required* anti-Judaism for the coherence of a philosophical doctrine, one must have a very good idea what the doctrine in question actually was. Without this internalist concern for the rational coherence of a philosophical argument, the suspicious practice of an ostensibly "exhaustive" contextualist or genealogical critique cannot disable in advance the possibility of redeeming from politically tainted texts arguments that may, *in principle*, transcend their past contexts of articulation. It is not hard to see that exhaustive genealogies of this kind are rationally indefensible. If one adopts a priori the suspicious interpretive posture that regards all philosophical argument as nothing else than ideology in disguise, one denies in advance the very possibility of rational argumentation itself: the result is a performative contradiction. This holds true for any philosophical text. It applies to any discussion of the troubled pairing of Kant and

Judaism and it applies, too, for any discussion of the even more vexed pairing of "Heidegger and the Jews."

The question regarding the place of anti-Judaism in Heidegger's philosophy cannot be resolved merely by collecting the most poisonous elements into one lethal draught. It can be resolved only if we ask how much the poison has circulated throughout the body of the philosophy and whether the body can survive if the poison is cleansed. I do not contest the fact that Heidegger was an anti-Semite. But, for a philosopher, the question of the longevity of Heidegger's philosophy *despite* his anti-Semitism is of more pressing concern. I doubt this is a question of a wholly different order from the ones that accompany all philosophical reading in a historical mode when the author of a given text has interlaced his argumentation with ideas we would not hesitate to recognize today as racist or sexist or in favor of slavery. Still, in the pages that follow, I want to suggest that the question of Heidegger's anti-Semitism casts in relief a certain methodological concern that bears directly on his critique of the metaphysical tradition.

I will begin by noting what I take to be a standard defense of Heidegger, a defense to which, I might add, I am not entirely unsympathetic. According to this defense, the case of Heidegger is no different from that of any other great thinker in the philosophical canon, insofar as one can draw a distinction between the empirical thinker and the philosophical arguments themselves. Whatever flaws or prejudices we ascribe to the empirical thinker, as historians of philosophy we are accustomed to the technique of bracketing (not unrelated to the bracketing or *epochê* of phenomenology), a technique by which the empirical facts are put out of play so as to better fix our attention on the immanent structures of philosophical argumentation itself. This is not to say, of course, that the historian of philosophy will disregard *all* empirical facts about the philosopher's life as if arguments were *necessarily* unrelated to those facts. Most historians of philosophy feel free to draw upon biographical and contextual considerations, but they do so *only insofar as they believe these considerations have some bearing on the integral or essential structure of the philosophical claims themselves.* If consulting the correspondence between Kant and Markus Herz permits us to understand an argument in the first critique better than we might have without this evidence, such consultation is warranted. Animating this methodological proviso, of course, is a strong commitment to the principle of coherence or rational reconstruction, according to which the historian of philosophy is enjoined to practice interpretive charity. The purpose of reading a given text in the history of philosophy, in other words, is to come up with the best possible reconstruction of a given argument so as to make that argument appear rationally defensible—at the very least, as defensible as it is possible for that argument to be.

One problem with philosophical charity has been expressed recently by the Spinoza scholar Yitzhak Melamed, who has noted that this kind of charity often turns out to be remarkably uncharitable, insofar as it has the tendency to turn a past thinker into a present contemporary who shares our own criteria as to what counts as a good argument.[5] The specific problem with philosophical charity is that its very idea of a defensible argument carries with it a host of specific philosophical commitments that a past philosopher may not have shared. Philosophical charity, in other words, tends to separate out a thinker's legacy into those arguments that are the embarrassing bits (which are discarded) from those arguments that admit of rational defense on our own contemporary terms. Melamed urges us to imagine a more charitable mode of reading that would leave us open to experiencing the truly different criteria that a past philosopher may have considered intrinsic to his argument, criteria that we too casually dismiss when they conflict with our own commonsense expectations of legitimate argument.

Now, if Melamed is right, a perverse consequence follows. For it is possible that philosophical charity itself would require that we take Heidegger's anti-Semitism as intrinsic to his philosophical argumentation. His critique of the Jews, according to this line of analysis, would be no less significant to his argumentation than his critique of technology, for example, or his general views on the unfortunate descent of philosophy when it traveled from the Greek to the Latin world as outlined in *Introduction to Metaphysics*. In my opening remarks I laid out what this sort of uncharitable reading might look like. However, for those who wish to salvage whatever can be salvaged from Heidegger's philosophy for the future, this sort of philosophical charity will hardly seem charitable at all. And, if this is right, we should probably return to the more conventional understanding of philosophical charity that permits us to bracket out certain embarrassing or contextual factors as extrinsic to the philosophical arguments under consideration.

But here I believe we need to consider what premises underwrite this practice of bracketing. The notion that the arguments of a past philosophy can present themselves as candidates for current philosophical consideration suggests that a philosophical work consists primarily in *arguments*, that is, claims that we, in our own time, may have good reasons to accept. Such reasons, however, will count as reasons only if they can retain this status *independent of* the contextual or biographical considerations we have bracketed out in advance. If an argument seems defensible only because it is grounded upon other evidence or beliefs that belong to the bracketed material, then this argument does not survive our salvaging technique, and, ipso facto, it cannot be a candidate for current philosophical consideration. If a given piece of philosophical writing presents me with a claim, and we justify that claim *only* by noting that "people in the philosopher's time and place commonly thought this way," such an observation regarding the original milieu in itself would hardly suffice as a reason for *me* to take that claim seriously as an argument today. It might serve, of course, for purposes of historical interpretation, if I am keen to understand why that philosopher exemplifies a certain way of thinking common to her world. But taking it as a philosophical argument demands something more. The idea of philosophical charity demands our commitment to the idea that a philosophical argument enjoys a certain kind of independence in relation to biography or history or in relation to (putting the thought in the most general terms) *the ambient context*.

The question we must ask, therefore, is just what is entailed by this idea of independence, since the very possibility of philosophy stands or falls with our commitment to this idea. I am not convinced that all of Heidegger's philosophy is now contaminated by Nazism or anti-Semitism (and I might add that I share Peter Trawny's sensitive warning on the dangers of pursuing philosophy according to metaphors of purity and contamination). But I am convinced that Heidegger's philosophy can no longer present itself for appraisal as an integral whole in the manner of the grand philosophical systems of the past. Nor can we sustain the old idea of the *maître-penseur* that awards to Heidegger an authoritarian and proprietary control over his own thoughts. Permit me to invoke a felicitous remark by Peter Trawny: "The freedom of philosophy counts for more than obedience to a beloved thinker."[6] If philosophy remains available to us today at all, it seems to me it remains available for thoughtful appropriation only where it can be redeemed, as Adorno might have said, in its fragments. The philosophical tradition itself appears to us today less as a monument unbroken in its grandeur than as a field of ruins that we can sift through in search of momentary insight.

But we might still ask about the quality of independence we assign to any one of those fragments. If we continue to believe that arguments are not wholly dominated by the local context of their initial articulation, and if therefore they make themselves available for reflection and, potentially, redemption within the ongoing projection of philosophical speculation, it seems to me we cannot avoid the methodological question as to the epistemic or metaphysical entailments that underwrite this very interpretative practice. My suggestion is that the attempt to isolate an argument from any number of ostensibly extrinsic factors suggests a pragmatic appeal to the context-transcendent rationality of argumentation itself.

Needless to say, this appeal is hardly consonant with Heidegger's philosophy, in which the law of situated hermeneutics disables the thought of a context-transcendent or critical rationality. In fact, one might say that much of what remains of value in Heideggerian thinking militates *against* the principles that nourish confidence in the possibility of a context-transcendent reason. This is true both for the early exercises in existential ontology as well as the later and more radical search for a different inception for philosophy beyond subjectivism and metaphysics. I have already noted how in *Being and Time* Heidegger associates critical rationality itself with the decontextualizing gesture that he calls a "deworlding of the world." The attempt to salvage an isolated strand of his philosophy from its own factical and historical world remains possible only on the transcendental-pragmatic supposition that philosophical argument exceeds any given horizon. Obviously this does not mean that such arguments persist in a metaphysical precinct "beyond" the confines of the world. It only means that these arguments remain available to us *as* arguments only on the condition that we commit ourselves pragmatically to the possibility of their validity within a hypothetically common world that is forged in a world-immanent fashion through nothing more than the ongoing process of argumentation itself. This does *not* imply metaphysical transcendence; it implies only the *postmetaphysical* gesture that Jürgen Habermas has called "transcendence from within."[7]

Needless to say, most Heideggerians do not have the resources to sustain such a gesture, since their pathologizing and self-sabotaging critique of deworlding reason refuses to grant such a quasi-transcendental power to rational argument. Indeed: from the Heideggerian point of view, the notion of argumentation on a shared terrain of intersubjective reason implies a breakdown of that holistic Umwelt which serves as the originary domain of analysis in Heidegger's existential phenomenology. It threatens nothing less than a metaphysics of "worldlessness." And Heidegger rejected this worldlessness of reason no less than the worldlessness of world Jewry.

I am therefore led to conclude that, on pain of self-contradiction, the orthodox Heideggerian must betray Heidegger to defend him. For one cannot simultaneously endorse the philosophical project of overcoming metaphysics while also insisting on the distinction in Heidegger's legacy between its worldly political entanglement and its enduring philosophical insight. Any successful destruction of metaphysics would seem to forbid just that distinction. More salutary would be to follow the paradoxical strategy that was first described by Jürgen Habermas in his *Frankfurter Allgemeine Zeitung* article from 1953: "Mit Heidegger gegen Heidegger denken," to think with Heidegger against Heidegger.[8]

The example of Habermas may suffice to remind us that there are various ways to take on board certain insights from Heidegger without subscribing in an unqualified or uncritical way to the entirety of his philosophical program. A cardinal example—one that remains of enduring value, in my opinion—is Heidegger's attempted dismantling of the metaphysical tradition, and I cannot see why this critical effort must be abandoned simply because Heidegger himself chose to yoke together his complaint against metaphysics with crude and counterfactual generalizations about the Jews. After all, this is a critical effort that is not without precedent: as Heidegger himself explained as early as 1929, the strike against metaphysics is anticipated in transcendental philosophy itself and might have succeeded had not Kant drawn back from the postfoundationalist radicalism of his own conclusions. And the polemic against ascetic rationalism as a species of nihilism is already prepared by Nietzsche, even if (according to Heidegger) this polemic only succeeded in celebrating the will to power as the culmination of metaphysics rather than as its undoing. Heidegger's mature turning against metaphysics (in the *Beiträge* and the Nietzsche lectures) has a great many sources of inspiration, and if we can discern a multiplicity of voices behind his achievement it seems odd to say that each one of those voices merits consideration while Heidegger's alone must remain forever damned. On the contrary, the obvious thing would be to say that the overcoming of metaphysics still deserves our attention even while we resist the grandiose verdict against modernity in which it is embedded. Hans Jonas may have been right to discern in Heidegger's philosophy traces of Gnostic despair regarding the destitution of our fallen world. But Jonas was still captive to the authoritarian ideal of a great philosopher whose work is embraced as a whole or not at all. A genuinely critical approach is different. Critique (as we know) derives from the Greek word for separation, and there is nothing more philosophical than the critical practice of separating and breaking apart the illusory unities of the philosophical canon. If Heidegger himself fashioned such unities in his own mythopoetic imagination, we should feel confident, I think, that we have the strength to resist his Gnostic conclusions while taking up what is philosophically insightful in his work. Indeed, if philosophy survives through acts of critical appropriation, the question as to how to redeem Heidegger is therefore nothing more than one occasion for posing the question as to the possibility of philosophy itself.

The recent movement by Jürgen Habermas toward "postmetaphysical thinking" serves as an apt illustration for such a critical appropriation.[9] Those who know of Habermas's earliest career will not dispute the fact that he was a youthful disciple of Heidegger's philosophy, as refracted through Schelling, and they will not blame him if he reacted with disillusionment and even anger in 1953 upon reading the published version of *Einführung in der Metaphysik* with its unrevised praise for "the inner truth and greatness of National Socialism" (GA 40:208/222). But we would be wrong if we neglected to note that Heidegger's own attempt at an overcoming of metaphysics helped to lay the groundwork for the theory of communicative action and for the "postmetaphysical" concerns that have preoccupied Habermas since the later 1980s. To be sure, the passage from the earlier project of "destruction" and the later project of postmetaphysical thinking is dialectical and at best indirect: the latter is animated by rationalist and emancipatory purposes Heidegger did not honor. Nor should we miss the fact that Heidegger's assault on the sovereignty of the Cartesian subject also helped to prepare the way for Habermas's attempt to overcome the philosophy of consciousness—a critique that is arguably the justification sine qua non for Habermas's analysis of language as a purely intersubjective (rather than monological) medium. The difference is that even while Habermas absorbed the critique of metaphysics (in both its general form as a departure from foundationalism and in its particular form as an assault on the sovereignty of consciousness), Habermas strongly resisted Heidegger's extravagant conclusion that this critique spelled the end of reason as such. Instead, Habermas inherited the latent energies of the first generation of critical theory (which had never surrendered its bond to the European Enlightenment) so as to develop a truly postfoundational and socially situated model of human reason. Whether this model is deemed successful is a question best left for another occasion. My only point is to suggest that in Habermas we can see at least one illustration of the way certain "Heideggerian" insights can survive if and only if they remain available for a truly critical appropriation.

I will conclude, however, by noting the important fact that the very idea of a critical appropriation is not entirely unknown in Heidegger's philosophy itself. In the well-known passage from *Sein und Zeit* (§74) on the "Fundamental Constitution of Historicality" ("Grundverfassung der Geschichtlichkeit"), Heidegger claims that Dasein comes into its authenticity only when, in resoluteness, it discloses the factical possibilities of its ongoing existence "*in terms of the heritage*" that, in its resoluteness, it appropriates for itself (*GA* 2:507/*SZ* 383). Such resoluteness, he writes, "involves handing oneself over to traditional possibilities, although not necessarily *as* traditional ones." (*GA* 2: 507/*SZ* 383, tm).[10]

Although Heidegger does not spell this out clearly, the passage seems to imply that the reappropriation of the traditions into which one is thrown need not be carried out in a wholly uncritical fashion. One needn't "hand down to oneself" the possibilities of a tradition with an unblinking acceptance of these possibilities simply because they belong to that tradition. For a tradition may contain latent possibilities that await interpretive realization and that will become authoritative only in the future. Now one could argue that Heidegger's original affirmation of heritage does not permit quite so bold an affirmation of a truly *critical* appropriation, since it lacks the crucial resource: even a resolute inheritance of tradition that *resists* understanding that inheritance as tradition does not necessarily make room for the rational scrutiny or outright *resistance* of that tradition. Because Heidegger rejects the notion of rational critique, his theory of authentic historicality remains locked in a conservative ethics of repetition even when that repetition is selective. The problem is that he does not— and perhaps he cannot—spell out the criteria by which this selection would occur. But we also know that critical reading of the tradition lay at the very heart of Heidegger's interpretative practice: under the general heading of a "destruction" of the history of ontology, a great many of his lecture courses (including, perhaps most famously, *Kant and the Problem of Metaphysics*) are devoted to working out the "unthought" in the thought of the canonical texts.[11] His work is distinctive for the vigor and determination with which he develops this interpretative method, and it would be inconsistent if one were to exempt Heidegger's own philosophical writing from the same transformative practice. To read Heidegger's own philosophy under the aegis of "destruction" seems consistent with Heidegger's own legacy.

We may therefore credit Heidegger with trying (however imperfectly) to develop a postmetaphysical theory of historical being, a theory, in other words, where the principles of historical selection are not distinct from the domain in which they are applied. Heidegger may not have resolved the problem (and in my judgment he did not). But perhaps the value of a philosophy is not best measured by the definitive solutions it provides so much as by the questions it manages to pose. And maybe we could even say that in laying out the question Heidegger was anticipating a critical appropriation of his own philosophical legacy.

What I have suggested, of course, does not absolve Heidegger's philosophy of its political complicities. But I would like to think it reminds us of an important dynamic in the history of philosophy: No thinker deserves unthinking devotion, and no philosopher survives if he is revered as a sage. Uncritical reading, in fact, is the death of philosophy, and an uncritical reading of Heidegger is the best way to assure that he is forgotten.

I would like to conclude on a note that I find somewhat uncomfortable, though for moral reasons I feel unable to avoid. The regime to which Heidegger swore allegiance murdered millions. But the nameless should be named. And this is so not only for reasons of commemoration but also because it is imperative that, in recalling the crime, we do not repeat its effacement of difference or what Adorno—deploying a musicological term—called "the totalitarian unison."[12] Among the dead was one of my aunts—a gentle woman, born with a disability, who spent her life as nursemaid and governess for a family in the Netherlands. Aunt Miriam was killed at Auschwitz when she was twenty-nine years old, and she belonged to that group which Heidegger, resorting to the collective singular, might have vilified as a mere exemplar of "world Jewry." Some scholars are drawn to the conceit that greatness errs greatly, but I do not feel there is any greatness whatsoever in this sort of chauvinism. To rescue Heidegger from oblivion is hardly of paramount concern for me, and it holds little personal appeal. I can even understand the temptation to declare that his name should be blotted out like Amalek, the ancient nation that attacked the weakest of the Israelites as they fled from Egypt. But oblivion is not criticism, and criticism demands philosophical engagement rather than forgetting. This is the chief reason why one must reject any proposal that we banish Heidegger from philosophy altogether. And it is the major reason—the moral reason—why most of us will continue to read Heidegger even as we do so in full awareness that his chauvinism forever stains his legacy.

Drawing back from this moral register, it is worth entertaining the point that no philosophy can proffer redemption from the complexities of modern life. In the concluding portion of *Negative Dialectics,* in the section labeled, "After Auschwitz," Adorno writes that "the capacity for metaphysics is crippled, because what occurred smashed the basis of the compatibility of speculative metaphysical thought with experience."[13] From the perspective of critical theory, Heidegger's attempt to overcome metaphysics, to seek another beginning in some precinct of ontological innocence beyond the realm of Machenschaft, was bound to fail. But its failure was not due to something illicit in the wish itself, since any such longing carries within it the correlative complaint that all is not right with the world. Its failure was due instead to its ideological character: its continued faith in the power of thought to think the whole of what there is. Heidegger betrayed a weakness for this faith, and not only in his Gnostic condemnation of all modernity as a realm that has fallen under the spell of technology, of "the gigantic," and of a world Jewish conspiracy. The master concept of being itself betrays the very same ambition of total mastery. And it is therefore a sign that Heidegger, no less than Plato at the beginning and Nietzsche at the end, remained under the spell of the metaphysical tradition he condemned. This should not surprise us, however, if we recall the famous dictum by Adorno: "Es gibt kein richtiges Leben im falschen."

10

HEIDEGGER AFTER TRAWNY

Philosophy or Worldview?

TOM ROCKMORE

n the 1940s, when the extent of Heidegger's relation with Nazism began to be known, French Heideggerians immediately began to circle the wagons. A scandalous French debate ensued when Victor Farías brought Heidegger's Nazi turn to public knowledge. It is possible that another such scandal is on the verge of occurring in the English-language debate.

An indication is provided in a recent op-ed article in the *New York Times*. Michael Marder argues for the right to read Heidegger in claiming that his critics, who are defending "the prevalent techno-scientific rationality," are seeking (unfairly) to smear him with Nazism and anti-Semitism.[1] Yet there is nothing resembling an anti-Heideggerian conspiracy, since Heidegger's critics are not limited to those committed to a certain form of rationality. They also include those who reject Nazism as well as its associated anti-Semitic doctrines. Surely, to employ Marder's term, it is not Heidegger's critics but Heidegger, as is apparent to anyone familiar with the recent belated publication of long-withheld parts of his *Nachlass*, who "smears" himself!

After many years of debate, it seems increasingly clear that Heidegger's philosophy, his turning to National Socialism, and his anti-Semitism are neither separate nor separable but rather inseparably linked. That does not mean his thought can be reduced to politics or the surrounding social context and therefore dismissed. But it also does not mean that his thought can fairly be understood apart from the surroundings in which it emerged.

Peter Trawny has obviously put us all in his debt through his pioneer analysis of Heidegger's anti-Semitism in the *Black Notebooks* as well as Heidegger's position in general. Trawny's study literally transforms this problem by providing a detailed, informed account of texts that were not earlier available, that are crucial to grasping Hegel's position, and that for-ever change our understanding of this theme in Heidegger's life and thought. Philosophy differs from other cognitive domains in that there is no decision procedure other than debate, which in practice, reputedly like psychoanalysis, simply cannot be brought to an end.

After Trawny it no longer seems plausible to defend Heidegger against anti-Semitism, which, if Trawny is right, is intrinsically linked to Heideg-ger's overall theory of being. The difficulty lies in assessing the precise nature and significance of this link. Here things become murky. The logic of the argument seems to be that if Heidegger is an anti-Semite then he can also be a Nazi in more than a passing sense, which in turn affects what one can say about his philosophy, but not otherwise.

Trawny argues that Heidegger's anti-Semitism, which was merely latent, later became explicit in the second half of the 1930s through his effort to carry further his analysis of being. I think the problem posed by Heideg-ger's anti-Semitism is wider and deeper than Trawny does. I will suggest two points: first, Heidegger's anti-Semitism is not confined to his effort either early or late to make progress with the problem of being, but runs in different ways throughout his writings; second, his anti-Semitism compro-mises the familiar philosophical distinction, which Heidegger is at pains to defend, between philosophy and a worldview (*Weltanschauung*).

ON HEIDEGGER, ANTI-SEMITISM, AND NAZISM

As concerns Heidegger, anti-Semitism is perhaps even more problematic than Nazism. An anti-Semite need not be a Nazi, but all Nazis are almost by definition anti-Semitic in one way or another. Heidegger's Nazism is an obvious danger to those interested in Heidegger's philosophy, since it sug-gests that his position is infected, hence compromised, by his politics. Yet anti-Semitism is somehow even worse for his defenders. According to Julian Young, Heidegger was "not viscerally anti-Semitic."[2] Yet adding the adverb, which is presumably intended to raise the bar so that Heidegger falls beneath it, is of no use in saving him. For anti-Semitism of any kind should be rejected.

The reason anti-Semitism is so crucial in the Heidegger debate is that once one admits that it is present anywhere in Heidegger's theories it almost immediately becomes visible elsewhere, in fact everywhere or almost everywhere. In that case, the carefully constructed edifice based on the supposed distinction between the man and his thought, or, on the contrary, on their supposed unity, begins to crumble. As concerns Heidegger, anti-Semitism presents an even deeper menace than Nazism, in that once the dam erected by Heidegger's defenders has been breeched, the whole edifice threatens to collapse.

In defense of Heidegger, a series of strategies were invented. The list is long and ingenious. Access to key documents was restricted. Everything that could be denied was denied. A distinction was drawn between Heidegger the unpleasant German writing in the twentieth century and Heidegger the great philosopher allegedly unrelated to time and place, a supposedly timeless thinker whose views are formulated within but do not depend on the historical moment. In his writings, important but embarrassing passages relevant to the discussion were often explained away, and observers were discredited as mean-spirited, incompetent, or worse. An indulgent version of his *Collected Writings*, which eschewed textual fidelity and also omitted possibly incriminating letters as well as various seminar texts, were later seen as unavailing and as only compounding the problem. Heidegger's writings were translated in ways that sometimes made difficult texts simply unintelligible. An instance among many is the infamous rendering of the ordinary German word *Ereignis* as the English hapax "enowning," a translation that is simply unintelligible to a native English speaker or perhaps to anyone else. Fanciful interpretations of key texts were offered, such as the suggestion that *Being and Time* is constructed along the lines of Kantian ethics. The motives of Heidegger's critics were impugned. And so on.

None of this is very plausible. Heidegger's anti-Semitism has been known for many years. One example is the publication of a previously unknown letter, written by Heidegger in 1929, that is, before the Nazis came to power. In this letter, his unfortunately typical German philosophical anti-Semitism is evident in his pointed rejection of the "Verjudung des deutschen Geistes."[3] More recently an earlier letter from 1916 to the woman he later married, in which he also used this term, has surfaced. It helps not in the least that other philosophers harbor similar views.[4]

Much of this looks like an effort at "philosophical misprision," that is, deliberate misinterpretation with a view to concealing rather than revealing the relations of Heidegger's thought to its context, including anti-Semitism and Nazism. In philosophy we must rely on the slender reed of interpretation. Interpretation is problematic, since, other than through fiat, there is no way of bringing it to an end, for instance in marshaling still more evidence to demonstrate that a particular interpretation one happens to favor is correct and all others are false.

This point is routinely exploited but only rarely explained. Paul de Man, who had things to hide, infamously observed there is no way to make out the distinction between history and fiction.[5] According to de Man, any reading, no matter how inconvenient, can always be "deconstructed," hence rendered inoperable. In that sense, philosophy is unlike chess, where moves elicit countermoves but finally the game comes to an end and someone wins. In philosophy, proverbially like psychoanalysis, the discussion cannot be brought to a close. This remark is brought home again in the debate about the *Black Notebooks*, which supposedly have nothing to do with Heidegger's anti-Semitism, which is no more than a publicity stunt, and so on. One wonders if philosophy has not here already reached the limits of useful dialogue.

ON HEIDEGGER AND ANTI-SEMITISM

"Anti-Semitism," which is not a natural kind, means different things to different observers. According to the dictionary, *anti-Semitism* is usually understood as prejudice, hatred, or discrimination against Jews as a national, ethnic, religious, or racial group. This view lies at the heart of Nazism. Someone who is not an anti-Semite cannot be a Nazi in a more than superficial sense, since this movement is almost by definition anti-Semitic. Yet only some anti-Semites are Nazis. This point is sometimes used to restrict criticism as well as to provide it, perhaps unfairly. For instance, to the Israeli government and their dwindling number of foreign supporters, all too often anti-Semitism seems increasingly to mean any criticism of Israel.

Anti-Semitism takes biological, religious, philosophical, and other forms. Trawny speculates that the entire conservative strand of German philosophy, from German Idealism over Nietzsche to Schmitt, Jünger, and Heidegger, is anti-Semitic.[6] There are many examples. Kant depicts Jews as forming a dishonest merchant class.[7] Fichte suggests Jews are a menace to the German nation and should only have civil rights if their heads were cut off.[8] Heidegger's anti-Semitism is both more and less open, more deeply rooted in his philosophical thought, and, since it was linked to Nazism, certainly more dangerous.

The refutation of the idea that Heidegger could even possibly be anti-Semitic is part of the general defense. In this defense, anti-Semitism seems to loom larger than National Socialism. There are many different forms of anti-Semitism, which varies in different times and places. The improbably strategic claim that Heidegger was not and could not have been anti-Semitic perhaps reflects a certain reality in largely Catholic France, where, during the Nazi occupation, there were many collaborators. For this political reason, in France anti-Semitism remains a highly sensitive topic even today. From a political perspective, it is arguably comparatively less significant elsewhere since, though a world war was not and never will be fought against anti-Semitism, one was indeed fought against Nazism.

The twin themes of anti-Semitism and Nazism have been part of the Heidegger debate for many years. Over a long period it was possible simply to deny Heidegger was a Nazi, at least in more than the most superficial sense. In the late 1940s the initial French debate on Heidegger and Nazism took place in the pages of *Les Temps modernes*. Sartre, who was generous but uninformed, suggested that we would later see that Heidegger's link to National Socialism was less significant than Hegel's connection with the Prussian state of his time. At this late date, when we know more than Sartre did at the time, probably no one denies that, as rector of the University of Freiburg, Heidegger was for a time Hitler's man in the German university.

In France a stout but not particularly intelligent defense of Heidegger against the charge of anti-Semitism has been associated over several decades with François Fédier, who calls attention to a casuistic distinction between anti-Judaism and anti-Semitism.[9] Other, more significant figures, also deny Heidegger was anti-Semitic. Thus Dominique Janicaud proposes a so-called iron triangle consisting of the *Führerprinzip*, anti-Semitism, and imperialistic nationalism, none of which he finds in Heidegger's position.[10]

Heidegger's anti-Semitism is in part well known and in part not well known at all. Since Nazism without anti-Semitism seems implausible, it is not surprising that someone who rallied to Nazism would be anti-Semitic as well. Yet, as concerns Heidegger, everything about this relationship except that it exists is subject to dispute. It has been asserted that Heidegger's anti-Semitism is philosophically insignificant, since the struggle concerning Heidegger is merely symptomatic of a weakness of contemporary thought. It has been claimed that Heidegger was not a Nazi, or at least not in any ordinary sense. It has been suggested that we must differentiate between Heidegger the thinker and Heidegger the man, for the former should not, indeed must not, be judged in relation to the latter. It has been held that everything that Heidegger ever did or wrote was Nazi to the core. It has been maintained that Heidegger's only problem was that he never said he was sorry. Finally, it has been maintained with all the seriousness of the professional scholar that Heidegger's thought is so difficult that only one wholly immersed in it—at the extreme only a true believer, someone unlikely to raise questions about it—could possibly understand it.

Anti-Semitism is, of course, in the eye of the beholder. There is no way to persuade someone who does not want to be persuaded. Even the publication of the *Black Notebooks* will leave some observers unmoved. Yet his philosophical anti-Semitism, which was widely current in the German philosophical establishment, has been known for many years. About a century ago, Heinz Heimsoeth, who complained in 1916 that *Kant-Studien* was *endgultig verjudet,* harbored similar views.[11]

TRAWNY ON HEIDEGGER'S ANTI-SEMITISM

Heidegger, whose activity was pluridimensional, intervened both politically and philosophically in German academic life. Trawny's careful reading of Heidegger's anti-Semitism assigns it a strictly philosophical role in the ongoing development of his thought in the second half of the 1930s, that is, after the rectorate and presumably after the obscure, never clarified turning in his thought. Trawny's useful account includes remarks on anti-Semitic representations of Judaism, types of anti-Semitism and anti-Judaism in Heidegger's position, a general claim for Heidegger's critical view of Nazism, and a specific claim for the philosophic relevance of anti-Semitism to Heidegger's later philosophical theories.

According to Trawny, Heidegger's anti-Semitism is based on ordinary anti-Semitic stereotypes and concerns a mythological figure in which the Jew incorporated everything he rejected.[12] Trawny's identification of different forms of Heideggerean anti-Semitism indirectly supports Derrida's claim for a plurality of Nazisms in Heidegger's thought.[13] According to Trawny, at a certain point Heidegger's "latent" anti-Semitism acquired a philosophical significance in respect to the history of being.[14]

In Trawny's narrative, Heidegger's anti-Semitism is pried loose from Nazism and assigned a crucial role as "an unavoidable step in the 'overcoming of metaphysics.'"[15] For Trawny, Heidegger's turn to anti-Semitism is not a mere accident, nor attributable to his Nazism, nor even due to the ongoing deterioration of the political situation. It is rather the result of an incessant, obsessive pursuit over decades of the meaning of being. In Trawny's mind, Heidegger's obsessive interest in being leads to a so-called *seingeschichtlicher Anti-Semitismus* resulting from a philosophical crisis in Heidegger's narrative concerning the German saving of the West.[16]

In the context of the evolving Heidegger reception, Trawny makes two crucial concessions. He suggests that Heidegger, like many other otherwise sophisticated German thinkers, including Frege, Fichte, Kant, and Schopenhauer, was prey to ordinary anti-Semitism. Heidegger was from this perspective not an ordinary anti-Semite but rather an ordinary philosophical anti-Semite. Trawny's further suggestion, that in the *Black Notebooks* Heidegger integrates his specific form of anti-Semitism into his still developing philosophy, suggests a need to surpass the usual distinction between the thinker and the thought in order to grasp the thought in the historical context.

ANOTHER NARRATIVE OF HEIDEGGER'S ANTI-SEMITISM

Trawny's account is useful in addressing the philosophical role of anti-Semitism in Heidegger's position, but problematic. In Trawny's narrative,

Heidegger illustrates the prevailing German academic anti-Semitism of the period. His anti-Semitism evolves as a function of the times and as he continues to work out his philosophical theories. Yet what if ordinary anti-Semitism were an ingredient in Heidegger's theories of being from the very beginning and throughout his philosophical career?

One problem in Trawny's view of Heidegger's anti-Semitism is that it obviously points in two directions: toward the overcoming of metaphysics as well as toward the German salvation of the West. A second difficulty lies in the restriction of Heideggerian anti-Semitism to the later 1930s, though it supposedly remained largely latent prior to this.

I think Heideggerian anti-Semitism is more complex than Trawny even now is willing to admit. My hypothesis is that Heidegger's anti-Semitism, was a factor in his life and thought, which were not enclosed in separate compartments in isolation from each other but rather integrally related over many years. In pointing to this link, I am not suggesting Heidegger's work is his life, but rather calling attention to the complex ways his life shaped his thought and his thought his life. For present purposes I will divide Heidegger's anti-Semitism into three phases, including his initial prephilosophical anti-Semitism, then the philosophical anti-Semitism in *Being and Time*, and finally the later anti-Semitic phase after the so-called turning (*Kehre*) in his thought. For reasons that will become clear later, I will discuss these phases in reverse sequence.

Trawny is concerned with anti-Semitism in Heidegger's *Black Notebooks* in the period when the German thinker, after what is widely but unclearly understood as the failure of the rectorate, was seeking to understand the political situation later culminating in the Second World War. Yet Heidegger's anti-Semitism, which did not suddenly arise in the *Black Notebooks*, and which is not or not only a product of the later evolution of his study of being, has a prior history.

There is a prephilosophical anti-Semitic phase as the young Heidegger was growing up in southwestern Germany in the last part of the nineteenth century, at a time when the rejection of Jews and Judaism on religious or other grounds was commonplace. We recall that, only slightly earlier in the nineteenth century, widespread German intolerance of Judaism led Karl Marx's father to convert the whole family and Heinrich Heine to go into Parisian exile. I suggest Heidegger's early anti-Semitic background in part explains his infamously fulsome praise for the anti-Semitic monk

Abraham a Sancta Clara.[17] In this phase Heidegger's anti-Semitism, which was not exceptional but rather typical, resembles the widespread anti-Semitism current in the Germany of the time, later leading up to the Weimar Republic.

The *Black Notebooks*, which were unpublished in Heidegger's lifetime, belong to his *Nachlass*. What about his published philosophical writings? Could it be that his philosophical writings, even before his Nazi turning, are anti-Semitic? Let us suppose that the distinction between philosophy and life is not watertight. If life influences philosophy, and philosophy influences life, then it is possible that Heidegger's philosophy, not only in the later 1930s but from beginning to end, throughout his career, depended on who he was, hence reflected his life, so to speak, including his typical form of early-twentieth-century conservative, religiously oriented, German anti-Semitism.

This thesis contradicts the familiar philosophical view, which is often invoked to defend Heidegger, on the grounds that the thinker and the ordinary person, in this case Heidegger, an important thinker, and Heidegger, the ordinary Nazi, are entirely unrelated.[18] Dilthey thinks that the distinction between philosophy and worldview cannot be maintained. Husserl contends, against Dilthey, that philosophy must be rigorous science. By implication, either philosophy is science or it is nothing at all. Heidegger, who shares this view, distantly follows Husserl on this point in various contexts, including *The Idea of Philosophy and the Problem of Worldview* (from the Kriegsnotsemester 1919) and *Basic Problems of Phenomenology* (1927), where he defends the view that philosophy is the science of being.

Not all philosophers deny the relation between philosophy and life. Fichte, who loudly but implausibly describes himself as in effect a perfect Kantian, breaks with the author of the critical philosophy at many points, including through his view that the kind of philosophy one formulates is not independent of but rather depends on the kind of person one is. This view of philosophy stands out as an exception in the debate, which largely favors the conception Fichte rejects: the idea that the philosophical subject is wholly independent of the surrounding context. Heidegger, for whom Dasein is always already in the world, arguably favors a version of the anti-Cartesian, Fichtean conception of subjectivity. Yet the familiar view that thought and life are unrelated is frequently but inconsistently enlisted

to defend, if not Heidegger's person, then at least the idea that his philosophical theories would be untimely and hence somehow independent of
time and place.

HEIDEGGER ON AUTHENTICITY, ROOTEDNESS, AND ANTI-SEMITISM

The defense of Heidegger's theories through denying a more than incidental relation between his life and thought takes two main forms: on the one
hand, I have already pointed to the familiar but implausible claim that the
life and the thought are distinct, in fact unrelated, so that the life does not
affect or in any way "compromise" the thought. On the other hand, there
is the claim that Heidegger's work was his life, and his life is his thought.[19]
This suggests there is simply no life outside the thought, so that thought,
or at least genuine philosophical thought, is simply independent of life. I
think, on the contrary, that Heidegger's life cannot be collapsed into his
thought, and his thought also cannot be reduced to his life, but rather that
both thought and life constitute a whole that is not entirely one or the
other.

Trawny concentrates on the link between the Jews and Heidegger's view
of being, which he dates from 1937,[20] though, as I have been suggesting, it is
plausible to think that Heidegger's anti-Semitism begins earlier. According
to Trawny, Heidegger very effectively hid his anti-Semitism, which only
became public knowledge through the publication of his *Black Notebooks*.
I believe, on the contrary, that his anti-Semitism was not hidden but rather
in plain sight, so to speak, before the public all the time for anyone who
wished to look.

This point is, of course, disputed. What counts as appropriate evidence
obviously depends on the specific audience. Most observers, that is, those
who are not Heideggerians and hence committed to any form of the
"defensive" view that Heidegger's position has nothing to do with anti-Semitism, were already convinced long ago by such instances as letters mentioning *Verjudung,* the virtually unknown but infamous endorsement of
the *Führerprincip,* praise for the so-called movement, the infamous passage equating the Holocaust and agricultural technology, and so on. For

such observers, there can be little doubt that for Heidegger the *Seinsfrage* and the *Judenfrage* are not unrelated but closely linked.[21] Others, like Günter Figal, require a higher standard of proof, which they regard as finally offered by the *Black Notebooks*. In my view, only such observers, namely those committed to Heidegger through a kind of blind philosophical faith, those who earlier thought that in the final analysis there was nothing damaging to reveal, or at least nothing "really" damaging, can possibly be shocked by the new material.

To support my view that Heidegger's philosophical theories are not unrelated to but rather linked to, even dependent on, his anti-Semitism, I will provide three examples drawn respectively from the late 1920s, from a letter written in 1933 and from a semipopular text published in 1934. All these instances are earlier than the time when Trawny thinks that, for reasons linked to his philosophical pursuit of the theme of being, Heidegger's position became tinged with anti-Semitism. Each of these examples manifests a familiar kind of philosophical nationalism linked with anti-Semitism, namely the defense of the Germans, or at least what I will be calling "real" or again "true" Germans, combined with the view that Jews are not and cannot be Germans in a more than peripheral sense. The main theme seems to be as follows: a German must have social roots that by definition a Jew cannot have, hence he (or she) cannot be German. This view was widely held during this period. Thus Bruno Bauch, the president of the Kant-Gesellschaft until 1916, notoriously held the opinion, which he published in *Kant-Studien* (1916), that a Jew simply could not become German no matter how long he lived in Germany.[22]

German philosophical anti-Semitism early in the twentieth century continues a tradition in which Fichte played a prominent role. In the *Addresses to the German Nation*, more than a century before Heidegger, Fichte distinguished between Germans, in his view those who speak German, and all others. Fichte, who does not seem to have any background in linguistics, thinks German is the only modern language that preserves the insights of ancient Greek and ancient Greece. Fichte's restrictive view, which once again distinguishes between authentic Germans and everyone else, was influential well into the twentieth century. According to Hans Sluga, Heidegger modeled his *Rektoratsrede* on Fichte's text.[23]

Nationalism and anti-Semitism are different. One can be a nationalist and not be an anti-Semite and conversely. Yet they are often combined.

In his *Addresses* Fichte combines a type of extreme nationalism with anti-Semitism. Heidegger seems to be combining nationalism with anti-Semitism on a Fichtean model. In most cases, being-historical anti-Semitism belongs less to the narrative about the history of being than to what one can call familiar German philosophical anti-Semitism.

In this period, that is, before the late 1930s, Heidegger seems to link his philosophical understanding of authenticity with what we can call being an "authentic" German. The Heideggerian view of authenticity seems to be largely borrowed from Kierkegaard. *Being and Time* includes numerous aspects that appear to be based on Kierkegaardian concepts, including fear, death, anxiety, repetition, and so on.

In *Being and Time* Heidegger suggests that authenticity amounts to choosing to repeat the past in the future. This view seems innocent, but loses its innocent veneer if we ask who is in a position to be authentic in this way. The answer is someone who belongs to this shared world, so to speak, not, say, someone who is worldless. In the *Black Notebooks* Heidegger at one point identifies the supposed worldlessness of Judaism (see GA 95:97). This view points to the difference between having a world, hence being rooted and capable of authenticity, and not having a world or being worldless, or again rootless as it were, thus incapable of authenticity.

Heidegger discusses concepts of world and worldlessness in the lecture course *Fundamental Concepts of Metaphysics* (1929). According to Derrida, he makes three basic claims: a thing, say, a stone, has no world. An animal is world poor (*weltarm*). A human being is world forming (*weltbildend*).[24] He again makes roughly the same triple distinction in "The Origin of the Work of Art" approximately a decade later.[25] This philosophical view of "world" is not harmful but harmless. But it loses its harmless character when it is combined with nonphilosophical, garden-variety, philosophic anti-Semitism, for instance, the view that only "real" Germans can be authentic.

We can infer that during the early 1930s Heidegger simply linked his preexisting view of authenticity, on loan from Kierkegaard and others, to German nationalism in stressing that Jews as such fall outside the circle of "authentic" Germans. I turn now to two further examples of the nationalistic perspective that Heidegger defended in the early 1930s, examples to the point when on Trawny's account Heidegger's anti-Semitism emerged.

Consider now a letter Heidegger wrote on June 25, 1933, when he was asked to evaluate Richard Hönigswald, at the time a widely known Jewish contemporary neo-Kantian. Heidegger wrote his letter as the National Socialist rector of the University of Freiburg, as a member of the NSDAP, in a period in which he was engaged in bringing about the *Gleichschaltung* of the German university with the projects of the Hitlerian state. Heidegger's political commitment arguably followed from his philosophical perspective.

Claudia Schorcht has reported in detail that, as Heidegger became interested in Hönigswald, the latter was under great pressure.[26] In 1930 he was called to the University of Munich as the successor of Erich Becher. In 1933, as a Jew, he fell under the law concerning the reinstitution of the status of professional civil servants (*das Gesetz zur Wiederherstellung des Berufsbeamtums*).

Dr. Einhauser, to whom Heidegger addressed his letter, was specifically appointed as *Oberregierungsrat* to carry out the application of the new Nazi law in ridding the German university system of Jewish professors. Einhauser requested letters about Hönigswald with supporting information from Heidegger, Johann Rieffert, and Hans Heyse. In comparison, Heidegger's letter was not only the most negative but also the first one to be received. Heidegger's attack on Hönigswald in his letter was linked not only to his support of Nazism but also to the vacancy created by Hönigswald's firing.

Here is the letter:

Dear Herr Einhauser!

I gladly accede to your wish and give you as follows my judgment. Hönigswald comes from the Neo-Kantian school, which represents a philosophy directly corresponding to liberalism [dem Liberalismus auf den Leib zugeschnitten ist]. The essence of man is dissolved, there in a freely floating consciousness in general, and this is diluted to a universally logical world reason. In this way, through an apparently rigorous scientific justification, attention is deflected from man in his historical rootedness and in his folkish [volkhaften] tradition from his origins from soil and blood [Überlieferung seiner Herkunft aus Boden und Blut]. Together with it went a conscious pushing back of all metaphysical questions, and man appeared only as the servant of an

indifferent universal world culture. Hönigswald's writings arose
from this basic attitude. It is however the case that Hönigswald
defends the thoughts of Neo-Kantianism with an especially dan-
gerous acumen and an idle dialectic [Scharfsinn einer leer-
laufenden Dialektik]. *The danger consists above all in that this*
drive awakens the impression of highest objectivity [Sachlich-
keit] *and rigorous science and already has deceived and induced*
many young people into error. I must also today again qualify the
calling of this man to the University of Munich as a scandal,
which can only be explained in that the Catholic system preferen-
tially favors such people, who are apparently ideologically indif-
ferent, because they are not dangerous with respect to its own
efforts and are "objective-liberal" in the usual way. I am always
available to answer further questions.

With best regards! Heil Hitler!
Your very devoted Heidegger (GA 16:132–33)

There are many different kinds of anti-Semitism, only some of which manifest themselves in crude remarks or insulting ethnic characterizations.
Heidegger's letter about Hönigswald is clearly not overtly, but very obviously covertly, anti-Semitic. In the historical context, Heidegger's use of
such terms as *Liberalismus, Scharfsinn,* or even *Dialektik* with respect to
Hönigswald are almost literal equivalents of *talmudistisch.* Yet, as has been
pointed out, it would be convincing to claim that Heidegger's letter is free
of both overt as well as covert anti-Semitism if, and only if, it could have
been written to describe an Aryan.[27]

I turn now to a third example. In 1934, a scant month after resigning as
rector, Heidegger published a semipopular three-page article entitled
"Why Do I Stay in the Provinces?" in which he emphasized his strong local
roots in pointing to his links to peasants.[28] This article apparently belongs
to Heidegger's strategic effort, after the rectorate, to create a public distance
between himself and the Nazi movement in disingenuously adopting the
pose of a simple peasant, whose philosophical work belongs, as he says, in
the midst of the peasant's work. It can also be read as identifying a mini-
mal condition of German "authenticity" turning on the difference between
Boden and *Bodenständigkeit.*[29]

It does not take much imagination to see in this contrast a familiar anti-Semitic distinction between the "real," "true," or "authentic" Germans, on the one hand, those with roots deep in the (German) soil, and the Jews, who in the anti-Semitic scheme of things are supposedly rootless and belong neither to the (German) soil nor anywhere else. Leo Strauss ascribes to Heidegger the view he shares with Nietzsche that every great age grows out of, hence presupposes, *Bodenständigkeit*.[30] This point is not unimportant if, as Emmanuel Faye says, *Being and Time* "is deeply structured by its opposition between rootedness in the soil and the absence of soil."[31]

In all three examples Heidegger's conception of authenticity for "real" Germans depends on the repetition of the past in the future, hence in reinforcing their intrinsic status or again who they always already are. This is an instance of the familiar conservative idea that, since things were better before, we need now to return to an earlier golden age. Understood in this way, Heidegger's strong opposition to Descartes is not merely an instance of the familiar philosophical struggle about which view of the subject as either Dasein or the *cogito* is acceptable, nor merely another chapter in the widely known antipathy between the French and the Germans. It rather points to a fundamental disagreement between a conception of the subject as transcendent to, hence as not rooted in, or, on the contrary, like Dasein, rooted in the world, the community and the soil. The social distinction Heidegger establishes, between those who are rooted in and hence belong to the world and those who are not rooted in and hence simply cannot belong to this world, is absolute. Only Germans in the full sense of the term, those who are rooted in their native soil, can possibly be authentic.

CONCLUSION: ON HEIDEGGER'S ANTI-SEMITISM, PHILOSOPHY, AND WORLDVIEW

In *Basic Problems of Philosophy* Heidegger says that dialogue with Hegel is a condition of the continued existence of philosophy (*GA* 24:254/178). Despite some gestures in this direction, this dialogue never took place. In part, this is due to the radically different philosophical approaches of these two thinkers. Hegel famously understands philosophy as the conceptual comprehension of its own times. This suggests three points: we live in our own time, our historical moment; we can at best comprehend that moment through philosophical reason; yet we cannot knowingly transcend it.

Hegel's view seems to undermine or perhaps relativize the distinction between philosophy and worldviews. According to Hegel, philosophy of all kinds, including his own, arises in and belongs to its own time. From this perspective, it follows that Heidegger's effort to renew metaphysics also belongs to its time and place. His philosophy influences his conception of life, including his view of Negroes, who supposedly cannot think, as mere things.[32] Further, his anti-Semitic preconceptions influence his apparent belief, which he seemed to share with Fichte as well as a number of other nineteenth- and twentieth-century thinkers, that only Germans in the full sense of the term could be "authentic." His philosophy and his life are not separable, but interrelated. His anti-Semitism and his philosophy are also interrelated, since each depends on the other. This complex interrelation in turn undermines the canonical distinction between the thinker and the thought as well as the canonical distinction between philosophy and worldview, which are separate in some theories but are in practice continuous.

11

ANOTHER EISENMENGER?

On the Alleged Originality of Heidegger's Antisemitism

ROBERT BERNASCONI

I
n 1988, in the wake of the publication of Victor Farías's book reigniting
the debate about the meaning and depth of Heidegger's involvement
with National Socialism, Emmanuel Levinas reaffirmed his long-standing
admiration for *Being and Time* but posed the troubling question of
whether there was not an echo of evil there. He explained the thought
behind the question as follows: "The diabolical is not limited to the wick-
edness popular wisdom ascribes to it and whose malice, based on guile, is
familiar and predictable in an adult culture. The diabolical is endowed
with intelligence and enters where it will. To reject it, it is first necessary
to refute it [*Pour le refuser, il faut d'abord le refuter*]. Intellectual effort is
needed to recognize it."[1] But precisely what kind of intellectual effort is
called for and where does this kind of questioning lead?

Levinas continued: "Who can boast of having done so? Say what you
will, the diabolical gives food for thought."[2] There is a certain modesty to
Levinas's statement. If anyone at that time had a right to boast of having
found the diabolical both in *Being and Time* and in Heidegger's later thinking it was Levinas. *Totality and Infinity* and other works by Levinas already
questioned, for example, the hostile implications of Heidegger's conception
of rootedness (*Bodenständigkeit*) for the Jewish understanding of human
beings as strangers on earth.[3] Levinas's suspicion is confirmed when we
read in the *Black Notebooks* Heidegger's repetition of the widespread characterization of Jewishness (*Judentum*) in terms of its "worldlessness" and

"rootlessness" (*Bodenlosigkeit*) (*GA* 95:97). Nevertheless, there was nothing modest about what Levinas attempted in *Totality and Infinity*, which, from its very first pages, amounted to an indictment of almost all of Western philosophy up until that time on account of its totalizing approach to being that seemed to offer only occasional glimpses of anything beyond it.[4]

This makes it all the more troubling to find Levinas accusing Heidegger of "paganism" and "primitivism" for his talk of "gods."[5] We have learned to be more sensitive in our choice of words than Levinas was when it comes to using such terms in the form of an accusation. The problem is even more marked when we reflect on Levinas's appeal to the notion of an "adult culture." The phrase is itself diabolical because it unwittingly evokes without any precaution the attempts to legitimate violence done to those who were judged to belong to allegedly primitive, childlike cultures by virtue of characterizing them as less advanced.

My point here is that once one opens up this line of questioning almost nobody is immune. One can never be sure where it might lead and whose reputation is in danger. This is not an argument against doing so. It is an argument for doing so in a measured way. Clearly Levinas's faults do not begin to compare with those of Heidegger, but the general point, which should always be insisted upon, is that the diabolical is easier to recognize in others than in oneself, just as it is easier to recognize in other traditions than in one's own, or in philosophers with whom one lacks an affinity. We have to be on our guard against participating in an inquisition where guilt is established simply by association and where the accusers feed their sense of self-righteousness simply by virtue of the fervor they can summon to the task: we are good because the others are evil. We equally have to be on our guard against anyone who accuses others of self-righteousness as a way of defending themselves against charges leveled against them, as Heidegger did in 1945 in his "Evening Conversation in a Prisoner of War Camp in Russia Between a Younger and an Older Man" when he suggested that a person's sense of their own "moral superiority" that derives from condemning others can blind them to the real evil and especially its pervasiveness (*GA* 77:209/134). But what does it mean to be measured when addressing such evils as slavery, genocide, and the Holocaust? It is not easy if one's sense of outrage is as overwhelming as it should be.

The greatest challenge scholars face when trying to decide the place of Heidegger's *Black Notebooks* within the history of antisemitism lies not in trying to determine which ideas were specifically Nazi ideas and which were commonplace expressions widespread throughout German culture or, more generally, the West at that time. Issues of that kind are not always easy to decide with precision, especially when dealing with historical periods different from our own, but they are readily open to investigation, and one can develop the necessary historical expertise so as to make it possible to establish within a certain context the originality of a given perspective, the availability of alternative perspectives, the intended audience and the intended effect on that audience, and so on. It is true that a number of commentators, both among Heidegger's critics and his defenders, imagine they know enough to make assessments about what counts as specifically Nazi when they clearly have not done the requisite research. That kind of ignorance can be exposed, but, even after one has determined the place of Heidegger (or whomever is being investigated) within the history of antisemitism, that leaves unanswered the question of how far the presence of those ideas contaminate their thought. That is what necessitates what Levinas calls "intellectual effort," even if he is not specific about what precisely he means by that. It includes developing the ability to identify those ideas that belong together. Some commentators, when setting out to defend a favorite philosopher, seem to think that it is perfectly legitimate to separate one idea from another simply by arguing that the one does not necessarily entail the other, but if we are concerned with the evil that does not immediately announce itself as such, then we must be more cautious and learn to be able to read between the lines.

A number of Heidegger's readers long refused to see what was staring them in the face. One could include among them all who waited until the publication of the *Black Notebooks* to acknowledge that Heidegger was capable of antisemitic remarks. So long as the issue was phrased as Heidegger's sympathy for National Socialism, there was no shortage of Heidegger scholars willing to serve as apologists or look the other way. As soon as the headlines in the newspapers came to focus on the charge of antisemitism, some of these same apologists rushed for cover, even though Heidegger's antisemitism had already been well established by commentators.[6] The frustration of Heidegger's critics toward these apologists is fully understandable, but it has equally been a problem that some of these same critics seem to have willfully misread Heidegger in an effort to prove themselves more critical—and thus more righteous—than anyone before them. Commentators who are concerned to give an accurate portrait of Heidegger have been forced to attack these critics and in the process have been made to look like apologists. It will likely be a long time before scholarly balance has been restored.

Nevertheless, what is frequently lost sight of is that the problem here is by no means unique to Heidegger or to this time period, but goes to the very core of philosophy's sense of itself, its long-standing pretense that thinking and moral insight were tied. Even Hannah Arendt succumbed to this temptation, in spite of her familiarity with Heidegger's failings.[7] The Eurocentrism, antisemitism, and racism of many of the canonical names of Western philosophy, including figures of the stature of Locke, Kant, Hegel, and Nietzsche, are now well documented, as is the fact that many of the standard responses, such as the "child of his/her time" defense or the denial that the statements at issue are central, are frequently applied without legitimacy. We know that the complicity of many of the major figures from that tradition with the evil of, for example, the enslavement and oppression of people of African descent in the Americas was extreme even by the standards of the time.[8] So the question that has to be posed is not only that of how we relate to Heidegger but also that of how we relate to the Western philosophical tradition more generally. To argue, as Emmanuel Faye does, that Heidegger should permanently be put to one side because of his politics and his antisemitic remarks is to assume that such faults automatically exclude one from being considered a genuine philosopher, but that is a proposition that is hard to sustain, given everything we know about the failings of so many of the canonical figures of Western philosophy.[9] Some people might see a choice: either we abandon the philosophical canon as presently constituted or we drop the long-standing presumption that a certain philosophical excellence can be associated with a certain moral excellence. I will not argue the case, but it is my view that we must do both. I will focus here on the task of learning to read others—and, above all, ourselves—more suspiciously, and, as I will show, we can find within the early history of opponents to antisemitism practitioners of this skill from whom we can learn.

Peter Trawny, in *Heidegger and the Myth of a Jewish World Conspiracy,* asks, "How could it be that one of the greatest philosophers of the twentieth century was an advocate not only of National Socialism, but also of anti-Semitism?"[10] The question might seem insufficiently precise, given that Heidegger never publicly advocated antisemitism and, as Trawny correctly observes barely three pages later, "hid his anti-Semitism from the National Socialists."[11] Trawny's most provocative claim in this context is that Heidegger introduced a new form of antisemitism to which Trawny gives the name of "being-historical anti-Semitism," *seinsgeschichtlicher Antisemitismus.*[12] Nevertheless, to the historian's eye, Heidegger's antisemitic remarks are all too familiar. They rest on long-standing tropes within antisemitism broadly conceived. The question is whether they become new by being repeated within the context of Heidegger's thought.

How are we to understand the history of antisemitism such that we can recognize what constitutes new forms of it? The term *antisemitism* was adopted by Wilhelm Marr, author of *The Victory of Jewry Over Germandom.*[13] It is frequently claimed that hatred of Jews to this point had previously been directed against them by Christians on account of their religion and that it was only at the end of the nineteenth century, through such writers as Marr, that they came to be hated because of their race.[14] One sees the shift very clearly in Eugen Dühring's *Die Judenfrage.* Describing a change that was already in the course of taking place, he wrote in 1881: "the basic understanding which sees in the Jew not a religion but a race [*Race*] is already making decisive breakthroughs."[15] Dühring drew the clear implication: "A Jewish question will exist even if all Jews turn their back on their religion and were converted to one of the ruling churches among us."[16] To be sure, the distinction between hatred of the Jews on account of their religion and hatred of them on account of their race is neither quite so straightforward nor so abrupt and could perhaps be dated earlier, but the main point is that we have a clear example here of what the introduction of a new form of prejudice against the Jews looks like.[17] There is an earlier case that is even more revealing in this context.

In 1794 Saul Ascher, a young Jew who had already aligned himself with Kantian philosophy, located in Johann Gottlieb Fichte the start of a new epoch of hatred of the Jews.[18] Ascher did so on the basis of his reading Fichte's A *Contribution to the Correcting of the Public's Judgments About the French Revolution,* where Fichte in the previous year had attacked Judaism as a state within a state, "a powerful, hostile state that lives with all others in constant warfare."[19] The young Fichte was pitting Kantian universalism against Judaism's alleged particularism, and it led him to propose that the condition of giving Jews civil rights should be "to cut off all of their heads at night and in their place put heads in which there is not a single Jewish idea."[20] It is quite staggering that anyone could employ that image in the context of a discussion of the French Revolution, written one year after the introduction of Joseph-Ignace Guillotin's guillotine. Ascher was also severely disappointed by Kant's portrayal of Judaism in *Religion Within the Boundaries of Mere Reason*, which was so very different from Ascher's own earlier attempt, in *Leviathan,* to apply what he took to be Kantian principles to Judaism, where he insisted that Judaism was for every individual and was valid at all times; even so, Kant was not Ascher's target in 1794.[21] Whether he was right to exonerate Kant can be debated. Perhaps he should have been more suspicious. Perhaps he would have thought differently of Kant if he had learned that in his lectures he had embraced Fichte's account of Jewish particularism as an obstacle to cosmopolitanism.[22] In any event, Ascher had found the diabolical within the Kantian philosophy of the young Fichte and for this reason he called Fichte by the name Eisenmenger the Second. This was a reference to Johann Andreas Eisenmenger, whose encyclopedic study of Jewish sources and calumnies against them, *Judaism Revealed*, was a sourcebook for those hostile to the Jews from the eighteenth century onward.[23]

There have been other forms of Jewish hatred and so other Eisenmengers, including the first person—whoever that was—to decide that the problem with the Jews was not that they *were not* cosmopolitan, as Fichte believed, but rather that they *were* cosmopolitan. This shows how complicated tracking new forms of antisemitism can be, because, as with forms of racism more generally, the old tropes often exist alongside the new even when they seem to conflict. It is worth recalling that Alfred Rosenberg in his first book repeatedly drew on Fichte's essay on the French Revolution, even though he could not have been more opposed to the cosmopolitanism in whose name Fichte had criticized the Jews.[24] The question here is whether Heidegger was another Eisenmenger in the sense of another person who introduced an original form of antisemitism, as Trawny maintains.

— ∞ —

Heidegger scholars have learned to be cautious about what they claim Heidegger never said, as they do not know what the next volume of the *Gesamtausgabe* will reveal, but I have so far seen nothing that suggests that he himself believed there was anything especially novel about his antisemitism. Nevertheless, Heidegger was clearly anxious about establishing his originality as a thinker. It was an obsession he shared with Kant.[25] In this section I will show the lengths to which Heidegger was willing to go in order to dismiss those whom he believed were not as original as he was. He was intent on pushing the boundaries. As he explained in his Nietzsche lectures: "There is no room for halfway measures in the present stage of the history of our planet" (*GA* 6.1:429; *N1* 6). This tendency is clearly exhibited in a polemical passage from *Considerations* VIII of the *Black Notebooks*, a passage that has thus far received attention only because it contains a passing remark about the Jews.

Under the heading "Descartes," Heidegger contrasted his own attack on Descartes in *Being and Time* with both previous and subsequent "critiques" of Cartesianism. Heidegger's own characterization of what he had attempted with his discussion of Descartes in *Being and Time* is tendentious insofar as he employed the phrase "a fundamental overcoming of metaphysics" to describe what he was doing there (*GA* 95:168), whereas in fact the discussion of Descartes in 1927 appeared under the very different label of a *Destruktion*, which, as most Heidegger scholars understand, operates differently.[26] In any event, the first point Heidegger emphasized was that his discussion of Descartes in *Being and Time* was not intended as a refutation (*Widerlegung*), but rather was an attempt to allow the one attacked "to stand properly in his historical unshakability" as the condition of a thoughtful questioning in the West, a questioning conducted through the question of being. Heidegger suggested in passing that his attack on Descartes had been exploited by people who did not understand the essential core of what he was doing. In this regard he mentioned both Jews and National Socialists, albeit without saying whom he had in mind. His specific target in this paragraph, whom he describes as an overhasty *Privatdozent* writing from a *völkisch*-political point of view, is also not identified by name, but it is clear that Heidegger has in mind here Franz Böhm, whose book *Anti-Cartesianismus* appeared at the very end of 1937.[27] In 1930 Böhm had published a short book on aesthetics and three years later a book on the ontology of history, both of which showed the influence of

Heinrich Rickert, with whom Heidegger himself had studied when in his early twenties.[28] However, by the time of the publication of *Anti-Cartesianismus*, Böhm had switched his allegiance to Ernst Krieck, who by this time was openly attacking Heidegger, although Heidegger chose not to defend himself against Krieck publicly in any significant way (see GA 94:179).[29]

That Böhm nowhere in *Anti-Cartesianismus* cited Heidegger's discussion of Descartes in *Being and Time* shows just how far the rift between Krieck's followers and Heidegger had gone. That omission must have irritated Heidegger, but his general complaint against Böhm was one that could easily have been predicted by anyone familiar with Heidegger's attacks on his contemporaries from the same period. The argument was that instead of successfully differentiating himself from Descartes, Böhm succeeded merely in reinforcing Descartes: however hard Böhm tied to establish his distance from Descartes, he remained locked into Cartesianism and its conception of the human being as *subjectum*. In other words, Böhm did not think sufficiently radically, and this was because he did not pose the question of being.[30]

Although Heidegger, from his own perspective, was totally justified in dismissing Böhm's turgid book, there are certain uncanny resemblances between it and some of Heidegger's own writings. In *Heidegger's Roots*, Charles Bambach already raised the question of whether Heidegger's thinking during the 1930s was not closer to that of Nazi philosophers of this period than many Heidegger scholars were willing to concede, and he offered a comparison with Böhm's *Anti-Cartesianismus* as his example.[31] Bambach was thinking not only of the standard Nazi tropes that everyone can recognize, such as those found, for example, in the rectoral address, but also of such seemingly quintessentially Heideggerian ideas as "another beginning" of thinking. This phrase has long been understood as a nuanced response to Husserl's attempt, inspired by Descartes, at a radical new beginning of philosophy, which in Heidegger came to be attached to a thinking that understood that in order to twist free from previous thinking it was not enough either to oppose oneself negatively to what went before or to embrace novelty for its own sake: another beginning can only take place with reference to the first beginning. But, as Bambach explained, a somewhat similar theme is present in Böhm, albeit without any of the same nuance. Indeed, Böhm began his book attacking Cartesianism by announcing the need for "a new beginning" that would proceed by finding resources in German philosophy that offered the opportunity of a kind of resistance to the idea of Descartes as the founder of modern philosophy.[32] In fact, the parallels go much further. For example, Böhm highlighted Jacob Böhme, and especially Meister Eckhart, both of whom Heidegger had celebrated in 1936 in his lecture course on Schelling (GA 42:54/31 and 204/117).[33] Like Heidegger, Böhm railed against the "rootlessness (*Bodenlosigkeit*) of rational absolutism."[34] Both authors were united in the conviction that the gods had abandoned the world.[35] These resemblances are enough to allow one to believe that a major reason for Heidegger's private polemic against Böhm was their superficial proximity. Heidegger was protective of his sense of his own originality, and it was perhaps with Böhm in mind that Heidegger later rejected as "childish" attempts to make a specifically German philosophy (GA 96:212), just as he had earlier explicitly rejected the possibility of a specifically Nazi philosophy (GA 94:509).

Heidegger's obsession with separating himself from his contemporaries repeatedly surfaces in the *Black Notebooks,* even if he did not always succeed in this endeavor. The fact that Heidegger decided not to flaunt his antisemitism in a context in which to do so would have been to his advantage shows that his antisemitism was not opportunistic. In the notebooks he also rejected "*vulgar* National Socialism" (GA 94:142), while at the same time developing his increasingly idiosyncratic "spiritual National Socialism" (GA 94:135). It is cold comfort to defenders of Heidegger, but what emerges most clearly from the *Black Notebooks* is that he was determined at every turn to be more extreme than his contemporaries in respect to the issues that preoccupied him. Judged on the basis of this criterion, antisemitism was not one of those issues.

I am inclined to believe the evidence currently available that even though Heidegger did at times integrate certain antisemitic tropes into his philosophy and into his unique vocabulary, thereby making the question of the originality of his antisemitism more difficult to answer definitively one way or the other, in the final analysis there is not much that is truly new there. Any suggestion that the crude antisemitism occasionally in evidence in the private *Black Notebooks* is also to be found coded in his lectures in the way politicians today code their anti-Black or anti-immigrant racism must be dismissed. Why would Heidegger in the context of Nazi Germany need to use what is sometimes called "sneaky rhetoric," especially when he was under attack from some of his colleagues for not being sufficiently Nazi?[36] The most likely reason why he was not more vociferous in expressing his antisemitism when the Nazis were in power is that he did not think that the position he took on the Jews was really that novel in context. The fact that he did not delete these comments from the *Black Notebooks* after the war was over, which some commentators find hard to fathom, is a clear indication that he was attached to these views and that he continued to think of them as very ordinary. I suspect he would have been surprised by the attention they have been receiving.

Heidegger seems to have found it relatively easy to introduce some familiar antisemitic tropes into the framework of his account of modernity. More challenging to the interpretive skills of his readers today is that he was also able to inject into this same framework a rejection of antisemitism, albeit this came after the war was over.[37] The passage in which he did this is worth examining in some detail because it is arguable that he was never more antisemitic than when he rejected antisemitism and that if his antisemitism was novel this is where its novelty is to be found. In an aside that he introduced after he had told himself that a note he had just written about the Jewish prophets was not antisemitic, he declared that antisemitism was as foolish and contemptible as Christianity's "bloody and above all un-bloody proceedings against 'pagans'" (*GA* 97:159). He went on to claim that although Christianity branded antisemitism as un-Christian, antisemitism was fundamentally Christian. This should be read in conjunction with an earlier passage where he suggested, according to a familiar logic, that whatever was opposed to Christianity derived from Christianity itself and so remained in its orbit: "The anti-Christian, like every anti-, stems from the same essential ground against which it is anti-. It stems from 'the Christian' ['*der Christ*']" (*GA* 97:20). Heidegger then added in the same place that Christianity stems from Jewry (*Judenschaft*). This suggests that whatever Christianity is against, including Jewishness, has its source in Jewishness, and this seems to have been what led him to the conclusion that Jewry was the principle of destruction (*Zerstörung*) within the Christian West, that is to say, within metaphysics (*GA* 97:20).[38]

The claim that Jewry was the principle of destruction lies behind the following deeply troubling claim: "When what is essentially 'Jewish' in the metaphysical sense fights against what is Jewish, the high point of self-annihilation (*Selbstvernichtung*) in history has been reached; assuming that the 'Jewish' has everywhere completely seized mastery, so that even the fight against 'the Jewish,' and it above all, falls under its sway " (*GA* 97:20). It should be noted at the outset that however strange the idea of Jewish self-annihilation might sound, it was another familiar trope within German antisemitism. It can be traced back at least as far as Richard Wagner's "Judaism in Music." Wagner had there called for the self-annihilation of the Jews and presented this as the going under (*Untergang*) of Ahasuerus, the Wandering Jew.[39] In the first edition of 1850 Wagner seemed to be joining the ranks of those advocating the conversion of the Jews, but in the revised edition of 1869 he seemed to be promoting what could, at least in part, become "a bloody fight of self-annihilation."[40] But whereas it seems quite possible to think of Jewish conversion as a kind of self-annihilation, as soon as the motif of violence is introduced it becomes unclear in what sense it is specifically a *self*-annihilation, except if it means that the Jews brought it upon themselves.

Heidegger's appropriation of the term *self-annihilation* in the context of the Holocaust is unconscionable. He seems to have done so in order to locate the Holocaust within the history of Western metaphysics and in the course of doing so to offer an explanation, in a way that Wagner did not, of the idea of a violent Jewish self-annihilation: according to a highly twisted, albeit in its own terms coherent, construction of what Jewishness meant, antisemitism is fundamentally Jewish. The context—a series of statements that bring Judaism and Christianity together—suggests that he is talking about Christian antisemitism. One is left wondering whether he believed that he could say the same of Nazi antisemitism, and, given his reluctance at this particular time to attribute much that was original to National Socialism, it would seem that he would have been willing to do so. So Heidegger was blaming the victim for both forms of antisemitism, even though his formulation cannot be reduced to a simple case of blaming the victim, who, after all, is always blamed for prejudice against them. This account is embedded in the larger narrative of the history of being and to this extent Trawny is on the right track, at least to the point of being able to say that Heidegger had fully integrated his antisemitism into his philosophy.[41] Heidegger had made antisemitism his own, even though one could not say, as Ascher said of Fichte, that he introduced a new epoch of hatred against the Jews. What one can say is that at the very point where Heidegger had seemingly succeeded in locating antisemitism within the history of Western metaphysics from which he was attempting to twist free, we find him relying on the antisemitic trope of Jewry as self-annihilating.

One must be clear that Heidegger's antisemitism was not of the racial kind that was no doubt dominant in Nazi Germany, although by no means the only kind to be found there. Heidegger was not biologistic, but many other Nazis were.[42] He dismissed the concept of race and did so very much on his own terms: racial thinking is tied to the modern thinking of the human being as subject (*GA* 96:48, also *GA* 69:71/66).[43] Furthermore, even though he had at one time embraced the notion of the *Volk* and sought to make sense of it in terms of the framework he had developed in *Being and Time*, he also abandoned that notion, again because it was tied to modern philosophy (*GA* 54:206/137 and 247/165).[44] Whereas Böhm had argued that one needed to depart from the rootlessness promoted by Cartesianism in order to restore the notion of the *Volk*, by the early 1940s Heidegger had come to believe that the modern idea of the *Volk* was developed in reaction against the Cartesian philosophy of subjectivity and so ultimately could be explained as a product of it.[45] With the same logic Heidegger still tried to use the principle of race to accuse the Jews of a form of self-contradiction: "The Jews with their *exaggerated ability for calculation* have 'lived' longest in accordance with the principle of race which is also why they are most strongly against the unrestricted application of this weapon" (*GA* 96:56). Heidegger was here referencing the idea, prevalent among the Nazis and their forebears, including Houston Stewart Chamberlain, that the Jews had embraced racial purity as an inflexible fundamental law.[46] Heidegger's argument was that by living according to the principle of race they had themselves promoted the very reasoning by which they were now being attacked and so they had no right to complain when it was being used against them by the Germans promoting their own racial purity. The use of scare quotes around the word *"lived"* is objectionable enough, but it is the gratuitous introduction at this point of the timeworn stereotype associating calculation with the Jews that is ultimately most telling.[47]

The argument about the Jews being on the other end of a principle that they themselves had held onto more rigorously than anyone was a familiar one at that time. What interested Heidegger was that, to the extent that there were both Jews and Germans who believed in racial purity as a biological law, their application of it involved what he would call "calculative thinking." His point, which he also made elsewhere ,was that not only the idea of race itself, but also, and even more, the eugenic practices based on it, belong to the age of machination (*Machenschaft*) from which his thinking seeks to twist free. And yet he then associated the Jews with the process of calculation itself as if they were the architects of their own fate. Here again one sees Heidegger integrating a familiar antisemitic stereotype into his narrative about modernity, and in a way that was intended to show his *distance* from a biologically based antisemitism. One can ask if Heidegger was against calculation because he thought it was Jewish, but the association Heidegger insisted on more often was the link between calculation and Descartes.[48] Again Heidegger seems to have been trying to depart from a certain kind of antisemitism (biologistic antisemitism) but doing so in a way that left him complicit with another form of antisemitism, one rooted in the stereotype of the Jews as calculating. Again the result is not an original form of antisemitism but an integration of antisemitism into Heidegger's thinking.

Let me offer one more example that seems to demonstrate that Heidegger had fully integrated his antisemitism into his thinking but without coming up with anything that was, strictly speaking, new. It occurs when Heidegger asked, as a metaphysical question, who might be capable of addressing the world-historical problem of the uprooting of beings from being (GA 96:243). Not surprisingly, the Jews were not considered plausible candidates, but, as with almost all of his references to the Jews, this was only a passing reference. It arose in the context of a discussion that started out being about the English. And yet by making Jewishness the principle of destruction within metaphysics, there was nothing marginal about the place of Jewishness, and thus of a certain nonracial antisemitism, in Heidegger's thought.

———— ✺ ————

The argument of Heidegger's critics is that one cannot isolate his antisemitism from other aspects of his thought. The attempt to do so is a path sometimes still taken by Heidegger's apologists, just as it is the path habitually taken by the defenders of Locke, Kant, Hegel, and Nietzsche. It is the analytic move: except where one idea necessarily entails the other, one can always discard from one's interpretations those ideas that one prefers to discount and keep only what one chooses to retain. It is an approach I reject because there are other kinds of connections between ideas that are familiar to the historian: ideas hunt in packs. It is these looser clusters of ideas that we need to investigate if we are committed to the philosophical task of challenging "antisemitism" and "racism." And there is also a need to come to a better understanding of how these prejudices operate in any given thinker. As I have tried to show in the previous section, in Heidegger's case that meant locating both the Jews and the opposition to them within the general narrative about Western metaphysics that belonged to the overcoming of metaphysics, while at the same time sometimes falling back into certain antisemitic formulae that were metaphysical, as assessed by Heidegger's own criteria.

When investigating Heidegger's narrative about Western metaphysics, with all its attacks on Bolshevism, Americanism, the English, Catholicism, and Jewishness, there is a serious risk of distortion if one singles out, as most commentators have done, the attacks on *Judentum* and cites them in isolation. To be sure, an attack on Jewishness in 1940 means something different from an attack on Americanness or Englishness at the same time for obvious contextual reasons, but if understanding what Heidegger is saying is at all at issue here, these attacks must be seen as conjoined. Not to do so would be another version of the analytic move that I have just referenced. One cannot isolate Heidegger's antisemitism from his broader critique of the West at a time when the Nazis generally, and not just Heidegger, were engaged in a "war against the West."[49] If there is anything especially distinctive about Heidegger's antisemitic remarks, it lies not in the fact that they are more extreme than anything one finds among his contemporaries but in the totalizing way in which his thought comes to operate. For Heidegger, almost everything belonging to Western metaphysics amounts to the same. This is what his narrative purports to demonstrate.

The importance of grasping Heidegger's larger vision can be demonstrated with a relatively straightforward example, the letter of June 25, 1933, in which Heidegger critically assessed Richard Hönigswald's suitability for a position at the University of Munich. The letter has frequently been cited as evidence of antisemitism because Hönigswald was a Jew, but Heidegger's objection to Hönigswald was that he belonged to the Neo-Kantian school that was cut from the same cloth as liberalism. There is no explicit reference to Judaism, but there is the remark that "the Catholic system has a preference for such people," whose "'objective-liberal'" manner renders them seemingly indifferent to worldviews (*GA* 16:132).[50] Heidegger might well have expected his objections against Hönigswald to be heard because Hönigswald was a Jew, but Heidegger's objections were clearly much broader.

It is a striking but often neglected fact that Heidegger's antipathy toward Roman Catholicism is much more prominent in the first two volumes of the *Black Notebooks* than his antisemitism. The Reich Concordat is today seen as a historic failure on the part of the Catholic Church, but Heidegger had problems with the concessions that *Hitler* made to the Catholic community. The hostility of some leading Nazis to Catholicism and the way they sought to develop a new religion was no secret, but seemingly what angered Heidegger was their failure to follow through on this. We are aware that Hitler was trying to downplay such moves for his own purposes, but for Heidegger this was an example of the lack of radicality of Nazi policies, their betrayal of the essence of "the inner truth of National Socialism."[51] During this period, Heidegger's anti-Catholicism was extreme when compared with that of his contemporaries, and by the same measure it was a great deal more extreme than his antisemitism, but they both belong to a much larger discussion from which they should not be separated.

There was a time when it seemed that Heidegger's relation during the 1940s toward both Judaism and Christianity, especially Catholicism, could be measured by their almost total absence from his account of the history of Western metaphysics.[52] It was as if their existence was irrelevant to the history of being, as could easily be demonstrated by reflecting on the positive content of Heidegger's history of being, where what remained worthy of thought was increasingly confined by him to the sayings of the so-called pre-Socratics and isolated words from canonical thinkers.[53] After the publication of the first few volumes of the *Black Notebooks,* it is clear that matters are a great deal more complicated and that, unless the remarks I discussed in the third section of this chapter were no more than passing fancies, Heidegger's antipathy to Judaism and Christianity played a much larger role in the construction of his account of the history of Western metaphysics than one would ever have recognized from studying the works he published in his lifetime.

———— ✤ ————

It is important to ask of any philosophy whether it lends itself to racism, antisemitism, or other forms of oppression, but it is also important to ask, albeit more difficult to determine, whether a philosophy has a potential for adequately exposing and combating those evils. Heidegger placed his thinking of the history of being on the largest stage imaginable. Terms like *Machenschaft* ("machination") and *Verwüstung* ("devastation") exemplify this, and they were part of his attempt to relate racial thinking to the history of Western metaphysics from which he sought to distance himself.[54] There is some merit to his diagnosis, which in some ways anticipated Foucault's account of biopolitics. Nevertheless, in the light of what I have written, it seems clear that, as Levinas insisted, we must leave behind the climate of Heidegger's philosophy. The question of whether this takes us back to Kant, as some commentators seem to want, or forward to a thinking that would not be "pre-Heideggerian" is what lies behind much of the current debate around Heidegger's *Black Notebooks*.[55] But reference to Kant reminds us that there are always possibilities of reading Kant against himself, whereas it is less easy to see what that would mean in the case of Heidegger, other than to declare that he still belonged to what he sought to overcome—Western metaphysics. To be sure, I am not convinced that, as I have argued elsewhere, inventing a "real Kant" who can allegedly get the better of the historical Kant, is any better than, for example, relying on the resources of the Declaration of Independence to overcome the legacy of the slavery.[56] Acknowledged there, given that it was a document designed to protect property interests. Honesty about history seems a better option than anachronistic interpretations.

Important though these questions are, they are not the only important questions that need to be explored. I am convinced that, for example, Locke, Kant, and Hegel all made major and new contributions to racism that go far beyond any contribution Heidegger made to antisemitism.[57] Indeed, insofar as Heidegger's account of *Machenschaft* highlights a certain technologization of biological life that is especially visible in what the

Germans called "racial hygiene," then he belongs less as a target of a history of racism in which he does not stand out and more as a contributor to the writing of that history. So one possible and, I would argue, compelling answer to the question of where the kind of investigation we have seen of Heidegger's antisemitism leads is that it leads to a broader questioning of the Western philosophical tradition. However, this would not operate with the broad strokes that we find in Heidegger (or, in his own way, Levinas), which form into a totalizing critique where everything is reduced to the same, with just a few exceptions noted. If all that we learn from studying Heidegger's comments on Judaism is the need to dismiss Heidegger, then we have not learned the most valuable lesson: it is time we investigate more thoroughly the suggestion that there are other, perhaps many, canonical philosophers who are tainted by their complicity with evil, including the evils of chattel slavery, colonialism, and colonial genocides, in addition to antisemitism. But this investigation must be conducted not by innuendo but by uniting rigorous historical investigation, raising the kinds of questions about originality, audience, and so on that I mentioned earlier, with the kind of intellectual effort that Levinas called for in "As If Consenting of Horror," where a hermeneutics of suspicion seeks to expose evasions, double-speak, and sneaky rhetoric.

My considered judgment on the basis of the evidence currently available at this time is that Heidegger's antisemitism, while fully integrated into his thinking of the narrative component of his history of being, even including his rejection of antisemitism, was not especially novel. Heidegger was no Eisenmenger, but even if he was, that would only succeed in placing him in the company of Kant and Fichte. This is not a defense of Heidegger, and I introduce the point here only to highlight the serious issues academic philosophy faces today because it continues to be complicit with the moral failures of past philosophers by ignoring them or dismissing them as irrelevant. There is today within the culture generally an almost universal condemnation of racism and antisemitism, at least as narrowly defined, and yet philosophy as an academic institution has not revised its canon according to this criterion any more than it has abandoned its naive convictions about the ethical efficacy of thinking. Perhaps these illusions are maintained because we mistakenly conclude that it is enough to show we are on our guard against the evil of philosophers with whom we do not share an affinity. As Levinas observed, the task is not as easy as some people try to make it, and complicity with the diabolical extends beyond the most compromised canonical philosophers to those who teach them without raising the requisite questions. When one extends the concern with antisemitism to include racism, sexism, and Islamophobia, then it becomes clear that the intellectual effort called for, including the task of scrutinizing our own practices as philosophers, has scarcely even begun. The question we must ask ourselves is whether scrutinizing Heidegger is to be the start of a larger inquiry or whether it is being conducted merely to make us feel morally superior.

12

THE PERSISTENCE OF ONTOLOGICAL DIFFERENCE

SLAVOJ ŽIŽEK

WHY HEIDEGGER SHOULD NOT BE CRIMINALIZED

One of the signs of the ideological regression of our times is the request of the new European right for a more "balanced" view of the two "extremisms," the rightist one and the leftist one: we are repeatedly told that one should treat the extreme left (communism) the same way that Europe after World War II treated the extreme right (the defeated fascism and Nazism). Upon a closer look, this new "balance" is heavily unbalanced: the equation of fascism and communism secretly privileges fascism, as can be seen from a series of arguments, the main one among them being that fascism copied the communism that preceded it (before becoming a fascist, Mussolini was a socialist, and even Hitler was a National Socialist; concentration camps and genocidal violence were practiced in the Soviet Union a decade before Nazis resorted to it; the annihilation of the Jews has a clear precedent in the annihilation of the class enemy; etc.). The point of this argumentation is that a moderate fascism was a justified response to the communist threat (the point made long ago by Ernst Nolte in his defense of Heidegger's 1933 Nazi engagement). In Slovenia the right is arguing for the rehabilitation of the anticommunist Home Guard that fought the partisans during World War II: they made the difficult choice to collaborate with the Nazis in order to prevent the much greater absolute Evil of communism. The same could be said for the Nazis (or fascists, at least) themselves: they did what they did to prevent the absolute Evil of communism . . . [1]

But the truly sad thing is that part of the liberal left is following a similar strategy in its eternal struggle against "French theory." Jürgen Habermas remarked apropos the famous Davos debate between Ernst Cassirer and Martin Heidegger in 1929 that we should rethink the common perception according to which Heidegger was the clear winner: for Habermas, Heidegger's "victory" was not so much a genuine philosophical victory but more the signal of a shift from liberal enlightened humanism to dark authoritarian irrationalism. Cassirer was effectively a figure like Habermas: his thought was simply not strong enough to grasp the horrors that threatened Europe (fascism in his time), in the same way that one looks in vain to Habermas for even the most rudimentary theory of the failure of that twentieth-century communism that culminated in Stalinism (if one's knowledge of post–World War II Germany were to be limited to Habermas's texts, one would never have guessed that there were two Germanies, BRD and DDR . . .). For Habermas and his followers (like Richard Wolin), it is as if Deleuze, Lacan, Bataille are all all protofascist irrationalists. They are uneasy even with Adorno and Benjamin who, in their view, often come too close to mystical "irrationalism," not to mention figures like Rosenzweig, who takes over Heideggerian motifs from a Jewish standpoint. Habermasians commit here the same mistake as those who dismiss Freudian psychoanalysis, a theory about the irrational foundation of the human psyche, as in itself irrationalist.

In 2014 a new Heidegger scandal exploded with the publication of the first volumes of the *Black Notebooks* (*schwarze Hefte*), handwritten notes of his intimate reflections from 1931 to the early 1970s that allegedly confirm his anti-Semitism as well as his continuing fidelity to the Nazi project.[2] (Heidegger himself planned that these notes should be published at the conclusion of his *Gesamtausgabe*, in a gesture that can be read either as a display of frank openness or a sign of his stubborn commitment to his pro-Nazi views.) Things are actually a bit more complex.

The volumes show that, after 1934, Heidegger effectively cultivated more and more doubts about Hitler and the Nazi regime; however, this growing doubt had a very precise shape of blaming the enemy. What Heidegger reproached Hitler for was not the Nazi stance as such but the fact that the Nazis also succumbed to technological-nihilist *Machenschaft*, becoming like America, Great Britain, France, and Soviet Union who are thereby always MORE guilty: "all well-meaning excavation of earlier *Volk*-lore, all conventional cultivation of custom, all extolling of landscape and soil, all glorification of the 'blood' is just foreground and smokescreen—and necessary in order to obscure what truly and solely *is:* the unconditional dominion of the machination of destruction."[3] Heidegger's critique of Nazism is thus a critique of the actually existing Nazism on behalf of its own metaphysical "inner greatness" (the promise of overcoming modern nihilism). Furthermore, Heidegger's growing reservations toward the Nazi regime have nothing to do with the eventual rejection of its murderous brutality; far from denying its barbarism, Heidegger locates in it the greatness of Nazism: "National Socialism is a barbaric principle. Therein lies its essence and its capacity for greatness. The danger is not [Nazism] itself, but instead that it will be rendered innocuous via homilies about the True, the Good, and the Beautiful."[4] Incidentally, the same debate went on at the beginning of modernity when Erasmus of Rotterdam, the Renaissance Catholic polyglot humanist, accused Martin Luther of barbaric primitivism—true, but Luther's break nonetheless opened up the space for modernity.

Second point: while anti-Semitism persists and survives Heidegger's disenchantment with Nazism, one should note that it doesn't play a central role in Heidegger's thought but remains relatively marginal, an illustration or exemplification of a central scheme that survives without it. However, although one may well rewrite Heidegger's scheme of growing Western nihilism without any mention of Jews, this doesn't mean that "Jewishness" (*Judentum*) just serves as a misleading example of a certain spiritual stance—such exemplification is never neutral or innocent. Ultimately, one can say the same about Hitler: is the Nazi figure of the Jew not merely an exemplification of the capitalist spirit of inauthentic profiteering and manipulation?—in both cases, the "example" irreducibly colors what it serves as an example of.

What is true is that one can reconstruct from Heidegger's dispersed remarks a consistent "theory" about the Jews. First, he performs the well-known operation of rejecting primitive biological racism: the question of the role of world Jewry is not a biological-racial question but the metaphysical question about the kind of humanity that, without any restraints, can take over the uprooting of all beings from Being as its world-historical "task." European nihilism, our forgetting of Being, culminates in modern Machenschaft, which "leads to total deracination, resulting in the self-alienation of peoples," and contemporary Jewry's "increase in power finds its basis in the fact that Western metaphysics—above all, in its modern incarnation—offers fertile ground for the dissemination of an empty rationality and calculability, which in this way gains a foothold in "spirit," without ever being able to grasp from within the hidden realms of decision."[5] "World Jewry" (*Welt-Judentum*) thus embodies the technological degradation of the totality of Being, which is why, as Heidegger observes in a related text, it would be important to ask: "What is the basis for the peculiar predetermination of Jewry for planetary criminality."[6] (And, incidentally, since this "Jewish worldlessness," their lack of roots in a *Boden*, is counteracted by the Israeli government's endeavor to make out of Israel a proper *Heimat* for the Jewish people, maybe today's Israel would find full approval of Heidegger as an attempt to decriminalize Jewishness . . .)

So how about the Holocaust? Here things get really dark. As Heidegger observed in 1942, with regard to Jews: "The highest type and the highest act of politics consists in placing your opponent in a position where he is compelled to participate in his own self-annihilation."[7] In an obscenely pseudo-Hegelian way, the elimination of European Jews must thus be understood as an act of Jewish "self-annihilation (*Selbstvernichtung*)": the Holocaust was as an act of Jewish "self-annihilation" insofar as, at Auschwitz and other death camps, the Jews—as the prime movers behind "machination" and the technological devastation of all of Being—themselves succumbed to industrialized mass murder. In this way, Europe's Jews merely fell prey to forces they themselves had unleashed, or, as Heidegger states in volume 4 of the *Notebooks*: "When the essentially 'Jewish,' in the metaphysical sense, struggles [*kämpft*] against what is Jewish [*das Jüdische*], the high point of self-annihilation in history is attained."[8] In short, the Nazis, in organizing the technological annihilation of Jews, merely turned the "essentially Jewish" stance of Machenschaft against the empirical Jews themselves . . . (Following an old cliché, Heidegger claims that Jews prefer to stay out of sight, manipulating events behind the scenes and leaving it to other nations, especially to Germans, to shed their blood in real struggles.)

What opened up the space for the Nazi-turn in Heidegger's philosophical edifice is relatively easy to discern. *Sein und Zeit* focuses on the individual's authentic existence with its structure of being-toward-death, and the problem it only superficially touches is how to expand this analysis onto collective modes of being, i.e., how to think authentic collective being beyond the inauthentic *das Man*, following the anonymous "one." It is here that Heidegger "takes a wrong turn" when he posits as the only way to break out of *das Man* the heroic assumption of one's historical Destiny. What this implies is that Heidegger's edifice cannot be reduced to some Nazi core—it would be absurd to dismiss Left Heideggerians like Caputo and Vattimo as closet fascists or as cases of a simple misreading of Heidegger: Heidegger's edifice is genuinely "undecidable," open to different political readings. There are even some black activists in the US and in Africa who, in their reaction to the *Black Notebooks* "scandal," insisted how a reference to Heidegger helped them to formulate their resistance to global capitalism and its ideological hegemony. And the ongoing attacks on Heidegger aim precisely at closing this undecidability and proving not only that Heidegger's thought is in its very core Nazi (an "introduction of Nazism into philosophy," as the subtitle of Emmanuel Faye's book on Heidegger says), but that the shadow of the same suspicion also falls on all who were influenced by him.[9] Markus Gabriel concludes his comment on *schwarze Hefte* with:

> Only now can the historical-critical resarch of Heidegger properly begin. Now we have gained the distance needed for this, and the texts are at our disposal. Furthermore, we should also inquire into the history of Heidegger's enormous influence. No other philosopher with his work has exerted more of an influence upon philosophy world-wide since the twenties of the last century—above all, albeit against his will, on existentialism, deconstruction, psychoanalysis, and the logically–schooled ontology. We should not close our eyes to all this.[10]

We should not close our eyes—to what? To this Nazi shadow which falls also on the most left of Heideggerians . . . this old story began in the 1980s when (among others) Lacan was attacked in the US for his alleged fascist links and when deconstruction was denounced as a justification of French collaborationism. And, maybe, this brings us to the true stakes of the ongoing attacks on Heidegger: to get rid of the "French theory" left by way of imposing on them a guilt by association. . . . But the ultimate target is here a tendency within critical theory itself: the theoretical complex called "dialectics of Enlightenment," with its basic premise according to which the horrors of the twentieth century (Holocaust, concentration camps, etc.) are not remainders of some barbaric past but the outcome of the immanent antagonisms of the project of Enlightenment. For Habermasians, such a premise is wrong: the horrors of the twentieth century are not immanent to the project of Enlightenment but an indication that this project is unfinished. (Incidentally, Adorno and Horkheimer also emphasize that the only way to overcome the deadlock of the Enlightenment is through further enlightenment, through enlightened reflection upon these very deadlocks.) We should make one step further here and recognize in this opposition between Enlightenment as an unfinished project and the dialectic of Enlightenment the opposition between Kant and Hegel: between Kantian progress and the Hegelian dialectic of immanent antagonisms.

Against the persistent calls for the direct criminalization of Heidegger's thought, for his simple and direct exclusion from the academic canon, one should insist that he is a true philosophical classic. A direct criminalization of Heidegger's thought is an easy way out—it allows us to avoid the painful confrontation with the proper scandal of his Nazi engagement: how was it possible for such a great authentic philosopher to get engaged in this way? When I asked a Heideggerian Jewish friend of mine how Heidegger could remain a key reference for him in view of his anti-Semitism and Nazi sympathies, he mentioned an old Jewish piece of wisdom according to which there are some deep traumatic insights that can only be formulated by a diabolical person.

AGAINST THE UNIVOCITY OF BEING

Which, then, is the dimension of Heidegger's thought that is worth fighting for and preserving? Perhaps the best way to discern this dimension is to render problematic the notion of the "univocity of being" whose main proponent in our times was Deleuze. The assertion of the univocity of being can play a positive role in enabling us to dismiss all notions of ontological hierarchy, from the theological vision of the universe as a hierarchical Whole, with God as the only full Being at the top, up to the vulgar Marxist hierarchy of social spheres (economic infrastructure as the only full reality, ideology as somehow "less real," part of an illusory super-structure). Along the same lines, one could interpret Dziga Vertov's (Eisen-stein's great opponent) *Man with a Movie Camera* as an exemplary case of cinematic communism: the affirmation of life in its multiplicity enacted through a kind of cinematic parataxis, a setting side by side of a series of daily activities—washing one's hair, wrapping packages, playing piano, connecting phone wires, dancing ballet—that reverberate in each other at a purely formal level, through the echoing of visual and other patterns. What makes this cinematic practice communist is the underlying asser-tion of the radical "univocity of being": all the displayed phenomena are equalized, all the usual hierarchies and oppositions among them, inclusive of the official communist opposition between the Old and the New, are magically suspended (recall that the alternate title of Eisenstein's *The General Line*, shot at the same time, was precisely *The Old and the New*). Com-munism is here presented not so much as the hard struggle for a goal (the new society to come), with all the pragmatic paradoxes this involves (the struggle for the new society of universal freedom should obey the harshest discipline, etc.), but as a fact, a present collective experience.

Univocity of being (directed against the Aristotelian ontology) found its greatest proponent in Spinoza, who draws the ultimate consequence from it: he radically suspended the "deontological" dimension, i.e., what we usu-ally understand by the term *ethical* (norms that prescribe how we should act when we have a choice)—and this in a book called *Ethics*, which is an achievement in itself. In his famous reading of the fall, Spinoza claims that God had to utter the prohibition "You should not eat the apple from the Tree of Knowledge!" because our capacity to know the true causal connec-tion was limited. For those who know, one should say: "Eating from the Tree of Knowledge is dangerous for your health." Adam thus

> perceived that revelation not as an eternal and necessary truth but rather as a ruling, that is, as a convention that gain or loss follows, not from the necessity and nature of the action done, but only from the pleasure and absolute command of the prince. Therefore that revelation was a law and God was a kind of legislator or prince exclusively with respect to Adam, and only because of the deficiency of his knowledge.

> It is for the same reason too, namely deficiency of knowledge, that the
> Ten Commandments were law only for the Hebrews.[11]

Two levels are opposed here, that of imagination/opinions and that of
true knowledge. The level of imagination is anthropomorphic: we are dealing with a narrative about agents giving orders that we are free to obey or
disobey; God himself is here the highest prince who dispenses mercy. The
true knowledge, on the contrary, delivers the nonanthropomorphic causal
nexus of impersonal truths. One is tempted to say that Spinoza here out-
Jews the Jews themselves: he extends iconoclasm to man himself—not
only "do not paint god in man's image" but "do not paint man himself in
man's image." In other words, Spinoza here moves a step beyond the standard warning not to project onto nature human notions like goals, mercy,
good and evil, and so on—we should not use them to conceive man himself. The key words in the quoted passage are: *only because of the deficiency
of his knowledge*—the whole "anthropomorphic" domain of law, injunc-
tion, moral command, etc., is based on our ignorance. What Spinoza thus
rejects is the necessity of what Lacan calls the Master Signifier, the reflexive signifier that fills in the very lack of the signifier. Spinoza's own supreme
example of "God" is here crucial: when conceived as a mighty person, God
merely embodies our ignorance of true causality. One should recall here
notions like "flogiston" or Marx's "Asiatic mode of production" or, as a matter of fact, today's popular "postindustrial society"—notions that, while
they appear to designate a positive content, merely signal our ignorance.
Spinoza's unheard-of endeavor is to think ethics itself outside the "anthropomorphic" moral categories of intentions, commandments, and the
like—what he proposes is *sensu stricto* an *ontological ethics*, an ethics
deprived of the deontological dimension, an ethics of "is" without "ought."
In clear contrast to Spinoza, Lacan (in *Encore*) emphasizes the "deontic"
dimension of being itself: to say that something "is" always implies that it
"has to be"—here is his comment on Aristotle's *to ti ên einai*, "what would
indeed have happened if it had quite simply come to be":

> What was to be. And it seems that here there is conserved the pedicle that
> allows us to situate from where this discourse of being is produced. It is
> quite simply that of being at someone's heel, being under someone's orders.
> What was going to be if you had heard what I am ordering you. Every

dimension of being is produced from something which is along the line, in the current of the discourse of the master who, uttering the signifier, expects from it what is one of the effects of the bond, assuredly, not to be neglected, which results from the fact that the signifier commands. The signifier is first of all and from its dimension imperative.[12]

At its most radical, disparity does not refer just to the gap between parts/spheres of reality—it has to be brought to a self-relation that includes the disparity of a thing with regard to itself or, to put it in another way, the disparity between part of a thing and nothing. A is not just not-B, it is also and primarily not fully A, and B emerges to fill in this gap. It is at this level that we should locate ontological difference: reality is partial, incomplete, inconsistent, and the Supreme Being is the illusion imagined in order to fill in (obfuscate) this lack, this void that makes reality non-all. In short, *ontological difference*—the difference between non-all reality and the void that thwarts it—is obfuscated by the difference between the "highest" or "true" being (God, actual life) and its secondary shadows.

THE HUMAN, THE POSTHUMAN, THE INHUMAN

From the Heideggerian standpoint, today's global scientific-technological civilization poses a threat to ontological difference—what Heidegger calls a "danger" immanent to our way of life. The popular expression of this threat is a more or less commonly accepted premonition that today we (humanity) are approaching a radical mutation, the entry into a "posthuman" mode of being. This mutation is sometimes described as a threat to the very essence of being human, while sometimes it is celebrated as the passage into a new Singularity (a collective mind, a new cyborg entity, or another version of the Nietzschean Overman). Furthermore, this mutation is both theoretical and practical, felt by all of us—who can measure the implications and consequences of biogenetics, of new prosthetic implants that will merge with our biological body, of new ways to control and regulate not only our bodily functions but also our mental processes?

Two opposed tendencies coexist within this orientation toward "overcoming humanity," posthumanism and transhumanism, which vaguely refer to the duality of culture and science. "Posthumanists" (Donna Haraway and others) are cultural theorists who note how today's social and technological progress more and more undermines our human exclusivity: the lesson of ecology is that we are ultimately one of the animal species on our Earth, that animality is part of our innermost nature, that there is no clear ontological gap that separates us from the animal kingdom, while contemporary science and technology make more and more visible the extent to which our innermost identity has to rely on technological devices and crutches—we are what we are through technological mediation. So while, for posthumanists, "humans" are a weird species of animal cyborgs, "transhumanists" (Ray Kurzweil and others) refer to recent scientific and technologial innovations (AI, digitalization) which point toward the emergence of a Singularity, a new type of collective intelligence.

This transhumanist orientation stands for the fourth stage in the development of antihumanism: neither theocentric antihumanism (on account of which US religious fundamentalists use the term *humanism* as synonymous with secular culture) nor the French "theoretical antihumanism," which accompanied the structuralist revolution in the 1960s (Althusser, Foucault, Lacan), but also not the "deep-ecological" antihumanist reduction of humanity to just one of the animal species on Earth, the species that derailed the balance of life through its hubris and is now facing the justified revenge of Mother Earth. However, even this fourth stage is not without its history. In the first decade of the Soviet Union, so-called biocosmism enjoyed extraordinary popularity: a strange combination of vulgar materialism and Gnostic spirituality that formed an occult shadow ideology, the obscene secret teaching, of Soviet Marxism.

Today it is as if biocosmism were reemerging in a new wave of posthuman thought. The spectacular development of biogenetics, with its scientific practices (cloning, direct DNA interventions, etc.), is gradually dissolving frontiers between humans and animals on the one side as well as between humans and machines on the other side, giving rise to the idea that we are on the threshold of a new form of Intelligence, a "more-than-human" Singularity in which mind will no longer be submitted to bodily constraints, inclusive of sexual reproduction. Out of this prospect a weird shame emerged: the shame about our biological limitations, our mortality, the ridiculous way we reproduce ourselves—what Gunther Anders called the "Promethean shame,"[13] ultimately simply the shame that "we were born and not manufactured." Nietzsche's idea that we are the "last men" laying the ground for our own extinction and the arrival of a new Overman is thereby given a scientific-technological twist. However, we should not reduce this "posthuman" stance to the paradigmatically modern belief in the possibility of total technological domination over nature—what we are witnessing today is an exemplary dialectical reversal: the slogan of today's posthuman sciences is no longer domination but surprise, (contingent, unplanned) emergence. Jean-Pierre Dupuy detected a weird reversal of the traditional Cartesian anthropocentric arrogance that grounded human technology, the reversal clearly discernible in today's robotics, genetics, nanotechnology, artificial life, and AI research:

> How are we to explain that science became such a "risky" activity that, according to some top scientists, it poses today the principal threat to the survival of humanity? Some philosophers reply to this question by saying that Descartes's dream—"to become master and possessor of nature"—has turned out wrong, and that we should urgently return to the "mastery of mastery." They understood nothing. They don't see that the technology profiling itself at our horizon through the "convergence" of all disciplines aims precisely at non-mastery. The engineer of tomorrow will not be a sorcerer's apprentice because of his negligence or ignorance, but by choice. He will "give" himself complex structures or organizations and he will try to learn what they are capable of by way of exploring their functional properties—an ascending, bottom-up, approach. He will be an explorer and experimenter at least as much as an executor. The measure of his success will be more the extent to which his own creations will surprise him than the conformity of his accomplishments to a list of pre-established tasks.[14]

The motor of this self-sublation (*Selbst-Aufhebung*) of man is the ongoing scientific progress in evolutionary biology, neurology and cognitivist brain sciences that holds the promise of the total scientific self-objectivization of humanity: evolutionary theory can explain how humanity gradually emerged out of animal life, and, in this sense, it can also account for itself (for the rise of cognitive mechanisms that allowed humanity to develop a scientific approach to reality). The question nonetheless persists: does this operation of closing the loop (accounting for oneself) really succeed? Here one should be absolutely clear: these accounts are, in spite of their imperfections, in a certain sense simply and rather obviously *true*, so one should abandon all obscurantist or spiritualist references to some mysterious dimension that would elude science. Should we then simply endorse this prospect? In philosophy the predominant form of resistance to the full scientific self-objectivization of humanity that, nonetheless, admits science's achievements is the Neo-Kantian transcendental state philosophy (whose exemplary case today is Habermas): our self-perception as free and responsible agents is not just a necessary illusion but the transcendental a priori of every scientific knowledge. For Habermas, "the attempt to study first-person subjective experience from the third-person, objectifying viewpoint, involves the theorist in a performative contradiction, since objectification presupposes participation in an intersubjectively instituted system of linguistic practices whose normative valence conditions the scientist's cognitive activity."[15]

Habermas characterizes this intersubjective domain of rational validity as the dimension of "objective mind," which cannot be understood in terms of the phenomenological profiles of the community of conscious selves comprised in it: it is the intrinsically intersubjective status of the normative realm that precludes any attempt to account for its operation or genesis in terms of entities or processes simpler than the system itself. (Lacan's term for this "objective mind" irreducible to the Real of raw reality as well as to the Imaginary of our self-experience is, of course, the big Other.) Neither the phenomenological (imaginary) nor neurobiological (real) profiling of participants can be cited as a constituting condition for this socially "objective mind." In the same Habermasian mode, Robert Pippin claims that, even if some day scientists do succeed in the total naturalization of humanity, explaining how self-consciousness emerged by natural evolution, this would have no consequences for philosophy: "Of course, it is possible and important that some day researchers will discover why animals with human brains can do these things and animals without human brains cannot, and some combination of astrophysics and evolutionary theory will be able to explain why humans have ended up with the brains they have. But these are not philosophical problems and they do not generate any philosophical problems."[16] What Pippin performs here is, of course, the basic transcendental turn: the point is not that self-consciousness is too complex a phenomenon to be accounted for in scientific terms but that, in this case, all psychoneuronal analysis is simply irrelevant since it moves at a totally different level from pure self-consciousness, which is not a psychological fact but an a priori that sustains all our activity inclusive of neurological research. Here we reach a certain limit: how do we relativize the truth-domain of science? Is the transcendental approach enough, or does this approach need to be sustained by a limitation at the level of content? In somewhat simplified terms: is it enough to state that positive science cannot account for its own possibility, that it has to presuppose the free argumentative procedure that characterizes science? Or should we supplement this transcendental point with some proof of the empirical limitations of scientific explanations ("no brain science can really explain how the human mind functions")?

One has to concede that some scientific experiments lead to results that cannot simply be dismissed as irrelevant. A recent experiment conducted by the Karolinska Institute in Sweden demonstrated that the experience of being inside one's own body is not as self-evident as one might think: neuroscientists "created an out-of-body illusion in participants placed inside a brain scanner. They then used the illusion to perceptually 'teleport' the participants to different locations in a room and show that the perceived location of the bodily self can be decoded from activity patterns in specific brain regions." The sense of "owning one's body" is therefore not to be taken for granted: it is "an enormously complex task that requires continuous integration of information from our different senses in order to maintain an accurate sense of where the body is located with respect to the external world."[17]

The signification of such experiments is double. First, they provide a clear argument against the spiritualist reading of out-of-body experiences by proving that our soul is not irreducibly located in our body since it can freely float outside it: if one can generate such an out-of-body experience through technological manipulation of our body, then our "inner" self-experience is strictly immanent to our body. Second, they also render problematic at least the notion, crucial to the philosophy of finitude, that we are irreducibly "embedded," that our self-experience as constrained to the standpoint of our (mortal) body is the ultimate horizon of our entire experience: the experiment indicates that our self-experience as "embodied" is the result of complex neuronal processes that can also go wrong. A more nuanced approach is thus needed, one that leaves Habermas's and

Pippin's transcendental-idealist position behind. Wilfrid Sellars gives the duality of (materialist) content and (transcendental) form a decidedly materialist twist. Accepting the gap between methodology (priority of transcendental horizon) and ontology (full naturalization), i.e., recognizing that direct naturalization is strictly pre-Hegelian, Sellars, in an unambiguously materialist way,

> upholds the *priority* of the scientific image by famously insisting that "in the dimension of describing and explaining the world, science is the measure of all things, of what is, that it is, and of what is not, that it is not." . . . Yet the manifest image remains indispensable as the originary medium for the normative. To the extent that this normative framework does not survive, Sellars warned, "man himself would not survive." . . . Science cannot lead us to abandon our manifest self-conception as rationally responsible agents, since to do so would be to abandon the source of the imperative to revise. It is our manifest self-understanding as persons that furnishes us, qua community of rational agents, with the ultimate horizon of rational purposiveness with regard to which we are motivated to try to understand the world. Shorn of this horizon, all cognitive activity, and with it science's investigation of reality, would become pointless.[18]

Along these lines, Ray Brassier defines materialism with the Marxist-sounding notion of the "determination in the last instance," which should be opposed to the similar notion of overdetermination: "determination-in-the-last-instance is the causality which renders it universally possible for any object X to determine its own 'real' cognition, but only in the last instance."[19] Overdetermination is transcendental, i.e., the point of transcendentalism is that a subject cannot ever fully "objectivize" itself, i.e., reduce itself to a part of "objective reality" in front of him, since such reality is always already transcendentally constituted by subjectivity: no matter to what extend I succeed in accounting for myself as a phenomenon within the "great chain of being," as the result determined by a network of natural (or supernatural) reasons, this causal image is always already overdetermined by the transcendental horizon that structures my approach to reality. To this transcendental overdetermination, Brassier opposes the naturalist determination in the last instance: a serious materialist has to presume that every subjective horizon within which reality appears, every subjective constitution or mediation of reality, has to be ultimately determined by its place within objective reality, i.e., it has to be conceived as part of the all-encompassing natural process . . . [20]

   The big question thus continues to haunt us: what—if anything—resists total scientific self-objectivization? Although, in contrast to scientific self-objectivization, ooo (object-oriented ontology) aims at reenchanting reality, it shares with the scientific view the notion that the ontological-transcendental horizon can be reduced to one among the ontic relations between objects-things. Levi Bryant is therefore right in naming his view "onticology" as opposed to ontology. Our problem is, on the contrary: how are we to be materialists without regressing to an ontic view? The answer is that the dimension that resists self-objectivization is not human self-experience but the "inhuman" core of what German Idealism calls negativity, what Freud called the death drive, and even what Heidegger referred to as "ontological difference," a gap or abyss that forever precludes the exclusively ontic view of humans as just another object among objects.[21] This dimension is beyond any transcendental horizon; it aims at reaching the In-itself. However, the In-itself is not "out there"; we do not reach it after we subtract from reality our subjective additions; the In-itself is "here" in the very subjective excess to what appears to us as objective reality.

   Nothing in the *Black Notebooks* changes the fact that Heidegger's thought provides a key contribution to our dealing with this ultimate question.

NOTES

EDITORS' INTRODUCTION

1. See Wolfgang Benz, *Was ist Antisemitismus?*, 2d ed. (Munich: Beck, 2005), 9–28.
2. Eberhard Jäckel, Peter Logerich, and Julius H. Schoeps, eds., *Enzyklopädie des Holocaust. Die Verfolgung und Ermordung der europäischen Juden* (Berlin: Argon, 1993), s.v. "Antisemitismus."
3. See Hugo Ott, *Martin Heidegger: A Political Life* (New York: Basic Books, 1993), 190; Martin Heidegger, "*Mein liebes Seelchen!": Briefe Martin Heideggers an seine Frau Elfride, 1915–1970*, ed. Gertrud Heidegger (Munich: Deutsche Verlags Anstalt, 2005), 51; English translation in *Letters to His Wife, 1915–1970*, trans. R. D. V. Glasgow (Malden, MA: Polity, 2010), 28.
4. The key term here, *Judentum,* could be translated as "Judaism" or "Jewry"; we have made no attempt to unify the authors' decisions on this point.
5. See Peter Trawny, *Heidegger and the Myth of a Jewish World Conspiracy*, trans. Andrew J. Mitchell (Chicago: University of Chicago Press, 2016), chapter. 2.
6. It does seem that some of the notebooks were given as gifts or lent to friends; *Anmerkungen* I, for example, was initially presumed lost only to be found in the possession of the family friend Silvio Vietta.
7. Martin Heidegger, *Eine gefährliche Irrnis. Jahresgabe der Martin Heidegger Gesellschaft* (Stuttgart: Offizin Scheufele, 2008).
8. Ibid., 11.
9. Ibid.
10. Ibid., 13.
11. Jacques Derrida, *Of Grammatology*, trans. Gayatri Chakravorty Spivak (Baltimore: Johns Hopkins University Press, 1974), 19.
12. Trawny, *Heidegger and the Myth of a Jewish World Conspiracy*, 12.

13. Jürgen Habermas, "On the Publication of the Lectures of 1935," in Richard Wolin, ed., *The Heidegger Controversy: A Critical Reader* (New York: Columbia Unviersity Press, 1991), 197.

14. Peter Trawny's presentation from the Emory conference has been replaced by a more recent essay. His Emory lecture has been published elsewhere; see Peter Trawny, "Heidegger, 'World Judaism,' and Modernity," trans. Christopher Merwin, *Gatherings* 5 (2015): 1–20.

1. THE UNIVERSAL AND ANNIHILATION

1. Marc Augé, *Non-Places: An Introduction to Supermodernity*, trans. John Howe (New York: Verso, 2009). Cf. also my book *Technik. Kapital. Medium. Das Universale und die Freiheit* (Berlin: Matthes & Seitz, 2015).

2. Paul Natorp, *Platos Ideenlehre: Eine Einführung in den Idealismus* (Leipzig: Dürr, 1903).

3. Emmanuel Levinas, *Autrement qu'être ou au-delà de l'essence* (The Hague: Martinus Nijhoff, 1974). English translation: *Otherwise Than Being: Or Beyond Essence,* trans. Alphonso Lingis (Pittsburgh: Duquesne University Press, 1998).

4. Wolfgang Benz, *Was ist Antisemitismus?*, 2d ed. (Munich: Beck, 2004), 192.

5. Adolf Hitler, *Mein Kampf*, trans. John Chamberlain et al. (New York: Reynal and Hitchcock, 1940), 666, tm; Theodor Mommsen, *The History of Rome*, vol. 4, trans. William P. Dickson (New York: Scribner, 1871), 643, tm.

6. Emmanuel Levinas, "Heidegger, Gagarin and Us," in *Difficult Freedom: Essays on Judaism*, trans. Seán Hand (Baltimore: Johns Hopkins University Press, 1990), 231–34, 232.

7. Ibid., 232–33.

8. Ibid., 233.

9. Ibid., 233–34.

2. COSMOPOLITAN JEWS VS. JEWISH NOMADS

1. See, for example, Ulrich Beck and Natan Sznaider, "Unpacking Cosmopolitanism for the Social Sciences: A Research Agenda," *British Journal of Sociology* 57 (2006): 1–23, as well as their "A Literature on Cosmopolitanism: An Overview," *British Journal of Sociology* 57 (2006): 153–64. Recently David Nirenberg, *Anti-Judaism: The Western Tradition* (New York: Norton, 2013) has raised the question of the projection of such spectral qualities onto the stereotype of the Jew.

2. Tim Brennan, *At Home in the World: Cosmopolitanism Now* (Cambridge: Harvard University Press, 1997).

3. John Dee, *General and Rare Memorials Pertayning to the Perfect Arte of Navigation* (London: John Daye, 1577), 54.

4. "Mitteilungen: Weltbürger," *Neuphilologische Mitteilungen* 27 (1926): 13.

5. Guillaume Lallement, *Choix de rapports, opinions et discours prononcés à la tribune nationale depuis 1789 jusqu'à ce jour*, vol. 15, *1794–1795* (Paris: Alexis Eymery, 1821), 231.

6.   Jay R. Berkovitz, *Rites and Passages: The Beginnings of Modern Jewish Culture in France, 1650–1860* (Philadelphia: University of Pennsylvania Press, 2004), 152.

7.   C. M. Wieland, "Das Geheimniss des Kosmopoliten-Ordens," in *Sämmtliche Werke* 30:113–48 (Leipzig: Georg Joachim Göschen, 1797), 122.

8.   Actually he wrote "Die Religionen Müsen alle Tolleriret werden und Mus der fiscal nuhr das auge darauf haben, das keine der andern abruch Tuhe, den hier mus ein jeder nach Seiner Fasson Selich werden!" Cited by Heribert Raab, ed., *Kirche und Staat: Von der Mitte des 15. Jahrhunderts bis zur Gegenwart* (München: Deutscher Taschenbuch Verlag, 1966), 194.

9.   C. M. Wieland, *Private History of Peregrinus Proteus the Philosopher*, translated from the German (London: printed for J. Johnson, in St. Paul's Churchyard, 1796), 2.32.

10.   Derek Penslar, *Shylock's Children: Economics and Jewish Identity in Modern Europe* (Berkeley: University of California Press, 2001).

11.   Sander L. Gilman, *Multiculturalism and the Jews* (New York: Routledge, 2006).

12.   Ulrike M. Vieten, *Gender and Cosmopolitanism in Europe: A Feminist Perspective* (Farnham: Ashgate, 2012), 7.

13.   Johann Gottfried Herder, *Outlines of a Philosophy of the History of Man*, trans. T. Churchill (London: printed for J. Johnson, by Luke Hansard, 1800), 658, a translation of *Ideen zur Philosophie der Geschichte der Menschheit*.

14.   Ibid., 351.

15.   Raymond Williams, *Keywords: A Vocabulary of Culture and Society* (New York: Oxford University Press, 1985), 89.

16.   Michaela Wirtz, *Patriotismus und Weltbürgertum. Eine begriffsgeschichtliche Studie zur deutsch-jüdischen Literatur 1750–1850* (Tübingen: M. Niemeyer, 2006).

17.   Johann Gottlieb Fichte, "Beitrag zur Berichtigung der Urtheile des Publikums über die französische Revolution," in J. G. Fichte, *Werke 1791–1794, Gesamtausgabe* I.1:193–404 (Stuttgart: Frommann-Holzboog, 1964), 292.

18.   Ibid., 295.

19.   Herder, *Outlines of a Philosophy of the History of Man*, 36.

20.   Michael Mack, *German Idealism and the Jew: The Inner Anti-Semitism of Philosophy and German Jewish Responses* (Chicago: University of Chicago Press, 2003), 5.

21.   Herder, *Outlines of a Philosophy of the History of Man*, 51.

22.   Ibid., 52.

23.   W. E. Tentzel, *Monatliche Unterredungen Einiger Guten Freunde von Allerhand Büchern und andern annehmlichen Geschichten. Allen Liebhabern Der Curiositäten Zur Ergetzligkeit und Nachsinnen heraus gegeben* 1 (1689): 833.

24.   Johann Christof Wagenseil, *Benachrichtigung wegen einiger die gemeine Jüdischheit betreffenden wichtigen Sachen : worinnen – I. Die Hoffnung der Erlösung Israelis. II. Wiederlegung der Unwahrheit als ob die Jüden Christen-Blut brauchten. III. Anzeigung wie die Jüden von schinden und wuchern abzubringen. IV. Bericht von dem Jüdischen Gebeth Alenu. V. Denunciatio Christiana, wegen der Jüden Lästerungen. Diesen sind beygefügt – Rabbi Mose Stendels, in Jüdisch-Teutsche Reimen gebrachte Psalmen Davids* (Leipzig: Johann Heiniche Witwe, 1705), 473–88.

25. Johann Jakob Schudt, *Judische Merckwürdigkeiten: vorstellende was sich curieuses und denckwürdiges in den neuern Zeiten bey einigen Jahrhunderten mit denen in alle IV. Theile der Welt, sonderlich durch Teutschland, zerstreuten Juden zugetragen: sammt einer vollständigen Franckfurter Juden-Chronick, darinnen der zu Franckfurt am Mayn wohnenden Juden, von einigen Jahr-hunderten, biss auff unsere Zeiten, merckwürdigste Begebenheiten enthalten: benebst einigen, zur Erläuterung beygefügten Kupffern und Figuren* (Leipzig: [s.n.], 1714), 470–512.

26. Ibid., 502.

27. Ibid., 504.

28. All references are from John K. Noyes, "Goethe on Cosmopolitanism and Colonialism: Bildung and the Dialectic of Critical Mobility," *Eighteenth-Century Studies* 39, no. 4 (Summer 2006): 443–62.

29. Karl Marx, *Capital* (New York: Penguin, 1976), 182–83.

30. Sidra DeKoven Ezrahi, "Considering the Apocalypse: Is the Writing on the Wall Only Grafitti?" in Berel Lang, ed., *Writing and the Holocaust,* 137–59 (New York: Holmes and Meier, 1988), 138–39.

31. George Simmel, *Philosophy of Money,* trans. Tom Bottomore and David Frisby (London: Routledge and Kegan Paul, 1978), 353.

32. Leon Pinsker, "Auto-Emancipation," trans. D. S. Blondheim (1916), in *Jewish Virtual Library,* http://www.jewishvirtuallibrary.org/jsource/Zionism/pinsker.html.

33. Ignaz Goldziher, *Der Mythos bei den Hebraern: Und Seine Geschichtliche Entwickelung* (Leipzig: F. A. Brockhaus, 1876).

34. Werner Sombart, *The Jews and Modern Capitalism,* trans. M. Epstein (New York: Dutton, 1913), 325.

35. Max Weber, *Ancient Judaism,* trans. Hans H. Gerth and Don Martindale (New York: Free Press, 1967).

36. Ibid., 438.

37. Ibid., 69.

38. The Hittite scholar Archibald H. Sayce was indeed philo-Semitic. In his 1903 Gifford Lectures he wrote that

> it is usually the fashion to ascribe this concentration of religion upon the present world, with its repellent views of Hades and limitation of divine rewards and punishments to this life, to the inherent peculiarities of the Semitic mind. But for this there is no justification. There is nothing in the Semitic mind, which would necessitate such a theological system. It is true that the sun-god was the central object of the Semitic Babylonian faith, and that to the nomads of Arabia the satisfaction of their daily wants was the practical end of existence. But it is not among the nomads of Arabia that we find anything corresponding with the Babylonian idea of Hades and the conceptions associated with it. The idea was, in fact, of Babylonian origin. If the Hebrew Sheol resembles the Hades of Babylonia, or the Hebrew conception of rewards and punishments is like that of the Assyrians and Babylonians, it is because the Hebrew beliefs were derived from the civilisation of the Euphrates.

The Religions of Ancient Egypt and Babylonia (Edinburgh: Clark, 1903), 295.

39. Houston Stewart Chamberlain, *The Foundations of the Nineteenth Century*, 2d ed. (London: John Lane, 1912), 369.

40. Adolf Wahrmund, *Das Gesetz des Nomadentums und die heutige Judenherrschaft* (Karlsruhe: Reuther, 1887), 91 (our translation).

41. Otto Gildemeister, *Judas Werdegang: in vier Jahrtausenden* (Leipzig: Weicher, 1921), 15.

42. For an example, see the German philosopher Christoph Meiners, "Kurze Geschichte der Hirtenvölker in den verschiedenen Theilen der Erde," *Neues Göttingisches historisches Magazin* 2 (1793): 654–85.

43. Friedrich Ratzel, *The History of Mankind*, vol. 3, trans. A. J. Butler (London: MacMillan, 1896), 548.

44. Ibid.

45. Ibid.

46. Cited by Vadim Joseph Rossman, *Russian Intellectual Antisemitism in the Post-Communist Era* (Lincoln: University of Nebraska Press, 2002), 8.

47. Felix Delitzsch, *Die grosse Täuschung, erster teil: Kritische Betrachtungen zu den alttestamentlichen Berichten über Israels Eindringen in Kanaan* (Stuttgart: Deutsche Verlags-Anstalt, 1921), 1.105.

48. Adolf Hitler, *Mein Kampf*, trans. Ralph Manheim (Boston: Houghton Mifflin, 1943), 300–11, 324–27.

49. C. G. Jung, *Interviews and Encounters*, ed. William McGuire and R. F. C. Hull (Princeton: Princeton University Press, 1977), 193.

50. I am indebted to Peter Trawny, *Heidegger and the Myth of a Jewish World Conspiracy*, trans. Andrew J. Mitchell (Chicago: University of Chicago Press, 2016).

51. Engelbert Huber, "Der Antisemitismus der NSDAP," in *Das ist Nationalsozialismus: Organisation und Weltanschauung der NSDAP* (Stuttgart: Union Deutsche Verlagsgesellschaft, 1933), 90–96.

52. Eberhard Jäckel and Axel Kuhn, eds., *Hitler: Sämtliche Aufzeichnungen 1905–1924* (Stuttgart: Deutsche Verlags-Anstalt, 1980), 88–90.

53. Joseph Goebbels, *Communism with the Mask Off: Speech Delivered in Nürnberg on September 13th, 1935, at the Seventh National Socialist Party Congress* (Berlin: M. Müller, 1935), 5.

54. Karl Baumböck, *Juden machen Weltpolitik* (Berlin: Propaganda-Verlag Paul Hochmuth, 1942), 29.

55. E. Günther Gründel, *Jahre der Überwindung* (Breslau: Korn, 1934), 93–94.

56. Max Brod, "Der Erfahrung in ostjüdischen Schulwerk," *Der Jude* 1 (1916–7): 35. "Man soll uns nicht eine Zentifugalkraft einimpfen und hintenach wundern, 'Nomadentum' und 'kritische Zersetzung' an unserm Leichnam konstatiren!"

57. Jacob Neusner, *Self-Fulfilling Prophecy: Exile and Return in the History of Judaism* (Atlanta: Scholars, 1990).

58. W. D. Davies, *The Territorial Dimension in Judaism* (Minneapolis: Fortress, 1991 [1982]).

3. METAPHYSICAL ANTI-SEMITISM AND WORLDLESSNESS

1. Peter Trawny, *Freedom to Fail: Heidegger's Anarchy*, trans. Ian Alexander Moore and Christopher Turner (Malden, MA: Polity, 2015). German edition: *Irrnisfuge: Heideggers Anarchie* (Munich: Matthes & Seitz Berlin, 2014).

2. See Alfred Denker, "Heidegger's Correspondence," in François Raffoul and Eric S. Nelson, eds., *The Bloomsbury Companion to Heidegger* (London: Bloomsbury, 2013), 67–73.

3. See my review of Victor Farías's Spanish edition of the Helen Weiss manuscript: Eduardo Mendieta, "*Lógica, Lecciones de M. Heidegger* (semestre verano 1934), en el legado de Helene Weiss, Introducción y traducción de Victor Farías (Barcelona: Anthropos: Editorial del Hombre, Centro de Publicaciones de MEC, 1991)," *Graduate Faculty Philosophy Journal* 16, no. 2 (1993): 516–24.

4. Theodore Kisiel, "Heidegger's Philosophical Geopolitics in the Third Reich," in Richard Polt and Gregory Fried, eds., *A Companion to Heidegger's "Introduction to Metaphysics"* (New Haven: Yale University Press, 2001), 226–49.

5. Peter Trawny, *Heidegger and the Myth of a Jewish World Conspiracy*, trans. Andrew J. Mitchell (Chicago: University of Chicago Press, 2016), 4–5.

6. There is now a massive, extensive, and meticulously documented study of the *Black Notebooks* in Italian by Donatella Di Cesare, *Heidegger e gli ebrei: I "Quaderni neri"* (Turin: Bollati Boringhieri, 2014), which, unfortunately, I became aware of only after I completed this text.

7. Domenico Losurdo, *Heidegger and the Ideology of War: Community, Death, and the West*, trans. Marella and Jon Morris (Amherst, NY: Humanity, 2001), especially chapter 4: "War, Revolution, and Conspiracy." See also David Nirenberg, *Anti-Judaism: The Western Tradition* (New York: Norton, 2013), which makes a persuasive argument that anti-Judaism is a better term to express all the types of pathological imaginaries that have been invented and mobilized to unleash genocidal violence on Jews.

8. It should be asked where I stand vis-à-vis Trawny's proposal that we see in Heidegger something like a being-historical anti-Semitism. My sense is that I am expanding on his work, but I also think that my work shows that Heidegger's attempt to marshal the powers of his philosophical thinking to develop his own nonbiological anti-Semitism leads to a *reductio ad absurdum*, i.e., that his categories do not allow for anti-Semitism, or, if they are to be used for anti-Jewish ends, they implode or become incoherent. I thus think that I partly agree and partly disagree with Trawny. I show that there is contamination, or rather attempts to use and translate concepts and paths of thinking for certain ends, but that elements in Heidegger's own categories deconstruct and dismantle the anti-Semitism that is hoisted upon them. Heidegger's thinking is its own *pharmakon*.

9. Robert Bernasconi, "Heidegger's Alleged Challenge to the Nazi Concept of Race," in James E. Faulconer and Mark A. Wrathall, eds., *Appropriating Heidegger*, 50–67 (Cambridge: Cambridge University Press, 2000), 61.

10. See Robert Bernasconi, "Kant's Third Thoughts on Race," in Stuart Elden and Eduardo Mendieta, eds., *Reading Kant's Geography* (Albany: SUNY Press, 2011), 291–318.

11. See Tom Rockmore, "Heidegger After Trawny: Philosophy or Worldview?" in this volume.

12. Stuart Elden, *Speaking Against Number: Heidegger, Language, and the Politics of Calculation* (Edinburgh: Edinburgh University Press, 2006), 129–30. It should be noted that these reflections on number should now be correlated with the reflection on the "gigantic"—a theme that runs through the *Hefte* but that is also present in *GA* 65.

13. Maurice Olender, *The Languages of Paradise: Race, Religion, and Philology in the Nineteenth Century*, trans. Arthus Goldhammer (Cambridge: Harvard University Press, 2008), 37.

14. Marion Heinz, "*Volk* and *Führer*," in Martin Heidegger, *Nature, History, State, 1933–1934*, ed. and trans. Gregory Fried and Richard Polt, 67–84 (New York: Bloomsbury, 2013), 80.

15. Trawny, *Heidegger and the Myth of a Jewish World Conspiracy*, 12.

16. Jacques Derrida, *Of Spirit: Heidegger and the Questions*, trans. Geoffrey Bennington (Chicago: University of Chicago Press, 1991), 45–46.

17. Of course this form of anti-Judaism is by no means any kind of confrontation with National Socialist anti-Judaism. In fact, it marches in lockstep with it. See Jeffrey Herf, *The Jewish Enemy: Nazi Propaganda During World War II and the Holocaust* (Cambridge: Harvard University Press, 2006).

18. Kisiel, "Heidegger's Philosophical Geopolitics," 248.

19. Here I would have also wanted to include a brief engagement with Andrew Benjamin, *Of Jews and Animals* (Edinburgh: Edinburgh University Press, 2010), but space constraints prevent me from doing so.

20. Eduardo Mendieta, "El Bestiario de Heidegger: El Animal sin Lenguaje ni Historia," *Revista Filosofía UIS* 11, no. 1 (2012): 17–43, and my forthcoming book, *The Philosophical Animal: Zoepoetics and Interspecies Cosmopolitanism* (Albany: SUNY Press, forthcoming).

21. I owe these remarks to Adam Knowles, who suggested that we ought to think of Dasein as also world destroying (*Weltzerstörend*).

4. "STERBEN SIE?"

1. Peter Trawny, *Heidegger and the Myth of a Jewish World Conspiracy*, trans. Andrew J. Mitchell (Chicago: University of Chicago Press, 2016), 44.

2. Ibid., 44.

3. I pay particular attention to Heidegger's *Contributions to Philosophy* (1936–38), posthumously published reflections contemporaneous with the first three notebooks. See *GA* 65:225–89/177–227.

4. Trawny, *Heidegger and the Myth of a Jewish World Conspiracy*, 24.

5. Robert Bernasconi points out that a biologistic reception of Nietzsche in 1930s Germany was largely the rule, even if "there was no uniform view about Nietzsche within National Socialism." See Bernasconi, "Heidegger, Rickert, Nietzsche" in Babette E. Babich, Alfred Denker, and Holger Zaborowski, eds., *Heidegger and Nietzsche* (Amsterdam: Rodopi, 2012), 160, see also 167–69. For sensitive discussion of Nietzsche's concepts of will to power, the *Übermensch*, and animality see Michel Haar, "The Ambivalent Unthought of the Overman and the Duality of Heidegger's Political Thinking," *Graduate Faculty Philosophy Journal* 14–15, nos. 2 and 1 (1991): 109–36.

6. Emmanuel Faye, *Heidegger: The Introduction of Nazism into Philosophy in Light of the Unpublished Seminars of 1933–1935*, trans. Michael B. Smith (New Haven: Yale University Press, 2011), 69. I am aware of the controversy that attended the publication of Faye's book. I use some of the historical research here, sparingly and for the purposes of contrasting Heidegger's university activities with the writings he did not publish until decades after the war. Faye writes:

> Heidegger posits as primary what he calls the effectiveness of life, which leads him to affirm the primacy of the ambient world, of the *Umwelt*. This term is not forged by him. It is borrowed from the non-Darwinian biology of Jakob von Uexküll, and, before Heidegger, it is found not only in Husserl himself but also, and especially, as early as 1923, in an author coming from phenomenology, Ludwig Clauß. Clauß, in *The Nordic Soul*, explicitly applies Husserl's method to the description of racial identity. . . . In 1925 Heidegger was certainly more moderate or less explicit than Clauß, but it is important to see what connotations, in that intellectual context, the substitution of surrounding world for consciousness, *Umwelt* for *Bewußtsein*, could have.
>
> Moreover, it is assuredly Uexküll that Heidegger has in mind when he alludes to the fact [in the 1925 Kassel lectures] that the knowledge of the correlation between life and its world has begun making its way into biology. It is essential to understand that if Heidegger always fought against Darwinian biology and what in the 1930s he would call "liberal biology," he was a great champion of what he called in a letter to Elisabeth Blochmann "the new biology"—that of Uexküll. It is worth noting that Uexküll was to become the editor of the race scientist, Houston S. Chamberlain.
>
> (ibid., 14)

On Heidegger's Kassel lectures, "Wilhelm Dilthey's Research and the Current Struggle for a Historical Worldview" (WDR), see the editors' introduction to their translation in Kisiel and Sheehan, eds., *Becoming Heidegger: On the Trail of his Early Occasional Writings, 1910–1927* (Evanston: Northwestern University Press, 2007), 238–41.

7. Eugen Fischer had many students at the Berlin Institute, of which one would achieve lasting notoriety, Josef Mengele. See Faye, *Heidegger*, 69–70. For a discussion of the transformation of the medical schools under the Nazis, see E. John, B. Martin, M. Mück, and H. Ott, eds., *Die Freiburger Universität in der Zeit des Nationalsozialismus* (Freiburg: Ploetz, 1991), 84, cited by Faye. Another important source is Arno Münster, *Heidegger, la "science allemande" et le National-Socialisme* (Paris: Kimé, 2002).

8. See Faye, *Heidegger*, 14. Ludwig Ferdinand Clauß, *Die nordische Seele: Rettung, Prägung, Ausdruck* (Halle: Niemeyer, 1923).

9. John Caputo has argued that the transformation of Heidegger's earlier Aristotelian and Neo-Testamentary emphases in *Being and Time* toward what Caputo calls a *Kampfphilosophie* can be discerned in his analysis of boredom and the "essential neediness" and

Leergelassenheit (void) of contemporary life. See "Heidegger's *Kampf*: The Difficulty of Life," *Graduate Faculty Philosophy Journal* 14:2–15: 1 (1991): 74–76.

10.   *GA* 2:455/*SZ* 344.

11.   I thank Andrew Mitchell for this insight.

12.   See, for example, Husserl's late essay "Universal Teleology," which discusses intersubjective drives "viewed transcendentally," in Peter McCormick and Frederick Elliston, eds., *Husserl: Shorter Works* (Notre Dame: University of Notre Dame Press, 1981), 335–37.

13.   He writes, in "The Origin of the Work of Art" (1935–36): "*All art*, as the letting happen of the advent of the truth of beings [*als Geschehenlassen der Ankunft der Wahrheit*], is, *in essence, poetry*" (*GA* 5:59/44).

14.   Heidegger writes: "World is 'earthly' (earthy), earth is worldly. Earth, because it is related to history, is in one respect *more originary* than nature. World is higher than merely 'created' things, because it is *formative of history* and so lies closest to the event [*Ereignis*]" (*GA* 65:275/216).

15.   Trawny, *Heidegger and the Myth of a Jewish World Conspiracy*, 34.

16.   On the previous page, Heidegger explicitly equated technology with Machenschaft (*GA* 65:274/216).

17.   Werner Marx, *Heidegger and the Tradition*, trans. Theodore Kisiel and Murray Greene (Evanston: Northwestern University Press, 1971), 140. Marx has a useful discussion of physis, arguing that being, as creative flourishing, appears to be the result of Heidegger's dialogue with Nietzsche. See ibid., 139–43, 258–59.

18.   Trawny, *Heidegger and the Myth of a Jewish World Conspiracy*, 31.

19.   Here and as late as 1942–43, in his Parmenides lecture course, where he seems first to consider the sense of humans as rational *animals*, Heidegger urged that no connection between Dasein and living beings could be made—and for precisely the same reasons. The animal is bound up in its "circle of food, prey, and sex" and is open to its world only in the sense of "the peculiar arousal of excitability." We cannot even ask what the lark "sees" as it flies into its open, because it does not see "the open" itself. If metaphysics called man "the rational animal," it missed both the mystery of the living being, construing it as "irrational," and the fundamental distinction between humans as able to see the open and animals as devoid of world. "In fact, an original poetizing capacity would be needed to surmise what is concealed to the living being, a poetic capacity to which more and higher things are charged, and more essential things . . . *versus* the mere hominization of plants and animals" (*GA* 54:238–39/160–61). As much as he attributed the poetizing capacity to Hölderlin, he denies it to Rilke, who confuses living beings with historical beings by *fusing* their two, distinct mysteries.

20.   Cf. Faye, *Heidegger*, 113–15.

21.   Faye reports: "On 13 April 1934, not many days before his resignation from the rectorship took effect, and therefore at a time when he was not obliged to any activism, Heidegger wrote to the ministry of Karlsruhe to demand the creation (and he reminds his reader that he has been demanding it 'for months') of a 'full professor chair in racial doctrine and hereditary biology' (*eines ausserordentlichen Lehrstuhles für Rassenkunde und Erbbiologie*)." See ibid., 69–70.

22. Compare Oswald Spengler's remarks on technology in his 1931 *Man and Technics:* "We cannot look at a waterfall without mentally turning it into electric power; we cannot survey a countryside full of pasturing cattle without thinking of its exploitation as a source of meat-supply; we cannot look at the beautiful old handwork of an unspoilt primitive people without wishing to replace it by a modern technical process. Our technical thinking must have its actualization, sensible or senseless." Oswald Spengler, *Man and Technics: A Contribution to a Philosophy of Life,* trans. C. F. Atkinson (New York: Knopf, 1932), 94. In 1931 Spengler saw no way out of a technologized world than *courageously* remaining at one's post, like the Roman soldier found, fossilized, in Pompei. The courage theme hearkens to Heidegger's theme of the decision in regard to beyng which, by *Überlegung* 6, he despaired of attaining. I return to Spengler at the end of this essay.

23. Hans Driesch wrote on embryology with a vitalist emphasis on a "mindlike" life force; see Hans Driesch, *Science and Philosophy of the Organism: The Gifford Lectures Delivered Before the University of Aberdeen,* vol. 2 (London: Adam and Charles Black, 1908). Although hostile to Nazism, his thought was swept up into the racial science of the "spirit" of a people in the 1930s. He died in 1941. See Heidegger's remarks on Driesch in *GA* 29/30:379–82/261–63.

24. The vigorous adherence of scientists from universities throughout Germany to the "new" National Socialist biology and its teaching imperatives (texts had to be accessible to all "German" readers, with special emphasis on high school students and university students in their initial years of study) can be seen from a survey of publications and articles in the heretofore respected academic journal, *Der Biologe,* from the years 1933–1934. Heidegger was clearly, if critically, aware of the normativity of the new biology, as he had discussed the work of von Uexküll (whose work was well represented in *Der Biologe*) five years before. Moreover, as most contributors were established academics and specialists, they set the tone for pedagogy and teaching material, from racial hygiene, race science, family planning, eugenics, ecology, political and legal theory (with race considerations), and a host of disciplines that no longer "exist" as such (e.g., *Erbgesundheitspflege, Rassenphysiologie,* and *Familienkunde*). Thus, in the single month of March 1934, some twenty-two reviews appeared on race science books published between 1933 and 1934. The following selection eloquently attests to the academic preoccupations one year after Hitler's election:

    1. "Grüne Woche, Berlin 1934" (Green week in Berlin), an article arguing that "blood and soil are the basic conditions for the life of our people . . . "
    2. H. W. Siemens, *Vererbungslehre, Rassenhygiene und Bevölkerungspolitik* (Inheritance theory, racial hygiene, and populations policy, 1934, 6th ed).
    3. J. Graf, *Vererbungslehre, Rassenkunde und Erbgesundheitspflege* (Inheritance theory, race science, and hereditary health, 1934).
    4. B. K. Schultz, *Erbkunde, Rassenkunde, Rassenpflege. Leitfaden zum Selbststudium u. für den Unterricht* (Science of inheritance, race science: outlines for self-study and for teaching, 1934).
    5. O. Steche, *Rassenkunde, Vererbungslehre u. Rassenpflege für die Oberstufe höhere Lehranstalten* (Race science, inheritance theory, and racial care for secondary school upper levels, 1934).

6. O. Steche, *Leitfaden der Rassenkunde und Vererbungslehre usw. für die Mittelstufe* (Guide for race science and inheritance theory, etc., for middle school, 1934).

7. E. Meyer and W. Dittrich, *Erb- und Rassenkunde* (Inheritance and race science, 1934).

8. H. Otto and W. Stachowitz, *Abriss der Vererbungslehre und Rassenkunde, einschl. der Familienkunde, Rassenhygiene und Bevölkerungspolitik* (Summary of inheritance theory and race science, including family science, racial hygiene, and populations policy, 1934).

9. E. Thieme, *Vererbung, Rasse, Volk* (Heredity, race, people, 1934).

10. R. Depdolla, *Erblehre, Rasse, Bevölkerungspolitik, Vornehmlich für den Unterricht in höheren Schulen bestimmt* (Heredity theory, race, populations policy, recommended primarily for instruction in high schools, 1934).

11. Freiherr E. von Eickstedt, *Rassenkunde und Rassengeschichte der Menschheit* (Race science and racial history of humanity, 1934).

12. Professor Dr. Otmar von Verschuer, *Sozialpolitik und Rassenhygiene* (Social Policy and Racial Hygiene, 1933).

12. Dr. Prinz von Isenburg, Priv. Dozent, *Das Problem der Rassenreinheit* (The problem of racial purity, 1933).

13. Reichsminister Dr. Goebbels, *Rassenfrage und Weltpropaganda* (Racial questions and world propaganda, 1933).

Most of these reviews were by Ernst Lehmann. See Anne Harrington, *Reenchanted Science: Holism in German Culture from Wilhelm II to Hitler* (Princeton: Princeton University Press, 1999), 195–99.

25. Trawny, *Heidegger and the Myth of a Jewish World Conspiracy*, 35–36. As Trawny relates, Heidegger inquires into the peculiar predetermination [*eigentümliche Vorbestimmung*] of Jewry for planetary criminality, including the calculation and machination resulting in the destruction of the world.

26. As Lacoue-Labarthe reminds us

> the political (the City) belongs to a form of *plastic art*, formation and information, *fiction* in the strict sense. This is a deep theme which derives from Plato's political-pedagogic writings . . . and reappears in the guise of such concepts as *Gestaltung* (fashioning) or *Bildung*. . . . The fact that the political is a form of plastic art in no way means that the *polis* is an artificial . . . formation, *but that the political belongs to the sphere of technē in the highest sense of the term*, that is to say in the sense in which *technē* is conceived as the accomplishment and revelation of *physis* itself.

This theme of rethinking *technē* in light of the German rediscovery of the Greeks as an "oriental" wisdom can be found passing from Winckelmann through Hölderlin and Hegel up to Heidegger. See Philippe Lacoue-Labarthe, *Heidegger, Art, and Politics: The Fiction of the Political*, trans. Chris Turner (Cambridge: Blackwell, 1990), 66–67.

27. Michel Morange, *Les secrets du vivant: Contre la pensée unique en biologie* (Paris: Découverte, 2005). Morange is professor of biology at the École Normale Supérieure, Paris.

28. Bettina Bergo, "The History of Anxiety in Nineteenth- and Twentieth-Century Philosophy" (unpublished MS).
29. In 1938–1939 Heidegger will go so far as to argue that, by assimilating humans to animals, Nietzsche had contributed to the domination of technology. See *Zur Auslegung von Nietzsches II Unzeitgemässer Betrachtung* (GA 46:218), cited by Michael E. Zimmerman, "The Development of Heidegger's Nietzsche Interpretation," *Heidegger Jahrbuch* 2 (2005): 97–116.
30. See Faye, *Heidegger*, 138–40.
31. See ibid., 259. Changing his attitude toward Spengler from criticism of his arguments for a decline of the West to his adaptation of Nietzsche's "will to power," Heidegger argues in 1939: "on the basis of a biological interpretation of the 'will to power,' he has become one of the leading and essential political educators [*politischen Erzieher*] of the decade between the years 1920 and 1930, in that he attempted to write history for the statesman and to present the art of statesmanship historically" (*GA* 47:75).
32. Heidegger writes: "Will the time of the gods then be *over and done* and a relapse into the mere life of *world*-poor creatures commence, ones for whom the earth has always remained only something to be exploited?" (*GA* 65:399/317). Also see *GA* 65:399/316. Just before that, in §251, he had announced, in what rings like the appropriation of biblical Judaism and its history: "A people [*Volk*] is a people *only* if it receives its history as allotted to it through finding its god" (*GA* 65:398/316).
33. Heartfelt thanks to Thierry Gendron-Dugré, Université de Montréal, for this insight.
34. Spengler, *Man and Technics*, 104, tm.

5. INCEPTION, DOWNFALL, AND THE BROKEN WORLD

1. Heidegger himself would reject the label *anti-Semitic*: "Note for jackasses: this comment [a postwar reflection on Jewish prophecy and the will to power] has nothing to do with 'anti-Semitism,' which is as foolish and abominable as Christianity's bloody and, above all, non-bloody attacks on 'heathens.' The fact that Christianity even brands anti-Semitism as 'un-Christian' is part of its highly developed and refined power technique" (*GA* 97:159). By "anti-Semitism," Heidegger appears to have meant the racist ideology invoked by most Nazis to justify the persecution and murder of Jews. His own views are distinct from this ideology. Most of them do not fit "anti-Judaism" either, if this is understood as enmity to Jewish religion. Nevertheless, the most dismaying passages express a general hostility to Jews, mixed with Heidegger's antimodernist world view; Peter Trawny's term *being-historical anti-Semitism* is not inappropriate. For an attempt to distinguish these various points of view, see Jesús Adrián Escudero, "Heidegger's *Black Notebooks* and the Question of Anti-Semitism," *Gatherings: The Heidegger Circle Annual* 5 (2015): 21–49.
2. Most of Heidegger's remarks on Jews and Judaism are directed against a supposed powerful and cosmopolitan Jewish elite and against the Judeo-Christian worldview. I believe the following to be a complete list of such remarks in *GA* 94–97, which I offer as a possibly convenient starting point for interpretations. The following references are prima facie anti-Semitic by my definition: Jewry's "groundlessness" (*GA* 95:97), its "worldlessness" (*GA* 95:97), its power and calculation (*GA* 96:46, *GA* 97:20), its exploitation of pacifism

and bellicosity (*GA* 96:133), its "uprooting of all beings" (*GA* 96:243). The reference to "intangible" Jewry that avoids having to fight while the Germans sacrifice (*GA* 96:262) seems, and probably is, anti-Semitic, but one should note that it is an item in a list of "'facts,' which are always only half true and are therefore erroneous" (*GA* 96:261). There is surely an anti-Semitic animus in the reference to "the Jew Litvinov" (*GA* 96:242). Heidegger's references to Jewish anthropology (*GA* 94:475; *GA* 95:322), the "Hellenistic-Jewish 'world'" (*GA* 95:339), ancient Jewish Phariseeism (*GA* 95:396), and Judeo-Christian monotheism (*GA* 97:357, 369, 409, 438) are generally negative. He compares Nazis to Jews, often appearing to be hostile to both, in his references to sociology (*GA* 95:161); anti-Cartesianism (*GA* 95:168); psychoanalysis (*GA* 95:258; *GA* 96:218); cultural politics (*GA* 95:326); racism (*GA* 96: 56); Barmat and Kutisker, Jewish swindlers denounced by Nazis in the 1920s (*GA* 96:234); and the supposed "Jewishness" of the very persecution of Jews (*GA* 97:20). Opposition to Nazi dogma does not imply agreement with Jews (*GA* 95:325).

3. For an explication of this interpretation of *Seyn*, see Richard Polt, *The Emergency of Being: On Heidegger's "Contributions to Philosophy"* (Ithaca: Cornell University Press, 2006), especially chapter 1.

4. Here is one affinity between Heidegger's thought and Jewish thought, as exemplified in early Christianity: in his interpretations of St. Paul, in the early 1920s, Heidegger focuses on the Judaic eschatological experience of time (e.g., *GA* 60:105/73).

5. Heidegger's focus on *Untergang* might suggest that he is "channeling Spengler," as Richard Wolin has put it: "National Socialism, World Jewry, and the History of Being: Heidegger's Black Notebooks," *Jewish Review of Books* (Summer 2014): 41. Heidegger does support Spengler's idea that Europe is "the realization of the downfall of the West" (*GA* 96:274) and says that this insight cannot be refuted by external signs of progress (*GA* 96:269–70). He gives Spengler credit for expressing "*a genuine force of his age*" (*GA* 95:140) and resisting historicism (*GA* 97:159). However, he also develops an extensive critique of various particular Spenglerian notions (*GA* 95:137–40, cf. *GA* 97:171–73, 410).

6. This seems to be how Heidegger sees China (*GA* 94:302, 432, *GA* 96:183).

7. Quoted in Peter Trawny, *Heidegger and the Myth of a Jewish World Conspiracy*, trans. Andrew J. Mitchell (Chicago: University of Chicago Press, 2016), 33. Trawny notes: "This sentence is lacking in the book [*GA* 69:78/66]. It stands in the manuscript, but is not included in the transcript of Fritz Heidegger, who indeed had thus 'struck it out.' In keeping with the plan for an edition of the 'last hand,' the editor and the estate executor decided at that time not to publish the sentence. In light of the *Black Notebooks*, the statement speaks differently. Chronologically, anyway, it belongs entirely in the context of the other anti-Semitic passages discussed here" (ibid., 120*n*39).

8. "*Der Spiegel* Interview with Martin Heidegger," in Günter Figal, ed., *The Heidegger Reader*, trans. Jerome Veith (Bloomington: Indiana University Press, 2009), 317.

9. See especially Robert Bernasconi, "Heidegger's Alleged Challenge to the Nazi Concepts of Race," in James E. Faulconer and Mark A. Wrathall, eds., *Appropriating Heidegger* (Cambridge: Cambridge University Press, 2000).

10. One possible interpretation of this thought is that European Jewry has brought the Holocaust upon itself. A rival interpretation is that the Nazis are futilely fighting against a

stereotyped image of Jewishness without understanding that they themselves exemplify that same image.

11. According to one passage in the notebooks (*GA* 94:429), "violence" is a trait of beyng itself; but it does not necessarily follow that we establish a proper relation to beyng when we carry out violent acts.

12. Even after the war, Heidegger imagines that the downfall of Europe could lead to a new inception; but, first, man must become the overman, the lord of the planet understood as mere raw material for his power (*GA* 97:366–67).

13. Thus I now consider the subtitle of my article on Heidegger's critique of Nazi ideology to be misleading: "Beyond Struggle and Power: Heidegger's Secret Resistance," *Interpretation* 35, no. 1 (Fall 2007): 11–40.

14. The 1934–35 course on Hölderlin also refers to the "inner truth" of National Socialism. The printed version of that text unfortunately misreads Heidegger's abbreviation for "National Socialism" as "natural science" (*GA* 39:195). See Julia Ireland, "Naming Φύσις and the 'Inner Truth of National Socialism': A New Archival Discovery," *Research in Phenomenology* 44, no. 3 (2014): 315–46.

15. Heidegger's letter to *Die Zeit* is found in the German editor's afterword to *Introduction to Metaphysics*. See *GA* 40:232/250.

16. Cited in the "Translators' Introduction to the Second Edition" of *Introduction to Metaphysics*, trans. Gregory Fried and Richard Polt, 2d ed. (New Haven: Yale University Press, 2014), xxi. Original: Christan E. Lewalter, "Wie liest man 1953 Sätze von 1935? Zu einem politischen Streit um Heideggers Metaphysik," *Die Zeit*, August 13, 1953.

17. Other passages question the concept of "barbarism" and link it to the equally problematic concept of "culture" (*GA* 95:280, 294, 322, *GA* 96:201).

18. According to one anecdote, Heidegger was angered by reports of killings of Jews in the East and fulminated against the foolishness of the "party bosses." See Latvian philosopher Paul Jurevics's recollection of a meeting with Heidegger in 1944, "Meine Begegnung mit Heidegger und seiner Philosophie," trans. Agris Timuška, in Alfred Denker and Holger Zaborowski, eds., *Heidegger und der Nazionalsozialismus I: Dokumente, Heidegger-Jahrbuch* 4 (2009): 264–67.

6. THE OTHER "JEWISH QUESTION"

My thanks go to Professor Marcia Sá Cavalcante Schuback for her detailed and helpful comments on an early draft of this paper.

1. Peter Trawny, *Heidegger and the Myth of a Jewish World Conspiracy*, trans. Andrew J. Mitchell (Chicago: University of Chicago Press, 2016), 2.

2. I am grateful to Richard Polt for his English translation of the key passages related to "the Jewish question" in *GA* 94–96.

3. Jacques Derrida, *Of Spirit: Heidegger and the Question*, trans. Geoff Bennington and Rachel Bowlby (Chicago: Chicago University Press, 1989), 9–10.

4. Karl Marx, "On the Jewish Question," in *The Marx-Engels Reader*, ed. Robert Tucker, 26–53 (New York: Norton, 1978), 28.
5. Ibid., 31–32.
6. Ibid., 36.
7. G. W. F. Hegel, *Early Theological Writings*, ed. and trans. T. M. Knox (New York: Harper, 1961), 204–5, em.
8. Marx, "On the Jewish Question," 45.
9. http://opinionator.blogs.nytimes.com/2014/07/20/a-fight-for-the-right-to-read-heidegger/.
10. Marx, "On the Jewish Question," 46.
11. Jean-François Lyotard, *Heidegger and 'the jews,'* trans. Andreas Michel and Mark Roberts (Minneapolis: University of Minnesota Press, 1990), 3.
12. Ibid., 22.
13. Marcia Sá Cavalcante Schuback and Michael Marder, "Philosophy Without Right? Some Notes on Heidegger's Notes for the 1934–5 'Hegel Seminar,'" in Peter Trawny, Marcia Sá Cavalcante Schuback, and Michael Marder, eds., *On Hegel's "Philosophy of Right": The 1934–35 Seminar and Interpretative Essays* (London: Bloomsbury, 2014), 84.

7. HEIDEGGER AND NATIONAL SOCIALISM

1. Rather than having merely a bad character, Hannah Arendt charges Heidegger with having no character whatsoever. Hannah Arendt to Karl Jaspers, September 29, 1949, in *Hannah Arendt, Karl Jaspers: Correspondence, 1926–1969*, ed. Lotte Köhler and Hans Saner, trans. Robert and Rita Kimber (New York: Harcourt Brace, 1993), 142. Richard Rorty attributes a "nasty character" to Heidegger. Richard Rorty, *Contingency, Irony, and Solidarity* (Cambridge: Cambridge University Press, 1989), 111. In addition to having a bad, absent, or nasty character, Heidegger was accused of having been "bewitched by Hitler" and of having "dreamed 'politically.'" Rüdiger Safranski, *Martin Heidegger: Between Good and Evil*, trans. Ewald Osers (Cambridge: Harvard University Press, 1998), 232, 234. Thus Heidegger also supposedly lacked a "minimum of necessary political reflection." Otto Pöggeler, *Philosophie und Nationalsozialismus—am Beispiel Heideggers, 39. Jahresfeier am 31. Mai 1989* (Opladen: Westdeutscher Verlag, 1990), 34. In the context of such considerations one can also find the idea that Heidegger never even developed his own political thought and was generally apolitical (at least before 1931). See Safranski, *Martin Heidegger*, 227, see also Hugo Ott, *Martin Heidegger: A Political Life*, trans. Allan Blunden (New York: Basic Books, 1993), 136–37. Also under discussion is the notion that Heidegger was mainly influenced by his wife Elfride, who inclined toward National Socialism. Ott, *Martin Heidegger*, 137–38, 174–78, 335. The upshot of these kinds of deliberations is the license to separate questions regarding Heidegger's philosophy from questions targeting his personality. In this vein Habermas has declared that "Heidegger's work has long since detached itself from his person." Jürgen Habermas, "Work and Weltanschauung: The Heidegger Controversy from a German Perspective," trans. John McCumber, *Critical Inquiry* 15 (Winter 1989): 434.

2.   It was one of the earliest criticisms of Heidegger's notion of *Sorge* that it seemed to have an essentially negative connotation and seemed therefore to be only applicable in situations of breakdown or failure. See, for example, Mark Michalski, "Terminologische Neubildungen beim frühen Heidegger," *Heidegger Studies* 18 (2002): 184. Heidegger tries to avert this result by distinguishing between an ontic and an ontological understanding of *Sorge*. Whereas the ontic understanding might contain negative connotations, his ontological notion does not, but reaches back to the Latin concept of *cura* and the Platonic formula of *epimeleia tês psychês*. It nevertheless remains true that even the "deep" philosophical notion of *Sorge* derives its meaning from the fundamental possibility of existential failure, since existence as a whole is always endangered and essentially risky. Inspired by Kierkegaard, Heidegger even employs the notion of *Ruinanz* in early approaches to the topic. Hans-Georg Gadamer, "Die Hermeneutik und die Dilthey-Schule" in *Hermeneutik im Rückblick, Gesammelte Werke* 10 (Tübingen: J.C.B. Mohr [Paul Siebeck], 1995), 196. A more pointed translation of *Sorge* as "sorrow" or "worry" is therefore not totally alien to the basic ideas inherent in the concept—especially since Heidegger himself historically connects ontic hardships to the ontological essence of Dasein.

3.   I am referring to Kant's statements from *The Conflict of the Faculties* where he regards the French Revolution as a historical sign. Kant's main point is that this sign gains its significance not through the objective fact of the revolution, but through the subjective enthusiasm this date provokes in the enlightened public. Immanuel Kant, "The Conflict of the Faculties," trans. Mary J. Gregor and Robert Anchor, in *Religion and Rational Theology*, ed. Allen W. Wood and George di Giovanni (Cambridge: Cambridge University Press, 2005), 301–5.

4.   See Hans Georg Gadamer, "Heidegger und Nietzsche: Nietzsche hat mich kaputtgemacht!" *Aletheia* 9/10 (1996): 19.

5.   Emanuel Geibel, "Deutschlands Beruf," in *Werke*, ed. Wolfgang Stammler, 2:219–20 (Leipzig: Bibliographisches Institut, 1918), 220.

6.   See Otto Pöggeler, "Den Führer führen? Heidegger und kein Ende," *Philosophische Rundschau* 32 (1985): 26–67.

7.   One might be inclined to point out that Heidegger's concept of technology from *Being and Time* largely proceeds from an analysis of handling actual utensils, while his concept of technology after the *Kehre* is more metaphysical and abstract. In the context of *Seinsgeschichte* (the history of being) technology is indeed a notion under which we can subsume the (doomed) thought of modernity. Arnold Gehlen's offer to understand technology as a "superstructure" is still helpful. Arnold Gehlen, *Die Seele im technischen Zeitalter: Sozialpsychologische Probleme in der industriellen Gesellschaft* (Hamburg: Rowohlt, 1957), 11. Such a superstructure allows us to combine Marx's critique of capitalism and Husserl's critique of the sciences with Heidegger's earlier ideas on the technological availability of the world. However, this does not validate a complete separation between the late metaphysical and the early (*Being and Time*) notion of technology in Heidegger. Both conceptions agree on the following: there is a chance to develop modern existence within the framework of modern technological possibilities. One could say that the later elevation of

technology into the worldview of modernity just shows to what extent Heidegger passed over the chance offered by the existential interpretation of technology in *Being and Time*.

9. PROLEGOMENA TO ANY FUTURE DESTRUCTION OF METAPHYSICS

1. Peter Trawny, *Heidegger and the Myth of a Jewish World Conspiracy*, trans. Andrew J. Mitchell (Chicago: University of Chicago Press, 2016), 18–19.

2. See my "Science, Realism, and the Unworlding of the World" in Mark Wrathall and Hubert Dreyfus, eds., *A Companion to Phenomenology and Existentialism* (Chichester: Wiley-Blackwell, 2006), 425–44.

3. Immanuel Kant, *Critique of Pure Reason*, ed. and trans. Paul Guyer and Allen W. Wood (Cambridge: Cambridge University Press, 1998), B xvi.

4. Nor does it help that Nirenberg, a brilliant historian but perhaps less knowledgeable in philosophical details, makes an occasional misstep in his philosophical exposition, as when he writes that for Kant sensible intuition, space, and time belong to "the pure forms of understanding." David Nirenberg, *Anti-Judaism: The Western Tradition* (New York: Norton, 2014), 392.

5. Yitzhak Y. Melamed, "Charitable Interpretations and the Political Domestication of Spinoza; or, Benedict in the Land of the Secular Imagination," in *Philosophy and Its History*, Moques Laerke, Justin E. H. Smith, and Eric Schliesser, eds. (Oxford: Oxford University Press, 2013), 258–77.

6. See Peter Trawny, "Heidegger, 'World Judaism,' and Modernity," trans. Christopher Merwin, *Gatherings: The Heidegger Circle Annual* 5 (2015): 1–20; 6.

7. Jürgen Habermas, "Transcendence from Within, Transcendence in This World," in *Religion and Rationality: Essays on Reason, God, and Modernity*, Eduardo Mendieta, ed. (London: Polity, 2002), 67–94.

8. "It appears to be time to think with Heidegger against Heidegger." Jürgen Habermas, "Martin Heidegger: On the Publication of the Lectures of 1935," trans. William S. Lewis, in Richard Wolin, ed., *The Heidegger Controversy: A Critical Reader*, 190–97 (New York: Columbia University Press, 1991), 197.

9. Jürgen Habermas, *Postmetaphysical Thinking: Philosophical Essays*, William Mark Hohengarten, trans. (Cambridge: MIT Press, 1993).

10. In the German original this passage reads as follows: "Das entschlossene Zurückkommen auf die Geworfenheit birgt ein Sichüberliefern überkommener Möglichkeiten in sich, obzwar nicht notwendig als überkommener" (*GA* 2:507/*SZ* 383).

11. *Kant and the Problem of Metaphysics* (*GA* 3) is the published version of the 1927–28 lecture course *Phenomenological Interpretation of Kant's "Critique of Pure Reason"* (*GA* 25).

12. Theodor W. Adorno, *Minima Moralia: Reflections on a Damaged Life*, trans. E. F. N. Jephcott (New York: Verso, 2005), 18.

13. Theodor W. Adorno, *Negative Dialectics*, trans. E. B. Ashton (New York: Continuum, 1990), 362 tm.

10. HEIDEGGER AFTER TRAWNY

1. See Michael Marder, "A Fight for the Right to Read Heidegger," *New York Times*, July 20, 2014, http://opinionator.blogs.nytimes.com/2014/07/20/a-fight-for-the-right-to-read -heidegger/.

2. Julian Young, *Heidegger, Philosophy, Nazism* (Cambridge: Cambridge University Press, 1997), 41.

3. For this letter and a discussion of it, see Ulrich Sieg, "Die Verjudung des deutschen Geistes," *Die Zeit*, no. 52 (December 22, 1989): 50. The vulgar term *Verjudung*, which is not contained in standard dictionaries, was common in contemporary forms of anti-Semitism and was used by Hitler in *Mein Kampf*, especially in his discussion of "Volk und Rasse," vol. 1, chap. 11. See, e.g., Adolf Hitler, *Mein Kampf* (Munich: Zentralverlag der NSDAP, 1935), 348–49: "Wie wir dabei die innere Verjudung unseres Volkes schon fortgeschritten ist."

4. See Peter Moser, "Die deutsche Philosophie an der Jahrhundertwende," *Information-Philosophie* 1 (April 2014): 76.

5. "It is always possible to face up to any experience (to excuse any guilt), because the experience always exists simultaneously as fictional discourse and as empirical event and it is never possible to decide which one of the two possibilities is the right one. The indecision makes it possible to excuse the bleakest of crimes because, as a fiction, it escapes from the constraints of guilt and innocence." Paul de Man, *Allegories of Reading: Figural Language in Rousseau, Nietzsche, Rilke, and Proust* (New Haven: Yale University Press, 1979), 293.

6. Peter Trawny, *Heidegger and the Myth of a Jewish World Conspiracy*, trans. Andrew J. Mitchell (Chicago: University of Chicago Press, 2016), 131n14.

7. See Immanuel Kant, *Anthropology from a Pragmatic Point of View*, ed. Robert B. Louden, trans. Mary J. Gregor (Cambridge: Cambridge University Press, 2006), 100nN.

8. See "Beitrag zur Berichtigung der Urtheile des Publikums über die französische Revolution" (A Contribution to Correcting the Public's Judgments About the French Revolution), in J. G. Fichte, *Werke 1791–1794*, *Gesamtausgabe* I.1:193–404 (Stuttgart: Frommann -Holzboog, 1964), 292–93.

9. See, e. g., François Fédier, *Heidegger: Anatomie d'un scandale* (Paris: Robert Laffont, 1988).

10. See Dominique Janicaud, "Farewell Heidegger?" in *The Shadow of That Thought*, trans. Michael Gendre, 12–30 (Evanston: Northwestern University Press, 1996), esp. 19–30.

11. Moser, "Die deutsche Philosophie," 76.

12. Trawny, *Heidegger and the Myth of a Jewish World Conspiracy*, 34.

13. See Jacques Derrida, "Heidegger, the Philosopher's Hell," trans. John P. Leavey Jr. in *Points . . . : Interviews, 1974–1994*, ed. Elisabeth Weber, 181–90 (Stanford: Stanford University Press, 1995), 186.

14. "Heidegger's being-historical Manichaeism, which increases at the end of the 1930s, his narrative of a history of the world and the homeland threatened by the un-history of worldlessness and homelessness (*Heimatlosigkeit*), formed a milieu in which his

anti-Semitism, long latent to be sure, could now take on its own being-historical significance" (Trawny, *Heidegger and the Myth of a Jewish World Conspiracy*, 92).

15. Ibid., 93.

16. Ibid., 94.

17. See Heidegger's 1964 speech "Über Abraham a Sancta Clara" (*GA* 16:598–608).

18. There is, as Sluga asserts, a difference between Heidegger the man and Heidegger the
philosopher, in virtue of which Heidegger's thought is unrelated to his political engagement. See Hans Sluga, *Heidegger's Crisis: Philosophy and Politics in Nazi Germany* (Cambridge: Harvard University Press, 1993), 6.

19. This view is formulated by Walter Biemel in *Martin Heidegger: An Illustrated Study*, trans.
J. L. Mehta (New York: Harcourt Brace Jovanovich, 1976), xi: "It is not his life from which
we can learn something about his work; his work is his life."

20. See Trawny, *Heidegger and the Myth of a Jewish World Conspiracy*, 20.

21. See Donatella Di Cesare, "Heidegger, das Sein und die Juden," in *Information-Philosophie*
2 (July 2014): 21.

22. Ulrich Sieg, *Geist und Gewalt. Deutsche Philosophen zwischen Kaiserreich und Nationalsozialismus* (Munich: Hanser, 2013), 130. "The ethnic stranger [*völkische Fremdling*] may
live among us for generations and speak no other language than our own. Nevertheless,
his language is not ours . . . [it remains] something foreign between him and us."

23. According to Sluga, who points to the themes of crisis, nation, leadership, and order,
Heidegger clearly modeled his carefully constructed speech on Fichte's *Addresses*. See
Sluga, *Heidegger's Crisis*, 41.

24. See Jacques Derrida, *Of Spirit: Heidegger and the Question*, trans. Geoffrey Bennington
and Rachel Bowlby (Chicago: University of Chicago Press, 1989), 48.

25. "The stone is world-less. Similarly, plants and animals have no world; they belong, rather,
to the hidden throng of an environment into which they have been put. The peasant
woman, by contrast, possesses a world, since she stays in the openness of beings" (*GA*
5:31/23).

26. See Claudia Schorcht, *Philosophie an den Bäyerischen Universitäten 1933–1945* (Erlangen:
Fischer, 1990).

27. Prof. Gereon Wolters brought this important point to my attention.

28. See Heidegger, "Why Do I Stay in the Provinces?" (*GA* 13:10–11/*HMT* 28).

29. The German *Boden* means ground, soil, floor, land, terrain, bottom, seabed, seat, base,
loft. This article clearly turns on the opposition between *Bodenständigkeit*, roughly, rootedness in the soil by someone who belongs to the land and by extension belongs, and
Bodenlosigkeit, or, equally roughly, the condition of someone who has no roots, or is rootless, hence does not belong.

30. Leo Strauss, "Philosophy as Rigorous Science and Political Philosophy," in *Studies in
Platonic Political Philosophy*, ed. Thomas Pangle (Chicago: University of Chicago Press,
1983), 33.

31. Emmanuel Faye, ed., *Heidegger. Le Sol, la communauté, la race* (Paris: Beauchesnes,
2014), 12.

32. See *GA* 38:81–83/71–73.

11. ANOTHER EISENMENGER?

1.   Victor Farías, *Heidegger and Nazism*, ed. Joseph Margolis and Tom Rockmore, trans. Paul Burrell, Dominic Di Bernardi, and Gabriel R. Ricci (Philadelphia: Temple University Press, 1989). Emmanuel Levinas, "As If Consenting of Horror," trans. Paula Wissing, *Critical Inquiry* 15, no. 2 (1989): 487–88.

2.   Levinas, "As If Consenting," 487–88.

3.   Emmanuel Levinas, "No Identity," in *Collected Philosophical Papers*, ed. and trans. Alphonso Lingis (Dordrecht: Martinus Nijhoff, 1987), 148–49.

4.   Emmanuel Levinas, *Totality and Infinity*, trans. Alphonso Lingis (Pittsburgh: Duquesne University Press, 1969), 102.

5.   Ibid., 142.

6.   To see just how much was known over twenty-five years ago, see Thomas Sheehan, " 'Everyone has to tell the truth': Heidegger and the Jews," *Continuum* 1, no. 1 (1990): 30–44. In addition, one must cite in this context Heidegger's now notorious call for the complete annihilation (*Vernichtung*) of the enemy of the people, which has been known since 2001. It is possible, given that the lecture course was delivered only a few months after the burning of the Reichstag, that he was talking about or was understood to be talking about the communists, but the phrase "Der Feind kann in der innersten Wurzel des Daseins eines Volkes sich festgesetzt haben" recalls the idea of the Jews as the so-called inner enemy (*GA* 36/37:91/73).

7.   See Robert Bernasconi, "Habermas and Arendt on the Philosopher's 'Error': Tracking the Diabolical in Heidegger," *Graduate Faculty Philosophy Journal* 14/15, nos. 2 and 1 (1991): 1–23.

8.   I have attempted to demonstrate this in a number of studies. See, for example, Robert Bernasconi, "Proto-Racism: Carolina in Locke's Mind," in Iris Wigger and Sabine Ritter, eds., *Racism and Modernity* (Berlin: LIT, 2011), 68–82; "Kant as an Unfamiliar Source of Racism," in Julie K. Ward and Tommy L. Lott, eds., *Philosophers of Race* (Oxford: Blackwell, 2002), 145–66; "Hegel at the Court of the Ashanti," in Stuart Barnett, ed., *Hegel After Derrida* (London: Routledge, 1998), 41–63.

9.   Emmanuel Faye, *Heidegger: The Introduction of Nazism Into Philosophy*, trans. Michael B. Smith (New Haven: Yale University Press, 2009), xxv and 316.

10. Peter Trawny, *Heidegger and the Myth of a Jewish World Conspiracy*, trans. Andrew J. Mitchell (Chicago: University of Chicago Press, 2016), 3.

11. Ibid., 6.

12. Ibid., 2. I would contest Trawny's account of *Seinsgeschichte* as "a narrative." I believe it is that, but I believe it is also more than that, as I try to explain in "Descartes in the History of Being: Another Bad Novel?" in *Heidegger in Question* (Atlantic Highlands, NJ: Humanities, 1993), 150–69. Because of the additional volumes in Heidegger's *Gesamtausgabe* that have subsequently been published, I would write it somewhat differently today, but I believe the fundamental point still stands. I mention it here also because Heidegger's interpretation of Descartes becomes important in section 3 of the current essay.

13. Wilhelm Marr, *Der Sieg des Judenthums über das Germanenthum* (Bern: Rudolph Costenoble, 1879).

14. See, for example, Hannah Arendt, *The Origins of Totalitarianism* (New York: Harcourt Brace Jovanovich, 1973), 238–43.

15. Eugen Dühring, *Die Judenfrage als Racen-, Sitten- und Culturfrage* (Karlsruhe: H. Reuther, 1881), 2. English translation in *Eugen Dühring on the Jews*, ed. and trans. Alexander Jacob (Brighton: Nineteen Eighty Four Press, 1997), 56, tm. In a subsequent edition of the book, Dühring changed the word *Race* to *Racenstamm*. See *Die Judenfrage* (Berlin: Nowawes-Neuendorf, 1901), 2.

16. Dühring, *Eugen Dühring on the Jews*, 57. Later he added the further possibility: "or if all religion were already destroyed." Dühring, *Die Judenfrage*, 4.

17. See, for example, Jonathan M. Hess, "Johann David Michaelis and the Colonial Imaginary: Orientalism and the Emergence of Racial Antisemitism in Eighteenth-Century Germany," *Jewish Social Studies* 6, no. 2 (2000): 56–101.

18. Saul Ascher, *Eisenmenger der Zweite. Nebst einem vorangesetzten Sendschreiben an den Herrn Professor Fichte in Jena* (Berlin: Hartmann, 1794), 32. See also Jonathan M. Hess, *Germans, Jews, and the Claims of Modernity* (New Haven: Yale University Press, 2002), 137–67.

19. Johann Gottlieb Fichte, "Beitrag zur Berichtigung der Urtheile des Publikums über die französische Revolution," in J. G. Fichte, *Werke 1791–1794, Gesamtausgabe* I.1:193–404 (Stuttgart: Frommann-Holzboog, 1964), 292.

20. Ibid., 293. Quoted by Ascher, *Eisenmenger der Zweite*, 24–25. For an interpretation of this passage, see Manfred Voigts, "Fichte as 'Jew-hater' and Prophet of Zionists," *Leo Baeck Institute Yearbook* 45 (2000): 87–89. Sven-Erik Rose argues that "the metaphor of decapitation seems perfectly chosen to finesse what remains an essentially insoluble problem of how to incorporate any instance of moral alterity into the absolute interiority of Kantian ethics." Sven-Erik Rose, "Lazarus Bendavid's and J. G. Fichte's Kantian Fantasies of Jewish Decapitation in 1793," *Jewish Social Studies* 13, no. 3 (2007): 89.

21. Immanuel Kant, *Religion Within the Boundaries of Mere Reason*, trans. George di Giovanni, in Allen W. Wood and George di Giovanni, eds., *Religion and Rational Theology*, 39–215 (Cambridge: Cambridge University Press, 1996), 154–57. Saul Ascher, *Leviathan oder ueber Religion in Rücksicht des Judenthums* (Berlin: Franke, 1792), 231.

22. Immanuel Kant, *Lectures on Ethics*, trans. Peter Heath (Cambridge: Cambridge University Press, 1997), 406. Nevertheless, so far as I am aware, Ascher did not comment when Kant publicly called for the "euthanasia of Judaism." Kant, *The Conflict of the Faculties*, trans. Mary J. Gregor and Robert Anchor, 233–327, in Wood and di Giovanni, *Religion and Rational Theology*, 276.

23. Johann Andreas Eisenmenger, *Entdecktes Judenthum* (Königsberg, 1711). The first edition of the book, published in 1700, was immediately banned. The second edition, posthumously published in 1711, runs to more than twenty-one hundred pages.

24. Alfred Rosenberg, *Die Spur des Juden im Wandel der Zeiten* (Munich: Deutscher Volks-Verlag, 1920), 24–25, 115, 160.

25. See Peter J. Park, *Africa, Asia, and the History of Philosophy* (Albany: State University of New York Press, 2013), 20–22.

26. See, for example, Robert Bernasconi, "Seeing Double: Destruction and Deconstruction," in Diane P. Michelfelder and Richard E. Palmer, eds., *Dialogue and Deconstruction: The*

Gadamer-Derrida Encounter (New York: State University of New York Press, 1989), 233–50.

27. Franz Böhm, *Anti-Cartesianismus. Deutsche Philosophie im Widerstand* (Leipzig: Felix Meiner, 1938). This Franz Böhm should not be confused with the economist and colleague of Rudolf Eucken of the same name who seems only to have escaped persecution from the Nazis because the Nazis confused the two of them.

28. Franz J. Böhm, *Die Logik der Aesthetik* (Tübingen: J. C. B. Mohr, 1930). *Ontologie der Geschichte* (Tübingen: J. C. B. Mohr, 1938). Heidegger, of course, was himself a student of Rickert.

29. Ernst Krieck, "Germanischer Mythos und Heideggersche Philosophie," *Volk im Werden* 2 (1934): 248–49.

30. This is the same critique Heidegger directed against Carl Schmitt between 1933 and 1935. See Robert Bernasconi, " 'The Misinterpretation of Violence': Heidegger's Reading of Hegel and Schmitt on *Gewalt,*" *Research in Phenomenology* 45, no. 2 (2015), forthcoming.

31. Charles Bambach, *Heidegger's Roots* (Ithaca: Cornell University Press, 2003), 21–23. It is ironic that Böhm seems mainly to be remembered only by Heidegger scholars. See also Pauli Pylkkö, *The Aconceptual Mind: Heideggerian Themes in Holistic Naturalism* (Amsterdam: John Benjamins, 1998), 249–51.

32. Böhm, *Anti-Cartesianismus,* 1.

33. See especially ibid., 22, 34, 133, and 184–87.

34. Ibid., 241.

35. Ibid., 246.

36. See, for examole, Ernst Krieck, "Germanische Mythos und Heideggersche Philosophie," *Volk im Werden* 2 (1934): 248–49; and Oskar Becker, "Nordische Metaphysik," *Rasse: Die Monatschrift der Nordischen Metaphysik* 5 (1938): 88.

37. One of the great frustrations of the *Black Notebooks* from a strictly scholarly point of view is that it is often difficult to date any given statement with as much precision as one would like.

38. Along the same lines, Heidegger associated destruction with uprootedness (*Entwurzelung*) at *GA* 65:101/80.

39. Richard Wagner, "Judaism in Music," in *Judaism in Music and Other Essays*, trans. W. Ashton Ellis (Lincoln: University of Nebraska Press, 1995), 100.

40. Ibid., 100*n*. For the German text, see Jens Malte Fischer, *Richard Wagners "Das Judentum in der Musik"* (Frankfurt: Insel, 2000), 173. The passage is discussed by Paul Lawrence Rose in *Wagner: Race and Revolution* (New Haven: Yale University Press, 2000), 177–84.

41. As I indicated at note 12, I would not reduce the history of being to the narrative that often accompanies it and, in a sense, belongs to it, but I will not insist on that point here because to do so would lead my insistence on the complexity of Heidegger's antisemitism into realms that might too easily open me to the charge of sophistry.

42. Robert Bernasconi, "Heidegger, Rickert, Nietzsche, and the Critique of Biologism," in Babette Babich, Alfred Denker, and Holger Zabrowski, eds., *Heidegger and Nietzsche* (Amsterdam: Rodopi, 2012), 159–80.

43. Heidegger did not renounce the term *race* in order to embrace the word *culture,* as the Boasian school of anthropology would have us do. Heidegger's obsession with the term *Kultur* is striking (e.g., *GA* 95:351). The term was an important one in the Nazi lexicon, but again especially powerful within Alfred Rosenberg's branch of the Nazi Party. Rosenberg was the first director of the *Kampfbund für deutsche Kultur,* which began in February 1929.

44. Robert Bernasconi, "Who Belongs? Heidegger's Philosophy of the *Volk* in 1933–34," in Gregory Fried and Richard Polt, eds., Heidegger, *Nature, History, State, 1933–1934* (New York: Bloomsbury, 2013), 109–25.

45. Böhm, *Anti-Cartesianismus,* 1–52. Emmanuel Faye attributes to Heidegger a position much closer to that of Böhm; see his "The Political Motivations of Heidegger's Anti-Cartesianism," in G. A. J. Rogers, Tom Sorell, and Jill Kraye, eds., *Insiders and Outsiders in Seventeenth-Century Philosophy* (London: Routledge, 2010), 184.

46. Houston Stewart Chamberlain, *Die Grundlagen des neunzehnten Jahrunderts* (Munich: F. Bruckmann, 1899), 1:273.

47. On the supposed relation of capitalism to *Rechnungsmässigkeit* and the talent of the Jews for calculation, see, for example, Werner Sombart, *Die Juden und das Wirtschaftsleben* (Leipzig: Duncker und Humblot, 1911), 187, 245–46, and 332–33.

48. Lilian Alweiss, "Heidegger's Black Notebooks," *Philosophy* 90 (2015): 305–16.

49. See Aurel Kolnai, *The War Against the West* (New York: Viking, 1938). Kolnai found in *Being and Time* a critique of the "average business and society man of Western civilization" (93).

50. See further Claudia Schorcht, *Philosophie aus den bayerischen Universitäten* (Erlangen: Harald Fischer, 1990), 160–61.

51. See Philippe Burrin, *Nazi Antisemitism. From Prejudice to the Holocaust,* trans. Janet Lloyd (New York: New Press, 2005), 82. The phrase, "the inner truth of National Socialism" is, of course, drawn from another context. See Julia Ireland, "Naming Φύσις and the 'Inner Truth of National Socialism': A New Archival Discovery," *Research in Phenomenology* 44, no. 3 (2014): 315–46.

52. See Robert Bernasconi, "Heidegger's Other Sins of Omission," *American Catholic Philosophical Quarterly* 69, no. 2 (1995): 333–50.

53. For a brief account of how I understand these words of being (*Sein*), see Robert Bernasconi, *The Question of Language in Heidegger's History of Being* (Atlantic Highlands, NJ: Humanities, 1985), 9, 39–44, and 81–90.

54. Robert Bernasconi, "Heidegger's Alleged Challenge to the Nazi Concepts of Race" in James E. Faulconer and Mark A. Wrathall, eds., *Appropriating Heidegger* (Cambridge: Cambridge University Press, 2000), 50–67. This is perhaps the context in which to remark on how shocking it is that most discussions of Heidegger's antisemitism entirely ignore his anti-Black racism. They are different but not unconnected.

55. Emmanuel Levinas, *Existence and Existents,* trans. Alphonso Lingis (Pittsburgh: Duquesne University Press, 2001), 4.

56. Robert Bernasconi, "Will the Real Kant Please Stand Up," *Radical Philosophy* 117 (January/February 2003): 13–22.

57.   See the texts cited in note 8 and, in addition, Robert Bernasconi, "Kant as an Unfamiliar Source of Racism," in Julie K. Ward and Tommy L. Lott, eds., *Philosophers on Race* (Oxford: Blackwell, 2002), 145–66.

12. THE PERSISTENCE OF ONTOLOGICAL DIFFERENCE

1.   The conservatives in Slovenia are pushing this equation of Nazism and the left to extremes: recently, one of their texts enumerated a series of programmatic requests that allegedly prove the closeness of the Slovene United Left to Nazism, and, among the items, one finds the demand for the progressive taxation of the wealthy. (Another commentator dismisses today's gender theory as a continuation of communism by other means, i.e., as an attempt to undermine the moral foundations of the Christian West.)

2.   Four volumes appeared by 2015 in the *Gesamtausgabe, GA* 94–97.

3.   *GA* 95:381–82.

4.   *GA* 94:194.

5.   *GA* 96:56, 46.

6.   Quoted from Peter Trawny, *Heidegger and the Myth of a Jewish World Conspiracy,* trans. Andrew J. Mitchell (Chicago: University of Chicago Press, 2016), 33. Acccording to Trawny, Fritz Heidegger struck this passage out from an early version of the manuscript.

7.   *GA* 97:19.

8.   *GA* 97:20.

9.   Emmanuel Faye, *Heidegger: The Introduction of Nazism Into Philosophy in Light of the Unpublished Seminars of 1933–1935,* trans. Michael B. Smith (New Haven: Yale University Press, 2011).

10.   http://www.welt.de/kultur/literarischewelt/article138868550/Heideggers-widerwaer-tige-Thesen-ueber-den-Holocaust.html.

11.   Benedict de Spinoza, *Theological-Political Treatise,* ed. Jonathan Israel, trans. Michael Silverthorne and Jonathan Israel (Cambridge: Cambridge University Press, 2007), 62–63.

12.   Jacques Lacan, "The Seminar of Jacques Lacan, Book XX: Encore 1972–1973," trans. Cormac Gallagher (unpublished translation), 101, http://www.lacaninireland.com/web/wp-content/uploads/2010/06/THE-SEMINAR-OF-JACQUES-LACAN-XX.pdf. Cited from seminar 4, January 9, 1973.

13.   Gunther Anders, *Die Antiquiertheit des Menschen* [The outdatedness of human beings] I–II (Munich: C. H. Beck, 1956).

14.   See Jean-Pierre Dupuy, "Le Problème théologico-scientifique et la responsabilité de la science," *Le Debat* 129, no. 2 (March–April 2004): 181. Quoted from Jean-Michel Besnier, *Demain les posthumains* (Paris: Fayard, 2012), 195.

15.   Jürgen Habermas "The Language Game of Responsible Agency and the Problem of Free Will: How Can Epistemic Dualism Be Reconciled with Ontological Monism?" *Philosophical Explorations* 10, no. 1 (2007): 31.

16.   Robert Pippin, "Back to Hegel?" *Meditations: Journal of the Marxist Literary Group* 26, 1–2 (Fall 2012–Spring 2013): 7–28, 13. Quoted from http://www.meditationsjournal.org/articles/back-to-hegel.

17.   Quoted from http://ki.se/en/news/brain-scan-reveals-out-of-body-illusion.

18.   Quoted from Ray Brassier, "The View from Nowhere: Sellars, Habermas, Metzinger" (unpublished MS).

19.   Ray Brassier, *Nihil Unbound* (London: Palgrave Macmillan, 2007), 138.

20.   The question one should raise here is also the one of discourse. Brassier concludes his outstanding *Nihil Unbound* with speculations about the death drive and the annihilation of reality—the type of discourse for which there is simply no place in his later Sellarsian preoccupations. The question is thus: is the duality of scientific discourse and its transcendental reflection the only option, or should we not keep the space open for a different type of discourse associated with names like Schelling and Hegel, Lacan and Deleuze, etc.?

21.   Ontological difference is, from our perspective, the very difference between the existing multiplicity of entities and the barred One: the One is barred, it doesn't exist, but the very void of its inexistence opens up the space for entities to arise. The illusion of metaphysics—the "forgetting" of the ontological difference, as Heidegger would have put it—is to obliterate the bar that makes the One inexistent, i.e., to elevate the One into the highest entity.

CONTRIBUTORS

BETTINA BERGO is professor of philosophy at the Université de Montréal, Canada. Her areas of specialization are phenomenology, psychoanalysis, Levinas, Nancy, and Jewish thought. She is the author of *Levinas Between Ethics and Politics: For the Beauty That Adorns the Earth* (Duquesne, 2003). Professor Bergo's work has focused on exploring and understanding the relationship between phenomenology and Judaism, as seen in her translations of Marlene Zarader's *The Unthought Debt: Heidegger and the Hebraic Heritage* (Stanford, 2006); translations of works by Emmanuel Levinas—*Of God Who Comes to Mind* (Stanford, 1998), *God, Death, and Time* (Stanford, 2000), *On Escape* (Stanford, 2003)—an edited volume on Derrida and Judaism, *Judeities: Questions for Jacques Derrida* (Fordham, 2007); and her translation of Jean-Luc Nancy's *Dis-Enclosure: The Deconstruction of Christianity* (Fordham, 2008).

ROBERT BERNASCONI is the Edwin Erle Sparks Professor of Philosophy and African American Studies at Pennsylvania State University. He is known for his work on Heidegger, Levinas, and critical philosophy of race. His books include *How to Read Sartre* (2007), *Heidegger in Question: The Art of Existing* (1993), and *The Question of Language in Heidegger's History of Being* (1985). Professor Bernasconi has published numerous articles on Heidegger and race theory including "Race and Earth in Heidegger's Thinking During the Late 1930s" in the *Southern Journal of Philosophy* (2010) and "The Policing of Race Mixing: The Place of Biopower Within the History of Racisms" in the *Journal of Bioethical Inquiry*.

MARTIN GESSMANN is professor for cultural and technological theory and aesthetics at the Hochschule für Gestaltung in Offenbach am Main, Germany. His work addresses the philosophical, political, and aesthetic dimensions of modernism and the role of technology therein. He is the author of the books *Montaigne und die Moderne* (1997), *Hegel*

(1999), *Zur Zukunft der Hermeneutik* (2012), and *Wenn die Welt in Stücke Geht: Warum Wir Philosophieren* (2014), among others, as well as numerous articles on Montaigne, Rousseau, Nietzsche, Heidegger, and Foucault. Professor Gessmann is also editor of the influential journal *Philosophischen Rundschau* and a member of the jury for the Raymond Aron translation prize in Germany.

SANDER GILMAN is distinguished professor of the liberal arts and sciences as well as professor of psychiatry at Emory University. A cultural and literary historian, he is the author or editor of over eighty books. His *Obesity: The Biography* appeared with Oxford University Press in 2010; his most recent edited volume, *The Third Reich Sourcebook* (with Anson Rabinbach), was published with the University of California Press in 2013. He is the author of the basic study of the visual sterotyping of the mentally ill, *Seeing the Insane* (Wiley, 1982), as well as the standard study, *Jewish Self-Hatred* (Johns Hopkins University Press, 1986). For twenty-five years he was a member of the humanities and medical faculties at Cornell University, where he held the Goldwin Smith Professorship of Humane Studies. For six years he held the Henry R. Luce Distinguished Service Professorship of the Liberal Arts in Human Biology at the University of Chicago and for four years was a distinguished professor of the liberal arts and medicine and creator of the Humanities Laboratory at the University of Illinois at Chicago. He has been a visiting professor at numerous universities in North America, South Africa, the United Kingdom, Germany, Israel, China, and New Zealand.

PETER E. GORDON is the Amabel B. James Professor of History at Harvard University. He specializes in modern European intellectual history from the late eighteenth to the late twentieth century. He has written a great deal about Martin Heidegger and has taught courses and published essays about the Frankfurt School, Theodor Adorno and music criticism, Weimar intellectuals, Hannah Arendt, political theology, theories of secularization, theories of historical ontology and historical epistemology, social theory after the Holocaust, and modern Jewish thought. His first book, *Rosenzweig and Heidegger, Between Judaism and German Philosophy* (California, 2003) won several awards, including the Salo W. Baron Prize from the Academy for Jewish Research for Best First Book, the Goldstein-Goren Prize for Best Book in Jewish Philosophy, and the Morris D. Forkosch Prize from the *Journal of the History of Ideas* for Best Book in Intellectual History. He is the editor of *Weimar Thought: A Contested Legacy* (Princeton, 2013). His most recent book is a major historical and analytical reconstruction of interwar German philosophy, entitled *Continental Divide: Heidegger, Cassirer, Davos* (Harvard, 2010), which received the Jacques Barzun Prize from the American Philosophical Society.

HANS ULRICH GUMBRECHT is the Albert Guérard Professor of Literature in the Departments of Comparative Literature, French and Italian, German, and Spanish and Portuguese at Stanford University. He is a Fellow of the American Academy of Arts and Sciences as well as directeur d'études associé at the Ecole des Hautes Etudes en Sciences Sociales (Paris), and professeur attaché au Collège de France. He has worked extensively on topics related to German literature, the history of ideas, aesthetics, and the intellectual history of the twentieth century. He is a frequent contributor to the *Frankfurter Allgemeine Zeitung* and *Die Zeit*, among other international journals. Professor Gumbrecht is a prolific author whose books include *Our Broad Present: Time and Contemporary Culture* (Columbia, 2014), *After 1945: Latency as Origin of the Present* (Stanford, 2013), *In Praise of Athletic Beauty* (Harvard, 2007), *Production of Presence* (Stanford, 2003), *In 1926* (Harvard, 1998), and *Making Sense in Life and Literature* (University of Minnesota Press, 1989).

MICHAEL MARDER is the Ikerbasque Research Professor of Philosophy at the University of the Basque Country, Vitoria-Gasteiz, and professor-at-large at the Humanities Institute of Diego Portales University, Santiago, Chile. His areas of specialization are phenomenology, ethics and political philosophy, philosophy of nature, aesthetics, and the philosophy of plant life. He has published many books including *Plant-Thinking: A Philosophy of Vegetal Life* (Columbia, 2013), *Groundless Existence: The Political Ontology of Carl Schmitt* (Continuum, 2010), *The Event of the Thing: Derrida's Post-Deconstructive Realism* (Toronto, 2009), as well as recent volumes such as *Phenomena—Critique—Logos: The Project of Critical Phenomenology* (Rowman and Littlefield, 2014), *Pyropolitics: When the World Is Ablaze* (Rowman and Littlefield, 2015), *Dust* (Bloomsbury, 2015), and *The Philosopher's Plant: An Intellectual Herbarium*, with drawings by Mathilde Roussel (Columbia, 2014).

EDUARDO MENDIETA is professor of philosophy and department chair at Stony Brook University. He is known for his work in global ethics, political philosophy, critical theory, postcolonial theory, and Latin American philosophy. He is author of *Global Fragments: Globalizations, Latin Americanisms, and Critical Theory* (SUNY, 2007), and is presently finishing another book on philosophy and war entitled "Philosophy's War: Nomos, Topos, Polemos." He has served on the editorial boards of *City, Environment and Planning D: Society and Space, Constellations*, and *Sophia*. He was the executive editor of *Radical Philosophy Review* until 2007 and founding member of the American Philosophical Association *Newsletter of Hispanics in Philosophy*. He has published a collection of political interviews with Richard Rorty entitled *Take Care of Freedom, and Truth Will Take Care of Itself* (Stanford, 2006), as well as a book of interviews with radical philosopher and prison activist Angela Y. Davis dealing with Abu Ghraib, mass incarceration in the United States, and torture as a weapon of the state, entitled *Abolition Democracy: Beyond Empire, Torture and War* (Seven Stories Press, 2006).

RICHARD POLT is professor of philosophy at Xavier University. He specializes in Heidegger, Greek philosophy, and continental philosophy. His books include *Heidegger: An Introduction* (Cornell, 1999); *A Companion to Heidegger's "Introduction to Metaphysics,"* edited by Richard Polt and Gregory Fried (Yale, 2001); *Heidegger's "Being and Time": Critical Essays,* edited by Richard Polt (Rowman & Littlefield, 2005); and *The Emergency of Being: On Heidegger's "Contributions to Philosophy"* (Cornell, 2006). His articles include "The Untranslatable Word? Reflections on Ereignis" (2014), "Hitler the Anti-Nihilist? Statehood, Leadership, and Political Space in Heidegger's Seminar of 1933–34" (2014), and "Beyond Struggle and Power: Heidegger's Secret Resistance" (2007).

TOM ROCKMORE is distinguished professor emeritus of philosophy at Duquesne University and currently professor of philosophy at Peking University. Dr. Rockmore's current research interests encompass all of modern philosophy, with special emphasis on selected problems as well as figures in German Idealism (Kant, Fichte, Hegel, Marx) and recent continental philosophy (Heidegger, Habermas, Lukács). He is continuing to explore the epistemology of German Idealism as well as the relation between philosophy and politics. His most recent work concerns a new theory of knowledge as intrinsically historical. He has published many books, including *On Heidegger's Nazism and Philosophy* (California, 1991), *Before and After 9/11: A Philosophical Examination of Globalization, Terror, and History* (Bloomsbury, 2011), and *Heidegger and French Philosophy: Humanism, Antihumanism, and Being* (Routledge, 1995).

PETER TRAWNY is the director of the Martin Heidegger Institut at University of Wuppertal and a specialist in political philosophy. He is the editor for all of Heidegger's *Black Notebooks* and author of the first book on them, *Heidegger and the Myth of Jewish World Conspiracy* (Chicago, 2015), as well as *Freedom to Fail: Heidegger's Anarchy* (Polity, 2015). His work on the *Black Notebooks* has been the subject of articles, interviews, and televised pieces across Europe. Professor Trawny is the author of numerous books in political philosophy, including *Medium und Revolution* (2011), *Adyton: Heideggers esoterische Philosophie* (2010), *Die Autorität des Zeugen. Ernst Jüngers politisches Werk* (2009), *Sokrates oder Die Geburt der Politischen Philosophie* (2007), *Denkbarer Holocaust. Die politische Ethik Hannah Arendts* (2005), *Heidegger und Hölderlin oder Der Europäische Morgen* (2004).

SLAVOJ ŽIŽEK is senior researcher at the Institute of Sociology and Philosophy at the University of Ljubljana in Slovenia, Global Distinguished Professor of German at New York University, international director of the Birkbeck Institute for the Humanities, Birkbeck College, University of London, and professor at the European Graduate School. He is author of over forty books in English, including *Disparities* (Bloomsbury, 2016), *Refugees, Terror, and Other Troubles with the Neighbors: Against the Double Blackmail* (Melville House, 2016), *Antigone* (Bloomsbury, 2016), *Trouble in Paradise: From the End of History to the End of Capitalism* (Melville House, 2015), *Trouble in Paradise: Communism After the End of History* (Allen Lane, 2014), *Absolute Recoil: Towards a New Foundation of Dialectical Materialism* (Verso, 2014), and *Event: A Philosophical Journey Through a Concept* (Melville House, 2014).

INDEX

Krieck, Ernst, 175
Kultur. See Culture
Kz. See Concentration camp

Lacan, Jacques, 190–91, 193–94
Lacoue-Labarthe, Philippe, 211*n*26
La Mothe Fénelon, François de Salignac de, 22
Lamprecht, Jakob Friedrich, 20
Lang, Beral, 41–42
Language, 45, 85–87, 100
Languages of Paradise : Race, Religion and Philology in the Nineteenth Century, The (Olender), 45
Last men, 16, 43, 72–73, 196
Latour, Bruno, 129
"Lazarus Bendavid's and J. G. Fichte's Kantian Fantasies of Jewish Decapitation in 1793" (Rose), 221*n*20
"Leap, The" (M. Heidegger), 59
"Leben, Das" (M. Heidegger), 60–61
Lectures on Ethics (Kant), 221*n*22
Left Heideggerians, 190–91
Legacy of the Question of Being, The (M. Heidegger), xxii
Lehmann, Ernst, 210*n*24
Leibniz, Gottfried Wilhelm, 59
Lessing, G. E., 20
Levels of being (*Stufen des Seyns*), 59–66
Leviathan (Ascher), 173
Levinas, Emmanuel, 5, 14, 15, 36, 52, 58–59, 168, 169, 202*n*3, 202*n*6, 219*n*n1–5, 223*n*55; intellectual effort called for by, 170, 183, 184–85; Jews in, 112–13; on philosophy, 183
Lewalter, Christian, 90–91
Life, 11–12, 53–54, 58, 59–66, 71, 209*n*19; Jewish law revolting against, 105; machination overpowering, 86, 105–6; philosophy influencing, 160–67
Lightning, Being as, 82, 123
Locke, John, 183–84
Logic as the Question Concerning the Essence of Language (GA 38; M. Heidegger), 38, 50–51

Losurdo, Domenico, 40, 206*n*7
Luhmann, Niklas, 121
Luther, Martin, 188
Lyotard, Jean-François, 112–13

Machination (*Machenschaft, Mach-schaft*), 6, 8–9, 12–13, 16–17, 76–97; agents of, 2; age of, 180; contemporary, 63; eugenic practices belonging to, 180; inquiry, 211*n*25; Jews participating in, 58, 189; life overpowered by, 105–6; modern, 71–72; nature destroyed by, 67; Nazis succumbing to, 187–88; nihilism culminating in, 189; philosophers and, 137–38; powers of, 107–8, 109–10; as principle of destruction, 3; race belonging to, 180; racism and, 183–84; sciences under sway of, 60–61, 71–72; technology equated with, 209*n*16; as true, 90–91; uprooting fostering, 11
Machtergreifung. See Seizure of power
Machtsteigerung des Judentums. See Power of Jewry
Macquarrie, John, 138
Man (*Das Man*), 84, 88, 109–10, 190, 214*n*12, 223*n*49; last, 16, 43, 72–73, 196; philosopher's difference with, 218*n*18
Das Man. See Man
Man and Technics: A Contribution to a Philosophy of Life (Spengler), 210*n*22
Man with a Movie Camera (Vertov), 192
Marcuse, Herbert, 127
Marder, Michael, xxvi, 98–113, 152
Marr, Wilhelm, 172
Martin Heidegger: An Illustrated Study (Biemel), 219*n*19
Martin Heidegger: Between Good and Evil (Safranski), 215*n*1
"Martin Heidegger: On the Publication of the Lectures of 1935" (Habermas), 217*n*6
Marx, Karl, 11–12, 25–26, 31–32, 159, 216*n*7. *See also* "On the Jewish Question"